Aircraft, Strategy and
Operations
of the
Soviet Air Force

Aircraft, Strategy and Operations of the Soviet Air Force

AIR VICE-MARSHAL R. A. MASON CBE MA RAF
and
JOHN W. R. TAYLOR

JANE'S

Copyright © R. A. Mason and John W. R. Taylor 1986

First published in 1986 by
Jane's Publishing Company Limited
238 City Road, London EC1V 2PU

Distributed in the Philippines and
the USA and its dependencies by
Jane's Publishing Inc,
115 5th Avenue,
New York, NY10003

ISBN 0 7106 0373 8

Typesetting by D. P. Media Limited,
Hitchin, Hertfordshire

Printed in Great Britain by
Butler and Tanner Ltd, Frome, Somerset

Contents

Acknowledgements

I am grateful for the extensive co-operation received from colleagues and other friends in the compilation of this book. The representation of facts, analysis, speculations and assertions in Part One are however mine alone and imply no endorsement from the United Kingdom Ministry of Defence or indeed from any other agency or individual. In addition to the formal attribution to other sources, especial thanks are due to Alexander Boyd for the example of his scholarship; to John Erickson and Air Commodore Ted Williams for their generous encouragement; to Chris Hobson at the RAF Staff College library for his regular identification and provision of sources; and to Jean Anne Bolton for preparation of the manuscript.

R. A. Mason
April 1986

Part One

CHAPTER 1

Evaluating the Soviet Air Forces

Sukhoi Su-27 Flanker air-superiority fighter. Assessing the capabilities of advanced Soviet types like Flanker is fraught with difficulties.

IN 1985 the Soviet Air Forces (SAF) were equipped with some 11,600 fixed-wing aircraft and helicopters.[1] In the previous year, according to a generally accepted US Government assessment,[2] the Soviet aircraft industry had produced some 1,250 military aeroplanes and 800 helicopters. Yet any attempt to describe the way those aircraft are incorporated into the Soviet Air Forces, how they train, how they contribute to Soviet operational doctrine and above all, how militarily effective they are, must be circumscribed again and again by conditions that apply in few other areas of military study.

There are four reasons why bald or sweeping statements about the Soviet Air Forces should be treated with a certain amount of caution. First,

Russia goes to great lengths to conceal evidence of a kind which in the West may be found in technical journals, obtained from conversations and observed on airfields. Second, much of the evidence which does become available is fragmented, sometimes contradictory and frequently open to varying interpretations. Third, interpretation of that evidence, like any other, is susceptible to the preconceptions of the analyst. Finally, even if the evidence was comprehensive and the analysis always well judged and objective, the factors making up the equation of Soviet military effectiveness are so variable that a wide range of solutions would still be possible.

Although Russian reticence about the disclosure of official information was well established before the October Revolution, it has since then assumed almost paranoiac proportions. There are for example no official publications to match the annual British Ministry of Defence White Papers, which conveniently list the major establishments and fighting units and detail the broad organisation of the armed forces. There is of course no public discussion of defence topics, or analysis of possibly competing programmes. Suspicion of foreign interest is aggravated by an atmosphere of incipient conflict and eternal vigilance, assiduously cultivated by means of anti-Western propaganda and continual references to the sacrifices endured during the Great Patriotic War. Security of information is further facilitated by the vastness of the Soviet Union's interior and its inaccessibility to either casual visitors or more professional seekers after military knowledge. Therefore tradition, political philosophy and a basic military inclination to conceal the realities of both strength and weakness from potential enemies continue to deny Western analysts the quantity and quality of information which they take for granted in their own environment.

Consequently, when fragments of evidence do seep out to the West they are avidly examined and interpreted until every conceivable implication has been wrung out of them. In the military bookshops of Moscow it is possible to buy copies of textbooks used in Soviet military training. Occasionally citations for awards for individual heroism or sustained devotion to duty appear in the national press. Photographs, carefully retouched, are regularly published to reinforce awareness of the debt owed by the Russian population to the military defenders of the revolution and the soil of Mother Russia.

In addition to the national civilian press, professional military publications such as the daily *Red Star* and monthly *Aviation and Cosmonautics* and *Air Defence Herald* publish technical, operational and ideological articles of interest to the armed forces, Air Forces and Air Defence Forces respectively. The military journals provide a forum for the floating of ideas, for thinly veiled

criticism of weaknesses in the current system or for examining developments in Western armed forces. It is however sometimes difficult to decide how significant any one particular article may be. The Great Patriotic War is consistently used to illustrate uses of air power regarded as having significance in modern combat operations. Occasionally a number of articles appear in different locations: examples are those published in the late 1970s to argue for greater flexibility in offensive air support operations and, more recently, several concentrating on greater freedom from close ground control for interceptor and air-superiority crews. Weaknesses of varying degrees of magnitude are concealed by expressions such as "in one or two cases" or "recently there was an incident in a squadron". More positive developments are introduced with formulae such as "recent successes achieved by such and such a squadron were attributable to . . .". In addition to the regular injunction to seek inspiration from the fashionable ideological mouthpiece of the moment, there may be hard words of a more practical nature. How widespread the weaknesses actually are has to remain a matter for Western conjecture.

Other items survey trends and equipment in Western air forces. Sometimes ideological hostility is paramount, but on many other occasions serious and well balanced analysis gives a clear impression that Western scenarios, aircraft and tactics are being taken into account in planning Soviet Air Force activities. In such circumstances the need to communicate within the Soviet Air Forces, and to keep the armed forces in the public eye, is presumably seen to outweigh the value of such subject matter to a potential enemy. On the other hand, it is reasonable to assume that the Soviet Union would rather have protected some of the evidence extracted. Data yielded by satellites and other sources of intelligence must come into this category. For example, stories of a new Russian aircraft carrier under construction were circulating in the West for many months before the dramatic photos of *Kremlin* which appeared in *Jane's Defence Weekly* in August 1984 confirmed the reports and at the same time illustrated the quality of satellite photography. Similarly, the advent of the 4th-generation Fulcrum, Flanker and Frogfoot com-

Blackjack strategic bomber prototype (bottom of picture) photographed in company with a pair of Tu-144 supersonic transports at Ramenskoye airfield near Moscow.

bat aircraft was forecast from diluted intelligence reports well before regular sightings of the aircraft in squadron service.

The Soviet Union is far from unaware of the analytical games which take place beyond its frontiers. As early as 1946 Yakovlev and Mikoyan were instructed to produce a small number of Yak-15s and MiG-9s in time to appear over the November 7 parade. In the event bad weather kept them grounded but at the following year's May Day ceremonies a handful of fighters were used to give the impression to the West that Stalin's air defences were already equipped with the most modern aircraft. The reality was very different. In 1981 a new Russian bomber was sighted at Ramenskoye field near Moscow. Not all Western analysts believed that its comparatively ready visibility to interested foreign observers was due solely to carelessness or indifference. Any country which relies heavily on military strength to project its influence abroad must be keen to capitalise on its apparent strengths and conceal the reality of its limita-

tions. Indeed, concealment and deception are significant elements in Soviet military policy, from the grand strategic concept down to the tactical innovation.

There is therefore no shortage of information about the Soviet armed forces in general, nor on the Soviet Air Forces in particular. But it does not emerge in coherent, co-ordinated, well documented form. Consequently, rather like the fragments from an archaeological excavation, information on the Soviet Air Forces can be made to fit the preconceptions of analysts who seek supporting evidence for a particular position. In their most clear-cut form such preconceptions have ideological roots. If one believes that the Soviet Union's foreign policy is driven by an urge for undisputed world domination, and that she is bankrupt of ideology, short of certain natural resources, threatened internally by demographic shifts and committed to reliance on military power, subject only to the risks provoked by her actions, then one's interpretation of the fragments will follow one readily predictable line. If on the other hand one views the Soviet Union as a land-locked power without natural frontiers, subject to repeated foreign invasions over the centuries, emotionally scarred by the losses of the 1941–45 war, fearful of Western capitalist adventurism in a nuclear age and simply seeking to protect her people and many thousand miles of frontiers, then the fragments are likely to "confirm" a very different hypothesis. Between these two extremes lie many shades of opinion held with varying degrees of objectivity.

Preconceptions can also be social in origin. It is possible for even the relatively experienced analyst to apply Western criteria when examining and interpreting Soviet activities. Any military organisation, and the Soviet Air Forces are

no exception, is the product of many factors and influences. The vastness of Soviet territory, the ready availability of large numbers of relatively unskilled personnel, habits of obedience to state discipline, a large but still unsophisticated technological base, a civilian existence still spartan by Western standards, a political philosophy which encourages conformity and inhibits initiative, a comprehensive and monolithic system of national and ideological indoctrination: these are some of the more obvious influences on the way the Soviet Union plans and trains to fight her wars. Observations by Western analysts that the Soviet airman endures primitive domestic conditions, is subject to harsh and unremitting discipline or bullying, and is constricted by close control and rigid operational procedures may or may not be accurate. But even if correct, they are not necessarily the symptoms of military weakness that they would be in Western air forces. "Mirror imaging" – this tendency to apply Western standards to Soviet phenomena – can make the most honest and superficially objective analysis a misleading basis for subsequent deductions.

Finally, there are the prejudices peculiar to

These Soviet NCO groundcrew probably lead less comfortable lives than their Western counterparts. Does that make them any less effective? (*Tass*)

professional military analysts. When a soldier analyses the potential of a possible adversary he is to a certain extent a paid pessimist; he has to be. In a Western democracy he is charged by the community to provide for the nation's defence. He must seek to identify all the military options open to the adversary and assess his ability to execute them. In peacetime he is vulnerable to charges of exaggeration. In wartime he is branded an incompetent if he has underestimated or overlooked anything. He knows that the friction inherent in all combat will reduce some of the opponent's theoretical capability. But his community will pay a heavy price for any overoptimistic, misdirected guesses about exactly what will not materialise. So even if the Soviet Union did believe in open government, if the evidence was not so fragmentary and the variables so numerous, the military analyst would still have every reason to make his assessment with great caution.

That caution has implications for the lay analyst and general reader. Outside the Eastern bloc air enthusiasts can read scores of professional journals and have access to full performance data on Western aircraft and weapon systems. Failures by contractors to meet specifications are rigorously exposed; operational shortcomings or accidents are widely publicised. The Western defence forces could not restrict access to such information even if they wished to do so. But Soviet secrecy means that most information on defence activities in the USSR is acquired by military or associated intelligence operations. Photographs of Backfire over the Baltic may be released by the Swedish or Norwegian air forces. Satellite photographs of Fencer at Soviet bases may be released by the United States Department of Defence. But for many reasons the release of such information is, or should be, tightly controlled. Western defence policies assume that the Soviet Union is a potential enemy. Soviet strategy is based on the principles of concealment, diversion, surprise and high-speed offensive warfare. If Western authorities were to reveal the full extent of their knowledge of Soviet strengths and weaknesses, the opportunities for swift exploitation of the latter and defence against the former would be reduced.

Sukhoi Su-24 Fencer all-weather attack aircraft photographed over the Baltic by the Swedish Air Force

Many of these strengths and weaknesses are widely known, but others, including details of aircraft and weapon performance, are closely guarded. Of particular sensitivity are technical data on electronic warfare. In the opening days of the October War of 1973 the Israeli Air Force was taken by surprise by the potency of the Egyptian and Syrian SA-6 missile batteries. Following swift US assistance, however, the Israelis' ECM pods were reprogrammed. Together with a tactical revision, this allowed the IAF to pursue its offensive air operations to a successful conclusion. In a European conflict the achievement of electronic surprise would yield an advantage which could be difficult to recover in the course of a short conventional war. Consequently there are many references to Soviet electronic operations in the Western press: it is known that they mix specialist ECM aircraft with their bomber formations, that they use converted transports such as the An-12 Cub to provide stand-off or barrage jamming, and that a variety of Bears and Badgers act as electronic intelligence-gatherers. Their effectiveness is however never discussed in Soviet publications, and no authoritative details appear in the West. Electronic warfare played a significant part in the Israeli annihilation of the Syrian Air Force over

the Beka'a in 1982, and since then speculation has abounded in the West. But the IAF and the USAF have remained extremely guarded in their comments, for obvious reasons, and so it is with Soviet ECM capabilities.

It is therefore important to bear in mind that any discussion of Soviet capabilities in the Western specialist press is in the last resort dependent on military sources which are unlikely ever to disclose the whole truth. Indeed, on occasion there may be good reasons to allow incomplete or inaccurate information to circulate widely. All this will be read not just by enthusiasts, but also by grateful Warsaw Pact military attachés, who avidly monitor the extensive range of Western defence publications.

In spite of all the above pitfalls it is possible to reach a net assessment and to make cautious forecasts about the future. When considering an air force the starting point is quantity and quality of aircraft and weapons. It is increasingly possible to make a confident assessment of numbers. But when pursuing the less readily definable elements of "quality" apologists for the Soviet armed forces frequently overlook the advantages in conventional warfare of numerical superiority. For as one senior Russian officer is alleged to have observed, "Quantity assumes a quality all of its own." Nonetheless, it is the application of the right degree of force in the right place at the right time that is decisive, and this is a product of more than just numbers.

Antonov An-12 Cub-B, Soviet Naval Air Force electronic intelligence version of the standard tactical transport. (*Swedish Air Force*)

Organisation provides the structure within which the other factors must coalesce. There is evidence to suggest that since the earliest days of Soviet military aviation its organisation has been more pragmatic than has often been the case in the West. In Europe and America the struggle by exponents such as Trenchard, Douhet and Mitchell to force an appreciation of the value of centrally controlled, independent air power on their army and navy colleagues has frequently left a legacy of disputed role priorities and resource allocation which has on occasion impeded the exploitation of the third dimension. By contrast, the most recent reorganisation of the Soviet Air Forces, in 1981, has created a structure in which, theoretically at least, offensive and defensive resources can be allocated according to the needs of the theatres of operations. The dominance of the Soviet Union in the Warsaw Pact, and this alliance's much greater homogeneity of equipment and procedures in comparison with NATO, could facilitate large-scale control and concentration of assets at the critical point. This could prove decisive in a confrontation in which the Warsaw Pact was able to choose the location, timing and scale of an offensive.

The organisation is however only as good as the staff which directs it and the men who carry out the operations. All of the Soviet Air Forces' most senior commanders are graduates of higher military schools and possibly of the Academy of the General Staff.[3] They may therefore spend up to six years preparing for their senior responsibilities. Whatever their basic speciality, they will become versed in political doctrine and, above all, combined-arms warfare. As will be shown later, however, the impact of the staff on day-to-day operations and exercises frequently leaves much to be desired, even according to Soviet publications.

The abilities of Soviet aircrew vary considerably. The defector Belenko, who presented the West with its first Foxbat in 1976, was by all accounts as competent a fighter pilot as many in the USAF. On the other hand, aircrew in all roles are frequently criticised in the Soviet press for shortcomings which are rare among their Western counterparts. An article by the Commander-in-Chief of Soviet Air Defence Forces Aviation (APVO) in *Air Defence Herald* for May 1984 was a very good example of the idiom used by the Soviet Air Force hierarchy to pinpoint weaknesses and indicate remedies. Too much should not be read into one article, but two assumptions could confidently be made about this one. First, it was unlikely to have been written to mislead the West. Otherwise some means would have had to be found to warn the several thousand aircrew in APVO to disregard the words of their commander-in-chief and to reassure them that the article, despite its detailed and specific content, was simply a piece of disinformation. Second, almost all the points made have occurred recently in similar articles about air defence in both *Air Defence Herald* and other publications such as *Aviation and Cosmonautics*, *Red Star* and *Military Review*.

Colonel-General Moskvitelev began by praising his men for their hard work and great sense of responsibility in ensuring a reliable defence of the nation's air borders. He made ritual obeisance to the guidance received from the Soviet Communist Party Plenum, the Supreme Soviet, the speeches of comrade K. U. Chernenko and the writings of Minister of Defence Marshal D. F. Ustinov. He summarised the complex challenges to air defences in recent years: radically new weapon systems, computers, improved fighter performance, and the rapid development of the "probable enemy's" air attack assets. The development of "complex forms of fighter aircraft tactical employment" had therefore become a matter of prime importance in APVO flying training. Specifically, the required tactics included low-level interception of small, low-flying targets; manoeuvring air combat, especially in groups (two aircraft or more); independent and semi-independent actions; long-range missile combat in jamming conditions; and "other tactics".[4]

The first clue that all was not well came when the Commander-in-Chief observed that the essential "good theoretical training" which should precede tactical exercises in the air was given by "the leading air units". This comment would be noted by the readers: not "all" units, just the "leading" units. There followed a very detailed description of exactly what such "theoretical" training comprised. In sum, the

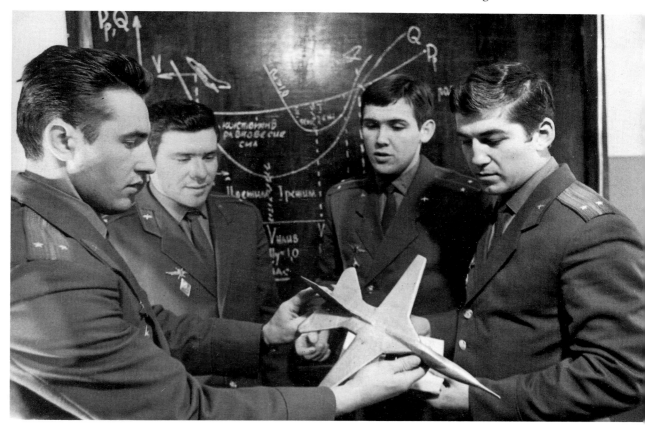

Left Soviet fighter pilots: well drilled in foreseeable combat situations but can they react to the unexpected?

Above Soviet squadrons are responsible for aircrew training down to a very basic level. These young pilots are talking through a tactical problem, using what looks like a model of the US F-111 strike aircraft. *(Tass)*

pilot was expected to think through all the combat manoeuvring situations likely to be met and to formulate his responses to them, thereby reducing the possibility of having to react to the unexpected. This approach, common throughout the SAF, is one of the factors which has led to Western assessments that Soviet training is over-dependent on drills, to the detriment of pilot responsiveness and initiative. According to the General, however, the underlying philosophy is more sophisticated:

A pilot is well trained in theory when he mentally "plays out" the plan of the impend-ing battle, graphically visualises the entire picture of the action, and correctly foresees the consequences of each manoeuvre and each error. The closer the real picture of the mission is to that which the pilot mentally constructed the day before, the more confidently he will perform each succeeding element of his combat actions.[4]

Subsequent combat flying training began with solo and pairs aerobatics at progressively lower altitudes before moving to actual combat manoeuvres. The Commander-in-Chief referred in detail to the problems involved. The training was carried out not at schools but "under the control of the flying personnel supervisor at the regimental air base where the squadron is located."[5] In fact all the regimental aircrew required such training in combat manoeuvres. Speculation on the operational effectiveness of the squadrons before such "innovations" took place is prompted by one specific criticism from the Commander-in-Chief:

There are well-known instances when, during the execution of a rather simple mission, wingmen have lost track of their leaders in a suddenly deteriorating situation and permitted close approaches within the group; all this bespeaks low psychological stability on the part of some pilots when faced with adverse flight factors.[6]

Before combat manoeuvre training could begin, all pilots had to show that they had fully mastered formation flying, separation, landings, and commands and signals. All this in a squadron alleged to be "a leading air unit," with a commander, Major M. Bolokov, singled out as having successfully carried out "ground training according to the uniform programme for manoeuvrable fighter aircraft of the Air Defence Forces." As usual, pilot achievement had been monitored by "instrument data," visual observations and, in common with units throughout the SAF, by sessions of the unit's "methods council". Sure enough, "live-fire tactical air exercises conducted on the range" ultimately proved that Squadron Commander Bolokov had instilled in his crews group manoeuvre combat skills.

But more than that was needed. Autonomous and semi-autonomous operations and combat under jamming conditions, involving "independent search" for the enemy, demanded that a commander instil a "creative approach" into his pilots. Any doubt that the readers might have retained up to this point about the oblique reference to "leading units" must have been sharply dispelled by the next few paragraphs:

> Regrettably, some air commanders do not pay enough attention to this form of fighter aircraft tactical employment. An analysis of the combat training of the Air Defence Forces shows that other forms of tactical employment of modern fighter aircraft are not practised sufficiently in certain units; this includes attacks using the weapons system's limits in adverse weather and during jamming, improving pilot skills in destroying small, low-flying targets, and others.[7]

Worse still, squadrons had not recognised the need for a new approach to training:

> . . . we still find commanders who continue

to work in the old-fashioned way when working out complex forms of tactical employment; they lack creative initiative and wait, as the saying goes, for prompting from higher up, and, in the event of failure, are prone to complain about so-called objective difficulties.[8]

One unfortunate deputy squadron commander was named. Lt-Col V. Nikonov had proceeded at "a snail's pace" in his weapon employment programme, over-simplified his low-level training, been neglectful and lacked a sense of responsibility, imagination and initiative. His career prospects did not look very promising.

In his concluding comments the C-in-C invoked the panaceas which have marked such perorations throughout the history of the SAF:

> Political and Party organisations should instill communists with the qualities of initiative and party high-mindedness, provide support for commanders and staff officers in their creative efforts, and assist in mastering and implementing progressive experiences in the training of pilots, as well as waging a persistent campaign against shortcomings.[9]

It was not explained how the encouragement of

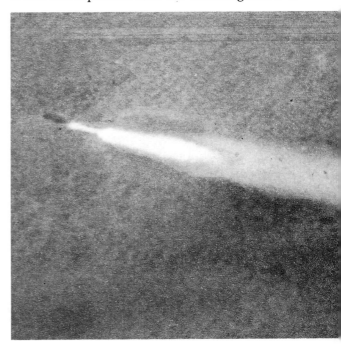

initiative and creativity could be achieved under a system in which conformity and acquiescence are the proven paths to privilege and power.

Soviet aircraft maintenance may also be inferior to that in the West. Groundcrew are largely three-year conscripts lacking the privileges of their officers and requiring regular reminders about even the most basic servicing routines. One implication of recent technological advances in Soviet aircraft and equipment not touched on by General Moskvitelev is the significant increase in demands on groundcrew in many specialisations. Routine servicing carried out in the West by enlisted men is frequently the responsibility of SAF officers and warrant officers. Though the numbers of technicians graduating from Russian schools and colleges are constantly increasing, there are grounds for believing that the conditions of service for SAF groundcrew are little incentive to long terms of engagement. The experience of Western air forces with conscript groundcrew suggests that the training bill is exorbitant, and even if the Soviet design principle of "make it simple, make

it work" has been applied, the maintenance requirements of fourth-generation aircraft such as Fulcrum, Flanker, Backfire and Blackjack are likely to be high. To a certain extent unserviceability can be offset by the possession of large numbers of aircraft, but the ability to sustain a high sortie rate for extended periods must be affected. Low serviceability may also lie behind what by Western standards is the small number of aircrew and aircraft hours flown per month in many Soviet squadrons. Published defector evidence on groundcrew competence is sketchy. Though enlisted men have criticised their working conditions and leadership, they nevertheless expected their unit to perform well in time of conflict and showed a certain pride in it.[10]

To sum up, the available evidence yields reasonably dependable conclusions about current and future SAF operational effectiveness. The potential contribution of air power to a combined-arms offensive on land has increased significantly since the 1960s. There is a harmony among the strategy, organisation, roles and equipment of the Soviet armed forces which would present severe problems to an opponent if they were ever allowed to conduct operations in the way for which they have planned and trained. Soviet Air Force commanders fully

On-the-squadron operational conversion culminates in live-firing exercises. This Sukhoi Su-17 Fitter-K has launched a pair of unguided air-to-ground rockets.

Left MiG-21 pilot gives an example of zeal to his maintenance man in the background. Probably a conscript, the latter will have undergone long and expensive training but is likely to be lost to the service when his term of enlistment ends. (*Tass*)

Below left The advanced systems embodied in types like the MiG-25 Foxbat have put pressures on the technical training organisation of the Soviet Air Forces.

understand the fundamental importance of air supremacy, not just for the success of air operations but also for the execution of operations on land and at sea. Lessons drawn from both the Second World War and Western experience and doctrine are assiduously studied. Political debate may be stifled, but there is plenty of evidence of keen professional military discussion about new tactics and role priorities. The ability of a monolithic, autocratic government to allocate resources to military procurement without any apparent internal disagreement means that deficiencies can be identified and remedied with a sense of purpose which Western air staffs can only envy. Moreover, there is also ample evidence to suggest that Soviet Air Force commanders are well aware of operational weaknesses resulting from inadequacies in aircrew training.

On the debit side, the weaknesses endemic in the Soviet political and industrial systems militate against the SAF balancing the quantity of its equipment against the quality achieved in the West. Aircrew initiative and professional competence; groundcrew skills and ability to work with the minimum of supervision; superior powerplant, avionics and airframe design; and personnel policies which reward traditional military virtues rather than political conformity: all these are priceless advantages denied to the Soviet Union. They could indeed be lost to the West, but surely only by default. Until then the Soviet air threat, while remaining a justifiable and serious source of concern to any potential opponent, should be kept in perspective. One suspects that NATO air force commanders would not change places with their Soviet equivalents, except perhaps to spare themselves the task of repeatedly persuading Western taxpayers that investing in air power in peacetime, however expensive, is far less painful than having to suffer from it in war.

Notes

1 *Soviet Military Power*, US Government Printing Office 1985, pages 77, 82, 101.

2 Ibid, page 87.

3 *The Armed Forces of the USSR*, H. F. and W. F. Scott, Westview Press 1979. Pages 331–374 give a comprehensive description of the philosophy and structure of Soviet higher military training.

4 ''Constant Attention Must be Given To Complex Forms of Tactical Employment,'' Col-Gen of Aviation N. Moskvitelev, *Air Defence Herald*, May 1984.

5 Ibid.

6 Ibid.

7 Ibid.

8 Ibid.

9 Ibid.

10 See for example *The Mind of the Soviet Fighting Man*, R. A. Gabriel, Greenwood 1984.

CHAPTER 2
Air supremacy

THE notion of "command of the air" has been central to the evolution of air power ever since its first recorded expression, by Major J. D. Fullerton of the British Royal Engineers at a meeting in Chicago in 1893. He prophesied that future wars might start with a great air battle and that command of the air would be a prerequisite for all land and air warfare.[1] Every so often a nation has overlooked that forecast, and as a result usually paid a severe penalty. Whatever their beliefs before 1941, Soviet leaders have since then had no doubts at all about the need for domination of the air, as witness the resources they have devoted to achieving this end.

There are however three fine but important differences between Soviet and Western theory

The MiG-29 represents a determined Soviet effort to match or even exceed Western technology in the competition for air supremacy. (*Hasse Vallas*)

and practice in relation to command of the air. First, the SAF tend to use the expression "air supremacy" rather than the broader term, probably because they regard full command of the air as unnecessary and possibly unattainable. The distinction was made before the Second World War:

Absolute air supremacy is generally unattainable. But temporary, local superiority is possible. However, it would be prejudice to think that air supremacy is achieved through the efforts of aviation alone. Both air and land forces participate in achieving this supremacy, in which case the latter not only defend but attack as well. The fight for air supremacy always goes in two directions: on one hand we support the work of our non-fighter and lighter-than-air craft, and on the other hand we take countermeasures against the work of the enemy's aviation and lighter-than-air craft. Air supremacy does not mean being able to fly a lot. Instead it means being able to fly with greater sense than the enemy, and this "sense," as I had noted above, is defined by the degree to which the air forces permit friendly troops to capitalise on the results of battle in the air and from the air and hinders the same on the part of enemy troops.[2]

Second, air supremacy is not a separate concept in the Soviet Union. Even in 1932, when the above was written, it was securely related to combined-arms activities rather than being the prerogative of the fighter pilot, as is so often the case in contemporary Western thinking. To maritime nations such as Britain or the United States command of the air implied totality akin to that associated with command of the sea. The Royal Air Force and the then United States Army Air Corps saw two distinct needs: defence of the national homeland, and freedom to operate in a combat theatre likely to be well beyond the national homeland. Command of the air was therefore not only a much broader concept than air supremacy, but it also did not necessarily imply combined-arms activities.

Finally, there seems to be no evidence that Western ground forces, unlike their Soviet counterparts, ever came to believe that air supremacy was anything to do with them, even though the most famous German fighter ace of the First World War, Manfred von Richthofen, was probably killed by ground fire.

These distinctions are extremely important when assessing SAF operational strength. To the Soviet Union air supremacy is not an exclusively defensive concept. Procurement of several thousand "fighters" does not presuppose a purely defensive posture, but rather reflects the traditional emphasis on the need to attain air supremacy over any kind of operations on land.

Two other influential writers exemplify the continuity of Soviet thought in this area. In 1970

> . . . the Air Forces were intended to be used both for independent air operations, and for support of ground operations.
>
> Foremost, in the independent air operations was the achievement of air superiority. Its basic aim was the destruction of enemy air power (the destruction of aircraft at airfields and in air battles) along a particular strategic axis or in the entire theatre of military operations. For achieving air superiority, it was planned to bring several air armies under a single command.[3]

Ten years later another senior SAF officer observed:

> Air supremacy implies a decisive superiority of one of the warring sides in the air over the theatre of operations or in the main direction . . .
>
> The Soviet Air Force fought the enemy intensively throughout the whole war period. Destroying enemy aircraft in the air and on airfields, the Soviet airmen strove to neutralise the enemy aviation and thus make it possible for the land and naval forces and also the home front to cope with their missions without enemy hindrance . . .
>
> Now, when deep qualitative changes have taken place in aviation equipment and the armament of planes and helicopters, in the struggle for air supremacy such air force features as high combat activity, offensive spirit and initiative in action continue to be of great importance.
>
> The experience of the Great Patriotic War convincingly proved that air supremacy is indispensable for success both in each military operation and in a war as a whole.[4]

In 1917 and during the Great Patriotic War air superiority over the battlefield or line of strategic thrust was synonymous with protection of the Soviet homeland. But the establishment of a *cordon sanitaire* in Eastern Europe in 1945 placed the Soviet Union in a position hitherto unique to Britain and the USA: protected from overland attack but vulnerable to long-range air power independent of combined arms. The Air Defence

Forces took on an extended responsibility: assertion of command of the air over Russian frontiers and territory. The idea was expressed in the aftermath of the Korean airliner tragedy of 1983:

> It is the sovereign right of every state to defend its borders, including its airspace . . . and in the future, if need be, [the Soviet armed forces] will also perform their combat tasks . . . .[5]

To discharge that responsibility . . .

Above It is believed that a Sukhoi Su-21 Flagon was responsible for the destruction of the KAL 747 in 1983. This Flagon-F is armed with Anab air-to-air missiles.

Below Soviet surface-to-air defences are now based on a massive overlapping deployment of missile systems. Illustrated here is SA-4 Ganef, ramjet-powered and capable of very long ranges. (*Tass*)

Every day, by regulation, aviators begin their combat alert duty in defence of the skies of the Soviet Union, the land and sea borders of which extend almost 67,000 kilometres.[6]

Thus Soviet air supremacy is largely tactical, and directly related to combined-arms activities even when described as "independent air operations". This designation is more accurately applied to operations in direct defence of the homeland against a threat offered by the strategic air arms of the potential enemy and aimed at the industrial, political and military heart of the country. While the two have frequently been interrelated, it is possible to trace the separate development of each since 1945. The contribution of surface-to-air defences (SAD) to both types of activity has fluctuated greatly over the past 70 years, but it is safe to say that their impact has not been confined to the era of the surface-to-air missile (SAM).

Origins of Soviet air defence

On the Eastern Front of the First World War, and in the Russian Civil War which followed it, tactical air supremacy was relatively insignificant to the land war. This was partly because there were, compared to the Second World War, few aircraft engaged, and partly because the vast distances involved kept air-to-air encounters to a minimum. Russian air activity was largely restricted to reconnaissance and limited offensive air support. Moreover, Western superiority in fighter design and armament was more than a match for Russian bravery, both in East Prussia before 1917 and in the Archangel region during the period of British intervention in the civil war. Nor is it likely that the "air defence" effort, as opposed to air supremacy, was much more noteworthy. It has however formed the basis of a mythology that has been deliberately fostered and imbued with modern relevance:

> Thus, when the enemy threatened Petrograd, the cradle of the Revolution, the Putilov (now Kirov) Works formed the country's first anti-aircraft armoured battalion on V. I. Lenin's direct instructions. The workers of the plant manned the guns and vehicles. On October 29, 1917, the battalion was sent to its firing positions, where it shot down its first aircraft. It should be mentioned that the 2nd Battery of this battalion formed the basis for a

unit that had a splendid war record. Today it is known as the Order of Lenin Guards Putilov-Kirov Air Defence Missile Regiment. By tradition it invariably participates in the military reviews in Red Square in Moscow.

It should be pointed out that from the very beginning the air defence system of the young Soviet Republic was organised on the principle of combining various fighting arms. Airmen, artillerymen, machine gunners and searchlight operators carried out their missions in close co-operation. Thus, the measures taken by the Party and Government made it possible to build up by spring 1918 the Air Defence Forces of 200 anti-aircraft artillery batteries and 12 fighter flights of six aircraft each.[7]

Not only have SAD been integral to the Soviet air defence system since 1917, but for the greater part of that period the Air Defence Forces, including the interceptors, have been commanded by a soldier, usually an artilleryman.

Between the two world wars Soviet fighter development was, like the rest of the country's military aviation, erratic and bedevilled by production problems, while the ranks of senior officers and designers were decimated by purges. In the Spanish Civil War the most advanced Soviet fighter, the Polikarpov I-16, was outfought by the Luftwaffe's Bf 109. Though three new fighters, the LaGG-1, Yak-1 and MiG-1, entered production in 1939, they were still available only in small numbers by the time of Operation Barbarossa, the German invasion of 1941. Meanwhile, no fewer than four successive chiefs of the air staff had been executed, with a fifth, Zhigarev, exiled to the Far East less than a year after the debacle of Barbarossa.

Any doubts the Soviet High Command might have had about the significances of air supremacy were settled in the first few days after the start of the Barbarossa offensive, on June 22, 1941. German sources had claimed 1,811 Russian aircraft destroyed by the evening of the first day, more than three-quarters of them on the ground, mainly at airfields in the Western and Kiev military districts. On October 5 an official Soviet statement conceded the loss of 5,316 aircraft.[8]

For 12 months Soviet fighters fought desperate defensive battles over Leningrad, Moscow and the Ukraine until the scale and intensity of the air war began to take its toll of Luftwaffe aircraft and crews. It was at this time that the practice of ramming German aircraft became common: one obsolete fighter for one Ju 88 or He 111 seemed a good exchange, even if the Soviet pilot did not always survive.

The PVO (Air Defence) Corps was created in June 1941 to provide air defence for Moscow, and by the end of 1941 it was part of a force of almost 2,000 fighters contributing to the defence of the capital.[9] The first Troops of National Air Defence (PVO *Strany*), including interceptors, anti-aircraft artillery, and air observation, warning and communications, were formed in November 1941. Previously all such units had been subordinate to army commanders in the military districts, a division of responsibilities which was later alleged to have weakened overall air defence provision and co-ordination.[10] Subsequently, as the Soviet aircraft industry began to produce more and improved aircraft, fighter regiments were reorganised with some 30 aircraft each. The original tactical formation, the three-aircraft *zveno*, was replaced by a *zveno* of two pairs. There is evidence to suggest that the morale of Soviet aircrew had, not surprisingly, been severely damaged during 1941. With the comparative exception of the regiments in the Odessa district, losses of aircraft and crews had been heavy, commanders had been instantly removed and executed by the NKVD, and the surviving crews had little confidence in their aircraft. One eminent British analyst has described the efforts of the Soviet High Command to counter this widespread loss of confidence and competence:

Throughout 1942, propaganda, exhortations, threats were liberally and doggedly applied in efforts to educate commanders and discipline aircrews. Fighter pilots had to be taught to be more aggressive, more determined, more capable of exploiting the potential of their new fighters and vanquishing their instinctive fear of the Luftwaffe. Against bombers they were instructed to hold their fire at extreme ranges and, as the premature expenditure of ammunition was only too common, to use short, well-placed bursts instead of prolonged, generally directed streams of fire while keeping safely clear of the rear-gunner. In combat with fighters they had to learn to fight on the dive and climb and develop skills in deflection shooting instead of relying perpetually on the stern chase. They had to be taught to use sun and cloud cover. Attack and cover groups were to be clearly allocated and adhered to, as escorting fighters had become notorious for deserting their charges at the first signs of trouble. Now disciplinary measures were to be enforced against fighter pilots who broke off

Ilyushin's Il-2 *Shturmovik*, the simple but durable type that allowed the Soviet Air Forces to hit back with ever-increasing effect after the initial defeats of Operation Barbarossa.

engagements or turned back without command instructions, and a sortie was only to be counted as such when the escorted bombers or shturmoviks got through to the target . . . . In 1942 and 1943 air commanders, endeavouring to provide the maximum fighter presence, often sent out too high a proportion of inexperienced new pilots on the same sortie, with disastrous results. Now the number was to be reduced and regimental commanders and squadron leaders were expected to fly with their units and keep a close eye on the well-being, performance and aptitude of their new pilots. Under attack, Soviet fighter formations tended to scatter and provide easy prey for the more confident and better organised Luftwaffe pilots; now they were educated to keep together and fight as a *zveno*.[11]

Forty years later Soviet commanders would still be emphasising similar themes, leading to speculation that a Second World War assessment by Luftwaffe pilots might still be valid:

> The characteristic features of the average Soviet fighter pilot were a tendency towards caution and reluctance instead of toughness and stamina, brute strength instead of genuine combat efficiency, abysmal hatred instead of fairness and chivalry. . . .[12]

From the Battle of Stalingrad onwards, however, the Soviet Air Force began to win air supremacy, slowly and spasmodically at first and then, with ultimate overwhelming numerical superiority, over most of the Eastern Front for most of the time. Ground control from advanced command posts on the main lines of advance was established, together with greatly improved ground-to-air communications, while deputy air commanders worked alongside their ground force colleagues at army headquarters. But even then the SAF considered it prudent to create large numbers of dummy airfields to decoy Luftwaffe counter-air operations, as during the battle of Kursk in 1943. By July 1944 the Soviet Air Force was in a position to support the Byelorussian offensive with 1,900 fighters, part of a total of 6,000 aircraft divided among six Air-Armies. In April 1945 the Soviet Union was estimated to have 17,000 aircraft, of which 8,000 were fighters, deployed against the Luftwaffe. Superficially at least, the air defence of the homeland was in far better shape than at any time in Soviet history. And yet, seen from the Kremlin, many weaknesses remained.

Establishment of a national air defence system

In August 1945 the awesome potential of combined air and nuclear power was demonstrated at Hiroshima and Nagasaki. The Soviet Union was secure from attack by land but could quickly come within range of America's B-29s. Hitherto, the defence of Moscow or Leningrad had been synonymous with the achievement of tactical air supremacy over the ground forces fighting for the cities. The same kind of aircraft, the same kind of warning and co-ordination could provide for both tactical and national air defence. But by the end of 1945 the wartime alliance had crumbled and both sides were beginning to fear that the next war would be between East and West, using nuclear weapons. Behind the numerical superiority of the Soviet Air Forces lay an aviation industry which had little experience of metal airframe construction, multi-engine design, electronics or gas turbines. There was no national radar early-warning system and, despite the pre-eminence of artillery generals in PVO *Strany*, co-ordination of and provision for surface-to-air defences were still inadequate. In the prevailing atmosphere of hostility between East and West, which was fully in accord with traditional Marxist-Leninist dogma about the inevitability of conflict, Western military capabilities and intentions, as perceived by the Kremlin, came to have a strong influence on the development of Soviet air power.

Ironically, the Anglo-American bomber offensive against Germany had provided an unexpected dividend for the USSR in that many German industries had been moved eastwards away from the bombing, only to fall into the hands of the advancing Soviet armies. It has been estimated that four fifths of all German aircraft production was acquired by the Russians in

1945, while by 1947 some 300,000 highly skilled airframe designers, project engineers, chemists, optical and electronic research staff and fuel specialists had been "relocated" in the Soviet Union.[14] Many examples of the Me 262 twin-jet fighter and the rocket-driven Me 163 were captured intact, as were production models of the Junkers *Schmetterling* radar-guided surface-to-air missile, which had a range of 50 miles and maximum operational altitude of 50,000 feet, the larger but experimental *Wasserfall* SAM, and various experimental air-to-air missiles. The German aircraft were thoroughly flight-tested by Soviet pilots, resulting in a decision to incorporate their characteristics in Soviet-designed aircraft rather than simply copying them. A. S. Yakovlev, in his autobiography *Aim of a Lifetime*, described a meeting with Stalin in December 1945 at which the aircraft designer argued in favour of incorporation rather than imitation on the grounds that mere copyism would have a stultifying influence on Soviet aircraft design. Moreover, he reasoned, the Me 262 was too complex to be copied and made too many demands of pilots and groundcrew.[15] Two Soviet-designed jet aircraft were subsequently built in a very short time. The Yak-15 and MiG-9, both using German engines, flew on April 24, 1946. The following day both designers were

The post-war strategic threat posed by America's Boeing B-29 – so recently demonstrated over Japan – stimulated the development of the Soviet air defences.

instructed by Stalin to build 15 of each to fly over Red Square on November 7. In the event, bad weather precluded their appearance. But by the 1947 May Day parade 50 of each were available to participate, and the aviation industry was beginning to examine the 25 Rolls-Royce Nene and 30 Derwent 5 jet engines provided free by the British Government.

Within two years of the end of the Second World War the three major Soviet post-war fighter design bureaux were well established. The subsequent contributions of Mikoyan-Gurevich, Yakovlev and Sukhoi are examined in detail elsewhere in these pages, but it was not long before the wisdom of Yakovlev's advice to Stalin began to be apparent. The MiG-15, for example, distinguished itself in Korea and also illustrated the skills of Soviet engineers, who increased the power of the original Rolls-Royce Nene by some 30%. It was however essentially a short-range interceptor, more suited to tactical dogfighting and with little endurance to apply to combat air patrols over the extensive Russian frontiers, and it was not until the appearance of the next generation that the Soviet air defences acquired long-range all-weather capability.

29

Though it served in very large numbers with the Soviet air defence forces, the MiG-21 left no lasting mark on operational thinking. (*Novosti*)

Meanwhile, and not for the last time in the evolution of Soviet air power, reorganisation was taking place to match the changing scope and responsibilities of the Air Defence Forces. At the end of the war air defence had been based on the four major fronts: Western, South-Western, Central and Transcaucasian. In 1946 the fronts were redesignated air defence districts, and two years later command of Troops of National Air Defence was removed from the Artillery Command of the Red Army. Gradually an increasingly integrated but still sparse infrastructure of early-warning radars, ground control units, anti-aircraft defences and communications was constructed and linked to the interceptor bases. Then, in 1954, the commander of PVO was elevated to the status of commander-in-chief and made a deputy minister of defence. At the same time the formal independence of the Russian "Fighter Command" was confirmed, as was its equality with the Army, Air Forces and Navy. Until 1981 Soviet air defence was to remain an independent service, with its own academies, training programmes and promotion patterns.

The 1950s were marked by the appearance of the second-generation MiG-21 and Su-9 fighters and, even more significantly, the first generation of Soviet surface-to-air missiles. Despite the numbers in which the type was deployed, MiG-21 operations have left no enduring mark on the modern SAF. But the habits developed by the Su-9 pilots and the advantages and complications of the SA-1 and its successors have had a major and lasting impact.

The disparaging German assessment of Soviet pilot initiative in the Second World War has often been repeated by Western analysts since then. Indeed, there is overwhelming evidence to suggest that the Soviet Air Forces themselves are aware of a constant need to encourage initiative. To be fair to Soviet aircrew, however, the advent and subsequent expansion of SADs, and the evolution of the "strategic" air defence partnership of ground radar control and interceptor, undoubtedly created operational conditions in which individual initiative could be severely circumscribed.

The first revelation to the West of the

capabilities of Soviet SAMs also illustrated an unexpected side effect of their entry into the race for air supremacy. The USA had presumably been aware of the first SA-1 deployment in the Moscow region in the mid-1950s. Nevertheless, U-2 reconnaissance flights continued to criss-cross the Soviet Union from bases such as Peshawar in Pakistan and Bodo in northern Norway. A second SAM system was reported to have been deployed in 1957, but the U-2 missions continued unmolested, flying well above the operational ceiling of the MiG-15 and 17. Then, on May 1, 1960, Gary Powers was shot down at a politically inopportune moment and the age of the manned bomber was pronounced to be at an end by Western cognoscenti. Certainly the hitherto invulnerable U-2 had been downed by a SAM, but, as Oleg Penkovsky subsequently reported, the success had not been achieved without cost. To begin with, of the 14 missiles fired at Powers, only one got near enough to blow his fragile aircraft apart. Moreover, he appears to have been "ambushed" by batteries sited beneath a regular flightpath. "They wanted to fire when the aircraft from Turkey flew over Kiev, but there was nothing to fire with and the aircraft escaped. Powers would

have escaped if he had flown a mile or so to the right of his flight path."[16] Powers was not the only SA-2 victim that day: a MiG-19 which was trying to intercept him was also shot down. Even modern SAMs are no great discriminators once launched towards a target; Western aircrew take a very keen interest in the degree of aircraft recognition taught to SAD crews. Clearly there was inadequate co-ordination between missile and interceptor controllers, or the MiG-19 pilot was unusually over-endowed with initiative, or both. In any event the principle was clear: the presence of friendly SAMs has a very inhibiting influence on free-ranging interceptors. Throughout the 1960s and 1970s the SAD umbrella spread steadily across the Soviet Union itself. But it was even more in evidence in the arena of the tactical fighter, covering the ground forces of the Soviet Union and her Warsaw Pact allies in traditional combined-arms manner.

During the 1960s NATO moved away from the "trip-wire" doctrine of nuclear dependence and towards the increasingly conventional posture of

The Lockheed U-2, first and most highly publicised victim of the Soviet SAM defences.

The SA-8 mobile SAM system is operated at divisional level. Seen here in Red Square are examples of the SA-8A variant, with four ready-to-fire rounds exposed on their launchers; SA-8B features six rounds in box launchers. (*Tass*)

"flexible and appropriate response". At the same time the threat of Soviet SAMs forced Western strike aircraft to exercise at ever lower altitudes. The resulting need for low-level air defence was met in the Soviet Union by a combination of radar-laid guns and SAMs. The SA-3 Goa was an early example, followed into service by a series of increasingly sophisticated and mobile weapons. These, usually under the control of the Soviet armies, have been well described elsewhere.[17]

The exact relationship between Soviet SADs and fighter aircraft is a closely guarded secret, and even if any NATO authority was aware of it such knowledge would itself carry the highest classification. The broad allocation of Soviet SADs within a front has however been well publicised in Western journals, from the platoon-held SA-7 and small arms, through the regimental ZSU-23 gun and SA-9 and 13, to the divisional SA-6 and 8 and the army-level SA-4 and 2. The fire and radar fields are in theory overlapping and complementary, and the organisation is expected to be mobile enough to accompany an armoured offensive. The whole is the responsibility of the ground combined-arms commanders. The ingredients of the ideal form of tactical ground-to-air defence were summarised by the then commander of PVO SV (Air Defence Troops of the Ground Forces) in 1976. First, co-ordination:

> It is possible to provide cover for troops against air strikes with sufficient reliability only through the combined efforts of all of the air defence resources when their operations are precisely co-ordinated with those of fighter aviation, with the air defence resources of the senior chief, and with the operations of adjacent units and subunits receiving cover. Co-ordination must be continuous.[18]

Second, the answer to the challenge presented by the high degree of mobility possessed by the air enemy, and by the rapidly changing positions of the ground forces to be defended:

All this, then, was the reason that manoeuvre was included among the most important principles of air defence, since without the capability to respond quickly to changes in the ground or air situation there can be no discourse on the reliability of cover for troops from air attacks.[19]

Implicit in this same article is an explanation of the very large numbers of SAD units deployed with the ground forces. Occasionally Western analysts seem to assume that NATO aircraft would be faced by all of them at the same time. But in practice there would, for example, be a need for one battery to cover another which is redeploying, as manoeuvrability is in fact

> . . . characterised by the time needed to tear down [redeploy] platoons, batteries, battalions, and resources for reconnaissance and control, and also by the mobility of equipment and its rate of movement on the march. One also must not forget the possibility that in the process of relocation air defence gunners will spend time firing at attacking aircraft and helicopters. . . .[20]

Nevertheless, manoeuvre can be sustained and surprise achieved against a low-flying enemy by "roaming air defence units," and the whole backed up by "faultlessly organised logistic support," if

> . . . the air defence officers are well acquainted with the situation and control subunits skilfully and without interruptions, and if warrant officers, sergeants and privates have been trained for manoeuvre operations.[21]

As in many other areas of Soviet military activity,

> . . . we need creative genius and initiative in personnel. Only with constant search for the best methods and techniques for accomplishing assigned missions will it be possible to ensure maximum utilisation of the high qualities of air defence missile and artillery equipment.[22]

These observations by the then commander-in-chief of Soviet tactical ground air defences reveal how complex the problem of airspace management over the battlefield has become. At any time friendly aircraft would be departing on or returning from missions behind the lines, providing close air support or complementing the SADs over ground forces engaged in a mobile offensive. The surface-to-air defences themselves would be deployed in ambush as well as along the line of march, with the emphasis on getting in the first shot. Capable of manoeuvring and changing position frequently, they would be covering large volumes of airspace with radar-guided missiles susceptible to jamming or spoofing, and they would be largely manned by conscripts and controlled at battalion level or above. Little wonder that Soviet fighter-pilots have become accustomed to the idea of close control in the combat zone. Traditional airspace management by means of safety heights, speeds, lanes, times or IFF are all called into question by such a ground environment.

There is however evidence to indicate that the troops of PVO SV may not present as much of a threat to their own aircraft or to those of a potential enemy as the quantity and quality of their equipment suggests. In 1979 a senior Tank Troops general considered it necessary to write at length on the need for army commanders to be more familiar with the combined-arms principles of tactical air defence, and to comment on weaknesses in organisations which by then had been in service for at least a decade. "Many combined-arms commanders did seriously and consistently concern themselves with questions of air defence . . . and persistently enhance their knowledge in this area. . . . In the majority of cases combined-arms commanders [in exercises] skilfully employed their AD resources . . . but unfortunately in training . . . examples of the other kind are still encountered."[23] Such examples included lack of knowledge of AD capabilities; failure to provide timely cover at water crossings; inadequate preparation and maintenance of equipment; lack of skill in group drills, tactical briefings, sub-unit command and control, and co-ordination with fighters; inadequate, unrealistic, stereotyped and simple exercises; inadequate combat training of gunners; and the need for improvements in the technical training of personnel, "especially officers". Twelve months later, in an even more widely

The modern Soviet fighter pilot has to reconcile the current policy of encouraging more aircrew initiative and the need for close control to avoid destruction by friendly missiles. (*Tass*)

circulated article, another army commander was even more explicit about training weaknesses, most of which stemmed from one fundamental failing:

> Unfortunately, not all commanders take pains to see that the air enemy during exercises behaves just as he would in real combat.

Sometimes the only thing the officer worries about is whether his subordinates will get high marks. He does not care so much about how they do it. Such a commander will be tolerant of simplifications and indulgences.[24]

The area of concern on this occasion was the training of the missile radar crews. Superficially, they looked efficient and creative and used their initiative. But

> . . . the concept of the exercise did not take into full account the capabilities of enemy air attack weapons. For example, no provision

The MiG-23 Flogger G typifies the third generation of Soviet tactical aircraft, with their bias towards fighter-bomber operations. (*Jahn Charleville*)

was made for targets attacking at low and extremely low altitudes using simultaneous diversionary groups and powerful electronic countermeasures. The situation was made more complicated mainly by increasing the number of targets and the density of the attack. While developing the exercise plan Major Zubrachev did not realise that the properties of the simulated targets bore little resemblance to actual ones, that their flight was not correlated with the topography. . . . As a result, the crews fought against a kind of abstract enemy and solved problems in situations which are extremely unlikely to occur in actual combat . . . we cannot be pleased by success attained at an exercise against a weak enemy.[25]

Thus while the comprehensive network of Soviet SADs would undoubtedly create difficulties for an attacker, it is not necessarily the impregnable barrier which its sheer size would suggest. Indeed it may present many problems to Soviet tactical aviation and could well inhibit free-ranging fighter operations close to friendly ground forces. Exhortations to fighter pilots to display more initiative and to embark on more free-ranging missions may be countered not just by residual reluctance and traditions of close control but also by the practical problems of airspace management in very fluid combat.

The spread of the SAD umbrella over the ground forces had one more important consequence for fighter aviation during the late 1960s and early 1970s. Though the numbers of air-superiority fighters were greatly reduced, those remaining were enabled to concentrate more heavily on offensive air-to-ground operations. At the same time the third generation of tactical aircraft – epitomised by the later marks of MiG-21, the Su-17 and 20, and the MiG-23 and 27 – were configured and exercised far more as fighter-bombers. The acquisition of, and heavy concentration on, tactical, surface-to-air defences therefore had a significant effect on the offensive capability of what was then Frontal Aviation.

Strategic air defence

Meanwhile, away from likely areas of combined-arms operations, Russian fighter pilots prepared for a very different kind of combat: under ground control against the long-range bombers of the USAF's Strategic Air Command

and the RAF's Bomber Command. The principles of ground-controlled interception (GCI) – based on ground radar and radio stations located at airfields, at air army headquarters, and with mobile groups of forces – had been established in the later stages of the Great Patriotic War. The radars could detect targets at ranges of 130–150km at heights of some 15,000ft.[26] The aviation commander on the ground was responsible for scrambling fighters from their airfields and vectoring them on to the incoming raid. Thereafter the airborne commanders, leading either flight, squadron or regiment, would assume control of the battle and the GCI post would fall silent unless further intruders or some other major change in combat circumstances were observed. Even if the squadrons broke down in combat into individual flights or pairs, they "continued to operate in conformity with the plan of battle developed earlier," which had "indicated targets for each flight, the distribution of duties in case of a change in the situation, and reorganisation of the battle formation by stages of the battle."[27] Such "advanced planning and co-ordination from the ground made squadron control in the air much easier, but did not constrain the initiative of the flight commanders."[28] In practice, however, even in the later stages of the war, things could be rather different when "intelligent initiative" was not always applied "within the overall concepts":

> The one who deserves a reproach is not the one who tries to destroy the enemy and fails but rather the one who, fearing responsibility, stays out of action and does not use all available forces and means at the necessary moment to achieve victory."[29]

But as ground radar detection ranges and heights were extended, so the opportunities for initiative were further reduced. The long-range bombers were expected to approach in small numbers or individually, by night or in bad weather, and probably protected by self-screening jamming or other forms of electronic countermeasures (ECM). During the 1950s and 1960s supersonic interceptors equipped with interception radars were deployed to hunt transonic bombers at heights, speeds and dis-

Right This Su-21 Flagon pilot's pre-flight preparation includes a round-the-cockpit conference. (*Tass*)

Below right The MiG-25 Foxbat seems to have proved something of a handful to its pilots when it first arrived on the squadrons, creating "emotional unbalance" among some of the less experienced.

tances perhaps three times greater than those of the Second World War:

> Fighter control was carried on primarily from the ground. The pilot flying alone strictly followed commands on changes of course, speed, and flight altitude given by radio and took the plane to the point of possible target acquisition by onboard radar. Practical success in aerial battle, or to be more precise, approach and detection of the target, began to depend on the ability of the command post to determine the flight parameters of the target and fighter, select the most advantageous intercept procedure in the particular situation, and determine the intercept point.[30]

One such practice mission was described in *Soviet Military Review* in 1972. Major Oleg Kuleshov was tasked, probably in a Su-15, to intercept at maximum range from his own base in ECM conditions and then recover to an unspecified airfield. "To secure success he had to carry out scrupulously every command coming from the aircraft controller and strictly maintain the flight conditions."[31] Kuleshov was placed by the GCI controller within AI radar range, apparently used electronic counter-countermeasures to burn through jamming, and made a simulated attack on his target. He was then vectored towards the recovery airfield and handed over to the controller there. The intruder was presumably not expected to be carrying defensive air-to-air armament, so any display of initiative by Kuleshov would have been not only unnecessary but also possibly counter-productive. Instead he was praised for his meticulous pre-flight preparation, particularly as it related to ECM procedures.

But not all Soviet pilots coped so professionally with the increasing challenges of long-range interception, especially following the arrival of the MiG-25 Foxbat-A in PVO *Strany* in 1970. Interceptor squadron commanders were advised to be on the look-out for signs of "emo-

tional unbalance" among less experienced pilots. This was ascribed to the "strain" and "uncertainty" stemming from "the additional psychophysical stresses which do not occur in flights near the airfield."[32] Of course the strain could not have been prompted by the aircraft, because "the pilots were now [1972] well acquainted with the splendid characteristics and reliability of the machine."[33] On the other hand,

> . . . there was a great difference between the aircraft they had been used to flying and the new interceptor fighter. It was different in everything: appearance, equipment, armament, performance characteristics and methods of employment.[34]

In fact, "inexperienced" pilots had difficulty with their navigation and could not cope with the pressure of time shortage in closing with targets, and, not surprisingly bearing in mind the endurance of the Foxbat,

> . . . the readings of the fuel gauge were also a source of tension when the pilot observed that the pointer was beyond the half mark, though the search for the target, attack, and approach to the landing airfield had not yet been executed.[35]

USAF F-105 Thunderchief, regularly on the receiving end of North Vietnamese high-speed, single-pass attacks during the Vietnam War.

The solution was sought by "a regular exchange of experience" with the best pilots of the squadron, as the younger ones were apparently keen to learn how to overcome "tension in flight" and "negative emotions". In 1972 at least, Soviet commanders seemed to believe that the answer to the problems posed to inexperienced pilots by the Foxbat lay in the triumph of mind over matter, with the result that "psychological training" of aircrew remained "a necessary element in each lesson in combat training and political education."[36]

There was however ample evidence in the early 1970s to indicate that Soviet commanders were concerned about the impact of close ground control on pilot "creativity" and initiative, quite apart from any temporary difficulties that inexperienced pilots had with new aircraft. Consistent emphasis was placed on the complementary nature of ground control and pilot activity. As usual, reference was made to the enduring relevance of experience in the Second World War. In addition, the air combat in South-east Asia between US air forces and North Vietnamese-flown Soviet aircraft was keenly observed. How to meld the air-to-air combat of the former period with the ground-controlled single-pass attacks of the latter obviously presented a problem. One solution was to aver that in fact there was no problem because the situation had been inaccurately analysed:

When aircraft began to be equipped with radar sights and missiles, when supersonic speeds were developed, some air force experts voiced somewhat one-sided views on the combat employment of aircraft in general and on fighter tactics in particular. Proceeding from the fact that it would be difficult to execute abrupt manoeuvres at such high speeds they assumed that, as a rule, the interceptor would attack in pursuit at small approach angles. In actual fact they denied the possibility of visual air-to-air search, formation air fighting and, what is more important, manoeuvrable air combat, which was a distinguishing feature of air warfare during the Second World War.[37]

In the subsequent paragraph the author, a Russian general, was unusually critical, by scarcely veiled implication, of the current condition of his fighter pilots:

This approach tended to water down the tactics of fighters. It attributed a passive role to the fighter pilot, sapped his initiative, independence and tactical resourcefulness, factors which, under all circumstances, constitute the elements of victory. However, life itself and the practical experience of combat

This pair of MiG-23 Flogger-Cs is setting off to practise formation air combat, a discipline that is winning new advocates at the highest level in the Soviet Air Forces.

training rejected these views. It became obvious that advanced flying and aerobatics, single and formation air fighting still retained their role. Such things as radar, missiles and various technical devices for crew guidance from the ground, far from ruling out special caution on the pilot's part, [actually emphasise] active air-to-air visual search, independence, initiative and resolve . . .[38]

His remedy was simple, traditional and, unusually from such a source, lacking any reference to the inspiration derived from the Party – although no doubt the required moral and psychological strength would flow from there:

To meet the new, much higher, requirements the pilot must train persistently, particularly in advanced flying and aerobatics. Profound knowledge of tactics, aerodynamics and aircraft multiplied by sound moral and psychological steeling constitute the bedrock of the pilot's professional skill and his readiness to fight the enemy at any moment and to emerge victorious from combat.[39]

Nor was this an isolated outburst against the practical consequences of "one-sided views". Two months earlier the same writer had reminded the same readership of the disasters which had befallen Luftwaffe pilots in the Great Patriotic War when their operations had become stereotyped and vulnerable to Russian surprise attack. "Nothing", he argued, "affects the correct solution of a combat mission more perniciously than stereotyped patterns, lack of initiative, passivity, repetition of the same tactical methods and use of the same flight routes."[40] Conversely, the pilot's creativity and initiative, together with his increasing degree of education and professional expertise, meant that his role continued to be decisive:

> An air battle will be won by a pilot who, all other conditions being equal, acts with greater purposefulness, can react swiftly and correctly to changes in the situation and profit by the slightest miscalculations in the enemy's actions to destroy the latter.
>
> But as is the case in every field of endeavour, the display of initiative in air combat will only lead to success if it is sound, if it draws upon deep knowledge and firm skills, upon accurate calculation and realistic assessment not of separate factors, but of their entire complex. Such qualities are inherent in pilots of the highest qualification and are attained by day-to-day painstaking work to improve one's knowledge and skills in an all-round way.[41]

The emphasis by the Soviet leadership on the need for aircrew initiative, creativity and "activity" is therefore not a phenomenon peculiar to the 1980s. Indeed, with the increased emphasis by NATO air forces on medium and low-level penetration, regularly supported by self-screening or accompanying jamming, the task of the Soviet fighter pilot, whether defending the national frontiers or seeking tactical air superiority in a combined-arms environment, has become progressively more complex since the above words were written. The Commander-in-Chief of PVO *Strany* summarised the situation in 1974:

> Success in destroying the air enemy at the maximum distance from the aerodrome depends on the time taken to launch the aircraft and their guidance to the interception line. The necessity and importance of such interception are dictated by the possibility of the enemy employing air-to-ground missiles possessing great range and speed. Even a rough consideration suggests that interception on a remote line includes all types of combat operations. Thus the enemy, approaching the launching line, can make use of extreme low altitudes, intensive jamming, manoeuvring and complicated weather conditions. At the same time these operations can be protected by the cover groups, diversions and other methods which will inevitably lead to manoeuvring formation air fighting.[42]

General Borovykh went on to emphasise that a commander's order did not require "blind obedience" but "creative thinking and initiative". Moreover, the pilot now had far more sophisticated aircraft to fly, with third-generation aircraft like the MiG-23, MiG-25 and Su-21 well into regimental service by 1974:

> Today Soviet interceptor pilots fly aircraft embodying the latest achievements of science and technology. They have to deal with automatics, radioelectronics, computers and transistor equipment. It is not fortuitous that today the interceptor pilot is at the same time an engineer. Now all-weather fighter-interceptors possess great fire-power and combat range and are capable of destroying an air enemy at any altitude and in any weather conditions. This enhances the combat capabilities of the interceptor pilot, his responsibility for each combat mission, for each interception. Combat actions in the air are now highly manoeuvrable and of fleeting character; the opposing sides pursue decisive objectives.[43]

But even then, in the opinion of the C-in-C, combat was still a "one-shot" affair: "To achieve victory one must strike down the enemy like a sniper, at the first attack, with a first missile."[44] He made no reference to dogfighting, even though "no two interceptions are alike". The context was still akin to that of South-east Asia:

initial sighting, superior position, and swift single-pass attack. Pilot initiative was required to ensure that the engagement began as, or was immediately transformed into, one possessing such favourable characteristics; hence the need for tactical awareness, rapid reaction and "creativity".

To add to his problems, the fighter pilot could rely on less and less help from ground control. Incoming low-level raids could be expected along certain headings, but they could be "fixed" by forward radars or other early-warning systems only if they intruded deeply enough. During the early 1970s, therefore, increasing emphasis came to be placed on "independent target search" by pilots who had no look-down pulse-Doppler radar capable of discriminating between moving targets and ground clutter. Junior squadron pilots progressed from two-seat low-level familiarisation flights to singleton, pairs and groups sorties relying entirely on visual search and navigation.[45] Again, however, the initiative of the individual pilot could be severely circumscribed by the need to maintain formation. In one exercise in 1972, for example, a squadron of ground attack aircraft was rescued

Soviet interceptor pilots have to cope with a growing array of systems, as indicated by this rare cockpit shot of an Su-21 Flagon

from enemy fighters by the intervention of a well drilled formation led by one Major Zerenkov, whose

> ... subordinates demonstrated adequate mutual understanding and concerted action plus excellent flying skills. Their faultless co-operation enabled the pilots to keep their place in formation confidently when executing the leader's most varied manoeuvres, carefully watch the air situation and strictly observe flight safety rules. This was of no small importance in achieving success.[46]

From the early 1970s formations increasingly comprised radar-equipped aircraft such as Flogger-B and its successors. Hitherto airborne squadron commanders had not been able to "see" the whole of the likely combat arena, hence the importance of the ground controller. The introduction of group formations not only made the ground controller's task more complex, whatever the height of the combat, but also

The introduction of radar-equipped types like the MiG-23 Flogger-B gave airborne commanders the ability to see the whole air combat arena.

meant that more responsibility could be left to the commander in the air. This in turn demanded powers of swift appraisal and improvisation, as well as leadership. Thus initiative became an essential ingredient of squadron command, if not among junior pilots.[47]

Throughout the 1970s the need for initiative among squadron commanders went beyond the question of leadership in the air. PVO fighter pilots joined their squadrons with no tactical training comparable with that enjoyed by RAF pilots at tactical weapons unit (TWU) and operational conversion unit (OCU). Consequently, every squadron had a blend of experienced pilots who could stand combat alert and who had to remain combat-ready, plus a number of pilots fresh out of training school who had to be brought up to operational standard. There are many accounts in the Soviet press of the methods employed within squadrons, in which responsibility for training was shared between squadron commander, Party commissar and regimental staff, with the latter apparently also responsible for squadron standardisation. Frequent criticisms have been directed against stereotyped, unrealistic training which takes account neither of individual pilot abilities nor of likely operational circumstances. Ideally, the

squadron commander would be guided by the unit's "methods council," comprising the head of the political affairs section, Party and Komsomol activists, and the squadron commander himself. The council would receive reports on the progress of individual officers and would advise on instructional methods on the ground and in the air. After a series of classroom sessions, in which the young pilots might be joined by flight controllers, radar landing system controllers and GCI controllers in the study of tactics and enemy capabilities, different examples of aerial combat would be "walked through," with the pilots carrying model aeroplanes. The novices would then move to the unit's two-seat trainer and ultimately to the squadron aircraft itself.[48]

Such training appears to lack the degree of centralised formulation, standardisation and supervision preferred by Western air forces, and to depend more heavily on the resourcefulness of the individual squadron commander and his senior pilots. Within the guidelines of "commander's documents, orders and instructions there are vast opportunities for initiative and creativity", the "decisive factors, not just in achieving victory but in all the activities of a leader who is training and indoctrinating young air combatants."[49] If however the training is unrealistic, without tactical setting,

. . . it means that your turns points are passed precisely on time, proper flight para-

Two-seat versions of combat aircraft play a far larger role in Soviet squadrons than in comparable Western units, which have far less responsibility for the airmanship training of new pilots. This is a MiG-23U Flogger-C.

meters are maintained and then, because you have no tactical assignment other than to observe the beauties of nature passing beneath the interceptor's wings, you're nothing but a sport pilot, and that's all![50]

In this case the unit's methods council decided to raise combat readiness and proficiency by "devising a plan with a specific tactical setting for each and every scheduled take-off."[51] Any pilot who then failed to meet the tactical requirements of the sortie could apparently expect to receive summary corrective treatment:

However, under no circumstances should the officer permit over-simplification in the air, as one pilot did when pursuing a target. Before reaching the pre-arranged intercept point he was supposed to execute a fighter evasive manoeuvre. For some reason, though, the officer "forgot" to do it. He continued his navigation flight without changing his routine, which naturally created the most favourable conditions for his attacking comrade to intercept him. He thought to himself: "Everything will work out." But after both pilots had landed, the picture immediately became clearer. Using the GCI controller's log and thoroughly analysing the flight

recorder data, the flight commander was able to firmly establish that the young officer had oversimplified the intercept for his friend. Both pilots were temporarily grounded. The commander as well as squadron Party and Komsomol activists then undertook the appropriate work with them. They didn't permit anything like that to happen again.[52]

The application of corrective measures by both operational commander and political activists epitomises their joint responsibility for training and discipline. This is true not just of PVO units but of all SAF squadrons. The balance of power between commander and activists is difficult to assess, depending as it does on the strength of the political directorate at C-in-C level or above and on the qualities of the individuals concerned. It is, however, highly probable that, just as there have been periods of tension between Soviet Army military theorists and political dogmatists, so any major trend towards greater individual creativity in the Soviet Air Forces must contend with traditional Party attitudes.

Such thinking lay behind a warning to fighter pilots in 1980. They were reminded that during the Second World War pilots who left their place in formation without permission to shoot down fascist airmen were arrested and brought before a military tribunal. Modern pilots, imbued with "a deep feeling of patriotism and proletarian internationalism . . . vigilantly love the socialist motherland, vigilantly guard the conquests of

Great October . . . carrying out the resolutions of the 25th Congress of the CPSU, firmly know that victory in modern combat is unthinkable without strict execution of the commanders' orders, [and of] the requirements of regulations, manuals and guidance documents regulating accident-free flight duties."[53]

The hero of this narrative was Capt T. Safyutdinov, who combined initiative in the air with strict flight discipline. He was rewarded by promotion, the award of the Sniper Pilot badge and selection for higher military academy. His virtue was however not "initiative," which is never mentioned again in the article, but his "air warrior's superior discipline". The theme is explicit: the relationship between flying discipline, military discipline and "established order," together with the responsibility of "political organs" and "Party and Komsomol organisations" for "combat and political training" employing "the entire gamut of political, military and moral education, following every day the historic resolutions of the 25th Congress of the CPSU and subsequent documents of the Party and leadership."[54] And lest anyone miss the point:

> The long experience of the best aviation squadrons clearly testifies that the actions of a military pilot during flight frequently determine the extent to which he, as an air combatant, is accustomed to strict observance of military discipline and established order on the ground, and the extent to which he, as an officer, serves as an example for his subordinates. Thus, flight discipline is a component of military discipline. They are united and indivisible.[55]

But, continued the article, some commanders had not always remembered their responsibilities; the spirit of socialist competition had not always been fostered, with the result that flying hazards had occurred and discipline become lax. Such officers were dealt with by the "unit Party bureau". Lest there remain any doubt about the bedrock on which combat effectiveness really rested, it was not initiative, or creativity, or independence of action but

> . . . the air warrior's discipline [that] is the most important factor in combat readiness of aviation units and subunits, a necessary con-

dition for attaining victory in modern warfare. High discipline and efficiency are inseparably linked with the moral fibre, heroism, steadfastness and courage of the air warrior, with his loyalty to the front-line traditions.[56]

In the West the responsibility for instilling such sterling qualities lies firmly with the squadron commander. Not so in the SAF:

> Therefore, the commanders, political organs, the staff, Party and Komsomol organisations must every day instil in the airmen these remarkable traits of the Soviet character, and strive so they may become the norm of daily life.[57]

The earlier reminder about the likely fate of the fighter pilot who broke formation or committed any other act of indiscipline contrasts with a contemporary analysis, suggesting that there was a strong divergence of opinion even within PVO *Strany* itself about "independent" fighter activity:

> But what is the current attitude in aviation to "freelancing"? Does this method, as they say, have the "right to exist"? Naturally the revolution in military affairs and the concomitant development of combat equipment, particularly equipment for electronic detection of aerial targets, have been a major force in changing tactical ways and means of combat operations. . . . Nonetheless, for testing the combat maturity of military pilots during tactical flying exercises, when the situation most closely approximates real combat, the use of freelancing in our view is not only possible but necessary. It is more appropriate because first-rate air combatants operating as though they're at the front employ some of the freelance combat methods with great benefit to their operations.[58]

The author of this piece dutifully pays homage to the historic resolution of the 25th Congress of the CPSU, but he is far more concerned with reality:

> In actual combat anything can happen. Let's assume that the enemy has destroyed some of the vectoring posts, has begun intensive

radar jamming, and has sent diversionary groups of aircraft to various altitudes. Then the aircrews in this zone use the old but formidable weapon of independent search for air targets, conducted both with onboard radar and visually. In the process the air combatants must carry out their assigned combat mission to the outermost intercept limits.[59]

Thus by the end of the 1970s there were strong influences at work both to encourage greater independence on the part of Soviet fighter pilots and to inhibit it. On the one hand the threat of dislocation or destruction of ground control, interference with air-to-air voice communications, low-level intruders below radar coverage, and group attacks faced by group defence conspired to make reliance on tight control and formation increasingly unrealistic. On the other, the need to co-ordinate meticulously with surface-to-air defences, to supervise inexperienced pilots on operational squadrons, to place supersonic interceptors at the right place and

The Komsomol organisation plays a significant part in preparing Soviet youngsters for military service. The slogan on the nose of the aircraft in the background means "Komsomol pledge".

time in front of supersonic intruders, and, above all, to maintain Party and military discipline would make the consequences of any loosening of control and development of initiative very unpredictable.

The challenges of the 1980s

By 1986 the Soviet air defences seemed truly formidable, which indeed they were when compared with those deployed only 25 years previously:

The Soviets have deployed massive strategic air defence forces that currently have excellent capabilities against aircraft flying at medium and high altitudes but much less capability against low-flying aircraft and

The Sukhoi Su-27 Flanker is one of the cornerstones of the new Soviet air defence system.

cruise missiles. Soviet air defences, however, are in the initial stages of a major overhaul geared entirely to fielding an integrated air defence system much more capable of low-altitude operations. This overhaul includes the partial integration of strategic and tactical air defences; the upgrading of early-warning and air surveillance capabilities; the deployment of more efficient data transmission systems; and the development and initial deployment of new aircraft, associated air-to-air missiles, surface-to-air missiles and an airborne warning and control system (AWACS). Currently, the Soviets have some 1,200 air defence interceptors and nearly 10,000 SAM launchers at over 900 sites dedicated to strategic territorial air defence. An additional 2,000 interceptors and some 1,800 tactical SAMs are deployed within the USSR's borders and could be made available for territorial defence.[60]

The significant weapon systems in this structure – MiG-31 Foxhound, MiG-29 Fulcrum, Su-27 Flanker, Il-76 Mainstay and the new SAMs – are described in detail elsewhere in these pages. Future weapon development is unlikely to differ from that of the West, although it is hoped that it will continue to lag behind. All-

aspect heat-seeking air-to-air missiles with finer temperature discrimination; more ECM-resistant radar-guided missiles combined with fire-and-forget multiple-launch equipment; longer-range missiles with mixed guidance systems; and laser weapons: all of these can be expected to enter Soviet service in the next decade. The introduction of the AEW&C Mainstay will improve low-level detection and control, while Fulcrum and Flanker should strengthen the Soviet bid for tactical air superiority.

It is however possible that a private Soviet assessment would not be quite so optimistic. Since NATO's adoption of flexible response in 1967 the Soviet Union has been faced with the problems of forcing a regional military victory against a possible combination of conventional and tactical nuclear weapons backed up by strategic deterrent forces. In the last decade the Warsaw Pact has reconfigured its ground forces, giving prominence to the operational manoeuvre group (see Chapter 3) as the spearhead of a large-scale highly mechanised ground offensive. Meanwhile, the potential contribution of NATO air power to the conflict has grown in both quantity and quality. The advent of the multi-role F-15 and F-16, Tornado GR1, A-10 and Alpha Jet, supplemented by the residual Harriers, and Phantoms, has made NATO air power a major, perhaps the major, potential obstacle to a Warsaw Pact offensive. The new aircraft, equipped with new families of stand-off and precision air-to-surface weapons, sup-

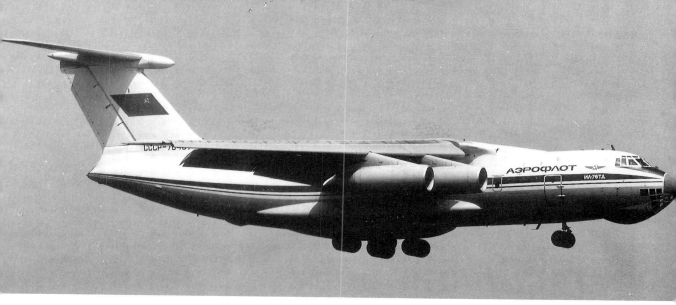

Though no photograph of the Mainstay AEW&C aircraft has yet become available, it is known to be based on the Il-76 Candid transport.

plemented by increasing numbers of combat support helicopters and supported by the E-3 AWACS, TR-1 and EF-111, have called into question Soviet reliance on precisely timed, thoroughly co-ordinated and multiple-echeloned combined-arms operations. The achievement of surprise may be denied by AWACS and TR-1 operations; communications and control dislocated by the EF-111 and other ECM platforms; and sustained pressure and co-ordinated air support could be seriously disrupted by many combinations of NATO air-to-ground and counter-air sorties. Air superiority is therefore even more critical to the outcome of Soviet operations on the ground than it was in the later years of the Great Patriotic War, when the Luftwaffe was both heavily outnumbered and increasingly matched in quality.

Nor can the Soviet Union continue to have unreserved confidence in its complex array of surface-to-air defences. The lessons painted by

New Western combat systems, co-ordinated by advanced command facilities such as the Boeing E-3A AWACS, represent a powerful threat to Soviet massed, multi-layered assaults. (*Robbie Shaw*)

their employment in Vietnam, in Egypt in 1973 and in Lebanon in 1982 must give cause for disquiet in the SAF. In Vietnam SA-2s were finally decoyed or suppressed by air attack. After the initial shock to the Israeli Air Force of carefully integrated ZSU-23s, SA-6s, SA-2s and SA-7s in 1973 the defences were breached by a combination of ECM and destruction by air and ground forces. In the Beka'a in 1982 Syrian SAMs were eliminated by ground and air fire combined with a wide range of ECM.

When moving, SAMs are more difficult to co-ordinate, complicate airspace management, and have difficulties in terrain which provides natural cover to ground forces. When accompanying a deeply penetrating offensive their rate of fire would place heavy additional burdens on logistic support. Moreover, as NATO air forces progressively rearm with stand-off air-to-surface smart weapons, the value of shorter-range surface-to-air defences will be steadily reduced. Further back in Soviet territory, the threat from the supersonic strategic bomber has been increased by USAF deployment of air-launched cruise missiles and will be made still more acute by the B-1B and stealth techniques. Finally, the Soviet Union must consider the threat of retaliation from the ground-launched cruise missiles deployed in Western Europe.

The Soviet Union has responded to this multi-faceted challenge with reorganisation, re-equipment and re-evaluation of tactics. But although the environment is changing rapidly, most of the new measures have a very familiar ring to them.

During the 1970s air defence of the armies was the responsibility of Frontal Aviation in the Soviet Air Forces; that of the homeland remained with the ten air defence districts of the independent PVO *Strany*. Consequently, when Frontal Aviation units were deployed in military districts of the Soviet Union, it was possible for fighter aircraft on neighbouring bases to be under different chains of command. At the same time the spread of surface-to-air defences released more interceptors for multi-role operations, a trend accelerated by the gradual introduction of the third-generation Flogger and Fitter and the imminent entry into service of Fulcrum and Flanker. It therefore increasingly made opera-

tional sense to put all regional defensive air assets under the one command. As a result interceptor units were reallocated on a geographical basis, so that the ground force combined-arms commander of each military district on the periphery of the Soviet Union assumed responsibility for all air defence.[61] Thus an air commander in a military district now has operational control of all his air assets except transport and Strategic Aviation. Not only should he be able to co-ordinate his air defences more thoroughly against low-flying aircraft or cruise missiles, but he could make fuller use of any multi-role capability his squadrons might have. Should his forces be required to advance into the theatre of operations to support an offensive – mounted for example by the armies of the Group of Soviet Forces in Germany – he would move, in theory at least, with fighter regiments which had trained alongside the ground forces and ground attack aircraft they would be expected to protect.

By 1980 the remainder of the former PVO *Strany* units had been retained in five air defence districts under the collective title of *Voyska* PVO (Air Defence Forces), covering strategically important regions such as Moscow and the Kola Peninsula as well as military districts with no Frontal responsibilities. This reorganisation, which preceded a wider regrouping of offensive units, offered opportunities for tighter control, simplified channels of command, greater concentration of force over a wider area, and more options for multi-role employment.

The re-equipment programme is explained in detail elsewhere, but the combined impact of three of its elements should be summarised. Radar installations manned by the air defence Radio Technical Troops have increased steadily in number since 1945, to an estimated total of 6,000 by 1984.[62] A three-layer chain comprising 3,000-mile-range Hen House radars, 1,500-mile Dog House installations, and Try Add close-in launch, control and target-tracking sites has been supplemented during the last decade by fixed-array battle-management radars at Pechora in Northern Siberia, Kiev, Abalakov in central Russia, and Komsomolsk in the Far Eastern Military District. Over-the-horizon radars and a major new PVO installation near Moscow have also been added to the network.[63] The

handful of Tu-126 AEW&C aircraft which have operated over North Russia, generally with the Tu-28 Fiddler long-range interceptor, are being followed into service by Mainstay. Some older radars are being retained in use, the effect of the new units is to improve both high and low-level warning and, by adding to the range of operating frequencies, to complicate opposing ECM. In addition, if Mainstay was to be deployed forward into Eastern Europe, it could contribute to early warning of attack by NATO tactical aircraft and would facilitate control of tactical air defences. Nevertheless, the vast extent of Soviet territory means that problems of timely warning and interception are likely to concern *Voyska PVO* for some years yet. Indeed, open-source reports of the two Korean airliner incidents – the 1978 fiasco and the tragedy of KAL 007 in 1983 – suggest that even after reorganisation and re-equipment there is still plenty of room for improvement in Soviet air defences.

After the April 1978 incident, when a Korean airliner wandered several hundred miles over

The Tu-126 Moss AEW&C member of the Tu-114 airliner and Bear strategic bomber family is being followed into service by the more capable Mainstay. (*Swedish Air Force*)

the Kola Peninsula before being intercepted, both the regional air defence commander and the C-in-C of PVO *Strany*, Marshal Batitskiy, appear to have been relieved of their commands. In 1982 Article 36 of Soviet Border Law was revised to allow Air Defence Forces to "Use weapons . . . against violations of the state border . . . when stopping the violation [if this] cannot be achieved by other means."[64] Exactly what happened in September 1983 may never be known because the details were so highly sensitive, in both East and West. The questions are many. Did Soviet radars detect and plot the progress of 007 over Kamchatka and the Kuriles? Did Soviet fighters in fact track the 747 for nearly two hours before shooting it down? Did the interceptor pilot really mistake the 747 for a much smaller and significantly different RC-135 intelligence-gatherer? Was the order to fire prompted by reflection on the fate of the Kola Peninsula commander five years previously? Was the flow of Soviet communications affected by awareness of the proximity of a USAF elint aircraft? Was there any confusion because the air commander in the Far Eastern Military District had assumed command of the ex-PVO *Strany* radars and interceptors only a few months before? Two things are certain, however: the United States Government will not have disclosed any information which could indicate the extent of its awareness of the effectiveness of Soviet air defences; and the Soviet High Command is not going to admit to a mistake or any other weakness. But circumstantial evidence strongly suggests at best military uncertainty, at worst gross inefficiency within the Soviet command, control and interceptor organisation.

The three most recent Soviet interceptors – Fulcrum, Flanker and Foxhound – should both strengthen the USSR's air defences and present interesting operational challenges. All three carry AI pulse-Doppler radars which can distinguish moving targets against background clutter.[65] The two-seat Foxhound, closely resembling Foxbat, is likely to be deployed against low-level supersonic intruders such as the USAF's B-1. The other two, similar in size and purpose to the F-16 and F-15, appear to be what would be described in the West as air-superiority fighters. As they come to be deployed in tactical air armies they will present an additional threat not only to NATO's offensive support, interdiction and counter-air operations but also to supporting aircraft which are not necessarily overflying the combat area, such as the E-3 AWACS, TR-1 and EF-111.

The problems posed by the recent improvements in Western air power have increasingly been the subject of analysis in Soviet military journals, as have the implications of the acquisition of aircraft such as Fulcrum and Flanker. During 1981 the theme of the need for initiative, creativity and "assertiveness" was re-emphasised in articles in *Aviation and Cosmonautics*, *Soviet Military Review* and other journals. But they differed in no longer concluding triumphantly with a successful first-pass attack. Colonel V. Babich, for example, in a series of articles in *Aviation and Cosmonautics*, extended the discussion of the 1970s by reflecting on the impact of new technology on old principles of combat, stressing the importance of "combat assertiveness, surprise, the skilful combination of manoeuvre and fire, and the constant search for the new in tactics. . . ." His broad context

The USAF's TR-1A battlefield surveillance aircraft will be increasingly threatened by the MiG-29 Fulcrum and Su-27 Flanker, with their clutter-rejecting radar and advanced missiles. (*Robbie Shaw*)

The growing flexibility of Soviet air-to-air missiles has led to debate about their effective use in complex dogfight engagements. This MiG-23MF Flogger-G is armed with AA-7 Apex (wing pylon) and AA-8 Aphid (air intake duct pylon).

was still that of the previous decade: the complementary nature of ground control and airborne leadership, but he also argued that to avoid premature disclosure of one's own position by early use of AI radar, it was possible to achieve surprise and enter into ''close air engagement with its own laws''. The objective was still however a first-attack success, achieved by ''a military strategem whose methods can be diverse and original''. Hence the need for fighter pilots who were not only experienced but also inventive, and commanders whose ''speed of thought out-distanced the speed of flight.''[66]

In a contemporary article a colleague of Colonel Babich stood back a little further from tactical details to reflect on the ways in which missile performance had affected the struggle for air superiority.

> At the initial stage of introduction of missile weapons their use was limited by stringent requirements as regards flight conditions of the carrier plane to ensure both the required accuracy and the necessary security. Therefore fighters equipped with air-to-air missiles were used at that stage mainly as interceptors. But in local wars the tactics of their employment changed: the methods and ways of attacking the enemy were determined to a great extent by attempts to adapt the interceptors and their weapons for group manoeuvre fighting. . . . How do the experts now conceive future air combat with participation of next-generation fighters? . . . Modelling of fighter air combat aimed at achieving air

superiority shows that the increased capabilities of weapons can change the tactical content of the attack stage. . . . It will become possible to launch the attack from a greater distance considerably exceeding the range of visual target detection. The probability of success will depend on the enemy's vigilance.[67]

Colonel Mikhailov's concluding paragraph introduced a very different idea, however. In addition to missile performance improvement, there was now a new generation of fighters:

> As regards the improvement in manoeuvre qualities of modern aircraft and the advent of new types of weapons, air combat is being modelled which incorporates transition from medium to small distances. Consequently, modern combat may include a fourth stage: manoeuvre to deliver a repeated attack in close combat.[68]

That ''fourth stage,'' essentially old-fashioned in-fighting, was the subject of a number of discussions in the Soviet professional press about how such close combat could best be achieved.[69]

The debate appears to have been opened by an article in *Aviation and Cosmonautics* in November 1981 which emphasised the detection range, all-aspect long-range missile capability and attack warning systems of modern interceptors, together with the relative difficulties of wingmen in long-range, low-intensity combat over wide areas. Subsequent articles disagreed strongly, emphasising the traditional effectiveness of two-ship and even larger formations. And lest anyone overlook the fact that air combat was only a means to an end, an account in December 1981 of a four-ship fighter-bomber sortie in Exercise Zapad-81 included a graphical account of the formation breaking into two pairs after a successful air-to-ground attack to deceive and draw a gun-camera bead on two enemy fighters.[70]

In 1984 the pressure for greater pilot autonomy was given the fullest expression in a practical analysis of the continued relevance of "freelance fighter combat".[71] First came reference to the successes of Second World War Heroes of the Soviet Union – and subsequently Marshals of Aviation – Pokryshkin and Golubev, followed by a quotation from Marshal Golubev himself:

MiG-27 Flogger-D pilots brief for a four-ship training sortie. (*Tass*)

Many pilots would like to fly freelance fighters, but not everybody could, due to a number of specifics . . . freelance fighter pilots must have the feel of a hunter in order to avoid falling prey themselves. He must be thoroughly familiar with the air and ground situation behind enemy lines, be skilled in instrument flying in clouds, and be an expert marksman in aerial gunnery. . . . There is no place here for uncertainty or confusion. . . .[72]

Then the article presented the "two main trends in the evolution of combat aviation," as analysed by a Western journal:

. . . increased mission orientation of strike aircraft, helicopters and air defence fighters through development of command and control systems (PLSS, AWACS), and efforts to provide a capability to deliver highly accurate stand-off cruise missile and air-to-surface missile strikes from friendly territory.[73]

Next, the statutory reference to the lasting value of ideological purity:

Because of this, bourgeois military theorists on the one hand seek to minimise the role of the human operator in battle, to take him out of the area where people's ideological conviction, will, and dedication to a just cause clash – the elements which in the final analysis determine the outcome of an armed struggle – while on the other hand they seek to ensure effective combat operations by their air forces, with the use of new equipment and tactics.[74]

In passing, those Western commanders who tend to forget the importance of manpower in air power might stop to reflect that, stripped of the ideological jargon, that sentence might just contain a point. The operational conclusions are similarly valid:

> . . . the fighter and air defence missile command and control system can be disrupted by ECM and fire suppression; but in order to combat the new offensive air weapons, it is necessary to destroy the weapons carrier and the command-control aircraft over enemy territory.[75]

Soviet commanders are fully aware of the significance to NATO of systems such as TR-1, EF-111 and AWACS, and of the resulting need for SAF interceptors to seek out their targets over NATO territory, using freelance fighter tactics. Moreover, aircraft such as F-14 and Tornado, carrying their own highly capable radar and

The Fairchild A-10A Thunderbolt II would be the NATO *Shturmovik* of any future European war, halting armoured assaults in their tracks while shrugging off battle damage that would put paid to a less rugged type. (*Robbie Shaw*)

fire-and-forget missiles, could operate autonomously in company with "lighter and smaller fighters". Thus, the writers conclude,

> . . . changes in the development of combat aircraft in modern conditions do not exclude extensive employment of fighter operations analogous to the freelance fighter combat practised in World War II.[76]

The scene is therefore set for the introduction and tactical employment of Flanker and Fulcrum, without any mention anywhere in the article of any Soviet fighter or tactics, and, more significantly, without reference to any kind of ground control, flight "discipline" or rigid formations.

A further air threat to Soviet ground forces has been the subject of debate: that from helicopters and other low-speed aircraft such as the USAF's A-10. The impact of the acquisition of Fulcrum and Flanker, with their look-down/shoot-down radars, and of Mainstay with its low-level detection ability, is indicated by the "suggested solutions" to the problem of low-speed, low-level air attack which appeared as recently as 1980, before the advent of pulse-Doppler-equipped fighters. Then pilots were advised to rely on "independent search" based on air patrol zones in which targets were likely to approach below radar. The problems of maintaining the correct height, bearings and position were to be minimised by training first over familiar terrain under close supervision. The adaptation of techniques used to attack ground targets was recommended, though the problem was acknowledged to be difficult because of "the capability of slow-flying targets to change the direction, speed and altitude of flight while the fighter manoeuvres and attacks . . . in operations over unfamiliar terrain, in all weathers, by day and night."[77]

The look-down/shoot-down capabilities of the fourth-generation fighters undoubtedly ease the problem, but by 1984 there was evidence that the SAF were considering another answer: the helicopter fighter. The discussion was again traditional, making reference to the "foreign press" and Western experience. Although the article's illustrations and conclusions ritually lambasted "the far-reaching marauding plans" of the US and NATO authorities, they were also factual and thought-provoking.[78] A combination of A-10s and AH-1 Cobra helicopters was reported to be three to four times as effective as a homogenous force in attacking tanks. Western experience had shown that high-speed fixed-wing interception of the helicopters had not been very successful, despite the improved lethality of heat-seeking air-to-air missiles. The fighters' high speed enabled them to close quickly, but restricted manoeuvre during aiming and firing at close range. Reaction time from airfields was longer and loitering more difficult than for helicopters, although on the other hand reaction time from a loiter zone was much shorter. Finally, the high cost of fixed-wing aircraft meant that they could not be deployed in larger numbers. Not only were helicopters cheaper by the unit but the training of their crews was less complex and crew replacement in combat that much easier. But above all, "fixed-wing fighters and ground attack aircraft have their own, more extensive missions, and to send them to engage helicopters violates the principle of economy of forces."[79]

Helicopters which are used to prevent enemy offensive suport helicopters from performing their mission should "work in close co-operation with airborne reconnaissance and control

entities in order to achieve success in combat". Moreover, the author went on, according to Britain's *Flight* magazine:

> . . . utilisation of the AWACS E-3A airborne command post and organisation of a long-range reconnaissance system employing high-altitude manned aircraft and drones will substantially expand capabilities to gather battlefield and air situation data on a real-time basis. Reconnaissance aircraft carrying synthetic-aperture radar should have the capability, without crossing the line of contact, to warn of the enemy forming a force of combat helicopters over his own territory, while an E-3A aircraft, with a radar operating in terrain-mapping mode, will track the movement of these forces (the effective radar cross-section of a combat helicopter is approximately equal to that of a fighter).[80]

On the face of it, that paragraph is nothing more than a perceptive analysis of the increase in NATO's ability to glean early information about impending helicopter attack. If however one reads "Mainstay" for "AWACS" and thinks of Foxbat-B or D and Foxhound then the outlines of a blueprint for yet another component of the Soviet air defences starts to emerge.

The blueprint is now beginning to acquire substance. A new military helicopter – the Mi-28 Havoc, likened to the AH-64 Apache – is undergoing trials, and Hokum, expected to be a dedicated air-combat type, is being developed.[81] Whereas previously Soviet combat helicopters have also been troop carriers, Havoc clearly is not. Its slim outlines are those of a weapon-carrier, whether air-to-ground or air-to-air. Press reports suggest that it is equipped with radar warning, infra-red decoy flares, a nose radar and forward-looking infra-red.[82] If so, its primary role could be offensive support. Equally, it could be armed with air-to-air variants of the SA-7 or SA-9 SAMs. In any event, it is beyond doubt that, as on several previous

Inset Foxbat-B would survey the battlefield from a stand-off position in the same way as Western types such as the TR-1A. (*Flug Revue*)

Right The Hughes AH-64A Apache is the Western equivalent of the Mi-28 Havoc. (*Hughes*)

occasions, ''theoretical'' discussion in the Soviet military press has foreshadowed the introduction of service hardware.

Summary

• Soviet provision for air supremacy over the combat areas, frontiers and heartland has attained a high degree of complexity and sophistication. The quality of the SAF's aircraft, weapons, early-warning systems, communications and organisation make it well nigh impossible for the Soviet Union, or her armies deployed in Eastern Europe, ever to be ravaged by conventional air attack on the scale of 1941.

The prestige and privileges associated with being a fighter pilot mean that the Soviet Air Forces have no shortage of candidates.

• The technological gap between East and West has been progressively narrowed.
• Soviet leadership is aware of the apparently endemic tendency in its armed forces towards over-rigid control, stereotyped operations, and disinclination to aggression and initiative, and is striving to eradicate them.
• It is possible that Russian thinking about the combined-arms nature of air supremacy is further developed than that of the West.
• In theory at least, extensive ground briefings are designed to consider as many airborne contingencies as possible to increase the chances of the right option being chosen at the right time.
• It is possible that responsibility for initial combat training is being switched from the squadrons to the flying training schools.[83] If so, experience and capability levels on the operational squadrons should increase, resulting in improved combat effectiveness.
• Evidence from defectors such as Belenko suggests that at least one award for aircrew achievement, the Sniper's Badge, is hard won

and highly prized, and that the best of Soviet pilots could individually be a match for their Western counterparts. This should not be surprising, given the prestige and perquisites enjoyed by fighter pilots and the resulting stiff competition for entry into the profession.

Fortunately for the West, there could be a sizeable gap between actual operational achievement and the theoretical potential outlined above. Several weaknesses have already been illustrated, notably in the areas of training and airspace management. Political interference persists, and there continues to be a need for perennial exhortations to greater initiative and aggression. The advent of new technology is sure to have brought additional problems to an air force which is still heavily dependent for groundcrew on short-service airmen and officers whose technological skills were already far below those of their Western counterparts even before the arrival of the third generation of aircraft during the 1970s. But the constant expansion of the Soviet national technological base, and of the colleges and universities which provide the manpower to sustain it, should gradually improve the quality of Air Force technicians.

As long as military expenditure is given its present priority, the Soviet Air Forces are unlikely to face the same economic constraints which occasionally force difficult choices of priority in the West. Moreover, the retention in Soviet service of equipment which would have long been obsolete in the West not only provides duplicated and overlapping systems but facilitates the recall and employment of reservists who had been familiar with them during their active service.

In any foreseeable contest for air supremacy the West should retain three priceless advantages: ability and character in depth among its aircrew; quality and professional expertise among its groundcrew; and superior aircraft, weapons and associated technology. But such is the priority given to air supremacy by the Soviet Air Forces that only if the West continues to nurture them will these advantages be maintained. Above all, it would be very foolhardy of the West to let images of Soviet rigidity, stereotyped behaviour, stifled initiative and inferiority of personnel and equipment obscure the fact of the SAF's single-minded drive to achieve and sustain air supremacy.

Notes

1 *Additional Insights* to *Billy Mitchell, Crusader for Air Power*, A. F. Hurley, Indiana Press 1975, page 142.

2 *The Air Forces in Battle and Operations*, A. N. Lapchinsky, Moscow 1932.

3 *On Features in the Development of Military Art in the Post War Period*, Maj-Gen M. I. Cherednichenko, *Military-Historical Journal* No 6, Moscow June 1970.

4 *Air Supremacy*, Lt-Gen P. Bazanov, *Soviet Military Review* 9–1980, pages 42–44.

5 Marshal of the Soviet Union N. Ogarkov, press conference, Moscow, September 9, 1983.

6 Col-Gen S. Golubev, *Aviation and Cosmonautics*, January 1984, page 1.

7 *Defending the Soviet Skies*, Marshal of the Air Force Y. Savitsky, *Soviet Military Review* 3–1977, page 11.

8 Statement by A. S. Shcherbakov, quoted by Alexander Boyd, *The Soviet Air Force*, Macdonald and Jane's 1977, page 111.

9 Boyd ibid, page 129.

10 E.g. *The Interaction of the Air Defence Forces of the Country with Air Defence of the Ground Forces in World War II*, Col-Gen of Artillery P. G. Levchenko, *Air Defence Herald* No 11 1976, page 144.

11 Boyd op cit, pages 148–149.

12 *The Russian Air Force in the Eyes of German Commanders*, Generalleutnant D. W. Schwabedissen, New York 1968.

13 Ibid.

14 *The Soviet Air Force*, Asher Lee, Duckworth 1961, page 72.

15 *Aim of a Lifetime*, A. S. Yakovlev, Moscow 1968, page 316.

16 *The Penkovsky Papers*, F. Gibney ed, Collins 1965, pages 265–266.

17 E.g. *Weapons and Tactics of the Soviet Army*, David C. Isby, Jane's 1981, pages 220–272.

18 *Air Defence and the Combined Arms Commander*, Col-Gen of Artillery P. Levchenko, C-in-C PVOSV, *Military Herald*, April 1976, pages 40–44.

19 Ibid.

20 Ibid.

21 Ibid.

22 Ibid.

23 *Air Defence Organisation, Important Mission of the Combined Arms Commander*, Col-Gen of Tank Troops M. Zaytsev, *Military Herald*, February 1979, pages 23–26.

24 *What kind of "enemy" is used in exercises?*, Maj-Gen of Artillery V. Zenchenko, *Red Star*, February 2, 1980, page 2.

25 Ibid.

26 *Controlling Planes in Aerial Combat*, Maj-Gen of Aviation L. Mikryukov, *Military Historical Journal*, September 1977, page 42.

27 Ibid.

28 Ibid.

29 *Fighter Aviation Tactics*, Moscow 1947, page 83, quoted by Mikryukov.

30 Mikryukov op cit.

31 *Difficult Attack*, Maj A. Fedotov, *Soviet Military Review*, August 1972, page 30.

32 *Interception Mission*, Lt-Col V. Belyaev, *Soviet Military Review*, June 1972, page 20.

33 Ibid.

34 Ibid.

35 Ibid page 22.

36 Ibid.

37 *Tactical Skill of a Pilot*, Maj-Gen A. Karikh, *Soviet Military Review*, June 1973, page 28.

38 Ibid.

39 Ibid.

40 *Initiative in Air Combat*, Karikh, *Soviet Military Review*, March 1973, page 24.

41 Ibid page 27.

42 *Pilots' Combat Readiness*, Col-Gen A. Borovykh, C-in-C PVO *Strany*, *Soviet Military Review*, January 1974, page 16.

43 Ibid page 18.

44 Ibid.

45 *Independent Target Search*, Lt-Col A. Fedotov, *Soviet Military Review*, April 1973.

46 *Group Co-operation in Flight*, Lt-Col Pryadko, *Soviet Military Review*, August 1972, page 35.

47 See for example *Air Combat Control*, Col A. Krasnov, *Soviet Military Review*, October 1975, pages 26–27.

48 Described in *Low-Level Intercept and Aerial Combat*, Maj M. Altynbayer, *Air Defence Herald* No 12 1978, pages 32–35.

49 *The Fighting Man's Initiative*, Lt-Gen G. Federyakov, *Aviation and Cosmonautics*, June 1979, page 5.

50 *A Tactical Setting for Every Flight*, Lt-Col G. Mikhailov, *Air Defence Herald*, 1983.

51 Ibid.

52 Ibid.

53 *Interceptor Fighter Pilot Discipline*, *Air Defence Herald*, January 1980, pages 30–33.

54 Ibid.

55 Ibid.

56 Ibid.

57 Ibid.

58 *Independent Search for an Airborne Target*, Col G. Mikhailov, *Air Defence Herald*, August 1979, pages 34–38.

59 Ibid.

60 *Soviet Military Power*, US Government Printing Office April 1984, pages 36–37.

61 Ibid page 55.

62 *Soviet Air Defense Systems Show Increasing Sophistication*, J. Bussert, *Defense Electronics*, May 1984, pages 75–86.

63 Ibid.

64 Quoted in Bussert, ibid,

page 76.

65 *Soviet Military Power* op cit, pages 37–38.

66 *Development of the Principles of Air Combat*, Col V. Babich, Lt-Col Yu. Kislayakov, *Aviation and Cosmonautics*, June 1981, pages 18–19.

67 *Air Combat*, Lt-Col G. Mikhailov, *Soviet Military Review*, July 1981, page 21.

68 Ibid.

69 The discussions are well illustrated in *Closing The Tactics Gap*, Capt R. J. Pennington USAF, *Air Force Magazine*, March 1984, pages 84–88.

70 *Flight Attacks the Battery*, Maj-Gen L. Supran, *Aviation and Cosmonautics*, December 1981, pages 6–7.

71 *Freelance Fighters*, Col Yu. Petrov, Lt-Col P. Isaev, *Aviation and Cosmonautics*, January 1984, pages 22–23.

72 Quoted by Petrov and Isaev ibid.

73 Petrov and Isaev ibid.

74 Ibid.

75 Ibid.

76 Ibid.

77 *Intercepting Low-Speed Targets*, Lt-Col G. Dovgalyonok, *Soviet Military Review*, July 1980, pages 21–22.

78 *Helicopter Versus Helicopter*, Maj-Gen (Res) M. Fesenko, *Aviation and Cosmonautics*, March 1984, pages 46–57.

79 Ibid.

80 Ibid.

81 *Soviet Military Power* 1985, page 65.

82 *The Soviet Mi-28 Combat Helicopter*, N. Cherikov, *International Defence Review*, 10/84, pages 1455–1458.

83 Pennington op cit. In August 1981 "an air firing and tactical training regiment under the command of Lt-Col V. Mamontov where students receive armament training" was reported to be at the Yeisk Higher School For Pilots, near Volgograd.

CHAPTER 3

Tactical offensive operations

DURING 1983 several Western defence journals identified a major reorganisation of the Soviet Tactical Air Forces. It was marked by an apparent disbandment of 12 numbered air armies deployed within the Soviet Union itself, together with three of the four deployed in Eastern Europe. Some observers postulated an outbreak of inter-service rivalry in which the Air Forces had been clearly subordinated to the Army. Others saw the reorganisation as a response to an increase in Western offensive capability. As is often the case when a major bureaucracy changes direction, the reasons are more likely to have been more complex, with roots well into the previous decade, if not even further back in the Bolshevik origins and Second World War experiences of the Soviet Air Forces.

As in the West, air power had little impact on the way that Russia fought in the First World War. Reconnaissance, interception and a limited amount of offensive support were peripheral to a conflict decided on land by ground forces, despite the publicity given to the single squad-

The Sukhoi Su-25 Frogfoot was designed to do the "down and dirty" close support work along the forward edge of the battle area. The type's credentials include an impressive load-carrying capability and flare dispensers for self-defence.

ron of Ilya Muromets four-engined "heavy" bombers. All activity was subordinated to the needs of the ground forces, and there was no move akin to British initiatives to establish an "independent" air force. When the "Field Administration of the Aerial Fleet" was subsequently established by the Bolsheviks after their 1917 success, it was largely manned by officers who had flown during the First World War and the subordination of air force units to army commanders was sustained. However, the Bolshevik commanders seemed to have a much sharper awareness of the potential of air power than had their Czarist predecessors, and in the revolutionary and counter-revolutionary campaigns of 1919 and 1920 aircraft dealt severely with cavalry, hit supply centres and strong-points, and dropped revolutionary leaflets. In the broad expanses of Russian territory even the relatively slow and cumbersome aircraft of the time could add a degree of mobility and concentration of force hitherto unknown. But there were few skilled mechanics available to service the aircraft, and the Bolsheviks quickly learned the value of rugged, standardised machines in simplifying maintenance. These three characteristics – close support of ground operations, organisation influenced by large geographical areas, and relative simplicity in aircraft construction – were to become the hallmarks of Soviet tactical aviation throughout the Second World War, known as the Great Patriotic War to the Russians, and beyond.

The Great Patriotic War, 1941–1945

Memories of the Great Patriotic War are assiduously fostered among Russians by the Soviet Government for a variety of political reasons. At the same time lessons from the war are used in the Soviet Air Forces as practical examples, along with studies of Western and Third World air activity since 1945, as guidelines for current operations and exercises.[1] The exception to this general pattern seems to be reorganisation, which is not usually accompanied by historical allusions. Were it to be so, the authors might have referred to the fact that before Marshal Timoshenko's shake-up of the military organisation in 1940, following the Finnish embarrassment, the tactical squadrons of the VVS (Soviet Air Forces) were assigned in brigade strength to the territorial military districts of the ground armies. Timoshenko's reorganisation included the formation of air divisions which could be assigned directly to an army or grouped to provide composite offensive support, air defence, and tactical transport to army groups to cover a major military district known as a "front". Below this "Frontal Aviation" were smaller divisional combinations: "Army Aviation" units were assigned to each ground army, with "Corps Aviation" units allocated at corps level. The "Timoshenko" organisation was designed to improve rapid response, co-ordination and

combined-arms control at all levels: the ideal sought by all tactical air forces. In fact the effect was to distribute the squadrons in penny packets, to the detriment of centralised command and concentration of force. After only nine months the operational weaknesses of the structure were repaired by a further reorganisation in March 1942. Tactical aviation was concentrated into air armies and allocated at frontal level only, with the air army commander assuming the position of air adviser to the front commander. The air armies comprised for the most part dedicated fighter, bomber and reconnaissance divisions which could be varied to match the requirements of the land battle. For example, the 16th Air Army, now well known in Eastern Europe, was formed with only 300 aircraft in August 1942 to defend Stalingrad; by the beginning of the battle of Berlin in 1944 it contained 2,183.[2]

Improved organisation was accompanied by improved aircraft, better training, more reliable communications and, above all, rapidly increasing numerical superiority. In 1942 the Soviet High Command had been forced to launch a campaign to improve morale and induce more confidence and aggression in both fighter and ground attack pilots. Considering their crushing defeats by the Luftwaffe over the previous 12 months and the inferiority and unreliability of aircraft such as the LaGG-3 and MiG-3, a certain diffidence among Soviet aircrew was not surprising. Over the next three years, although the Soviet aircraft industry could never match the quality of its German counterpart, its mass production made inferiority of performance largely irrelevant. By January 1945, 11 air armies and 155 air divisions comprising 15,815 aircraft faced a total Luftwaffe strength of 1,960.[3]

With numerical superiority came refinements to combined-arms operations. Tactical aviation's contribution to them took the form of reconnaissance information for the army commander; air cover for Soviet forces during the preparatory stage of the offensive and throughout its entire course; the winning of local air supremacy; close air support during the tactical breakthrough; destruction of enemy battlefield forces; blocking of enemy operational reserves; and cover for Soviet mobile groups while they destroyed the enemy's tactical reserve.[4]

The II-2 bore the brunt of the close support efforts accompanying the offensives which drove the Germans from Soviet territory in the latter years of the Second World War.

The continued emphasis on air supremacy has been dealt with in Chapter 2. Of equal significance to the post-war evolution of Frontal Aviation, culminating in the reorganisation of 1983, was the increase up to 1945 in the scope and effectiveness of offensive support in its various forms. While the majority of operations were launched against targets in the immediate area of the battlefields, an increasingly significant proportion attacked lines of communication, airfields and reinforcements up to 100 miles behind the front. Three related but distinct kinds of air support were used in the combined-arms offensives designed by the Soviet High Command to expel the German armies from Russian territory and drive them back across Eastern Europe. They are typified by the contribution of Frontal Aviation, and bomber units from the Long Range Air Force (LRAF), to the Byelorussian offensive in summer 1944. A total of 6,683 aircraft, almost 50% of available VVS strength, were deployed in five air armies and 16 LRAF divisions to support an offensive designed to destroy the German Army Group Centre and smash through Byelorussia to Poland and the Baltic States.

The attack was to be carried out by four fronts concentrating heavily on narrow sectors along a

488-mile section of the German line.[5] The first, "preparatory," air attacks were directed against heavily fortified German positions, artillery, tanks and reserves beyond Soviet artillery range. The second phase, close air support, comprised air cover and integrated attack on German units in close contact with the advancing Russian armies, much in the fashion of traditional Western close air support. In the third phase, known as "accompaniment," aircraft provided support for mobile groups exploiting penetrations of the German defences and moving up to 70 miles or more ahead of the main armies. At such times the tank armies were increasingly vulnerable to counterattacks from both flanks and, lying well beyond the range of their own artillery, were heavily dependent on aircraft for fire support. In fact, during the 1944 campaign the tanks outran the ability of the Frontal Aviation units to redeploy forward and sustain longer logistic lines, leaving themselves vulnerable to German counterattack. Nevertheless, the Byelorussian offensive was the clearest example of the ability of the Soviet High Command to concentrate offensive and defensive aircraft in large numbers on relatively small areas of major thrusts and to switch them swiftly and successfully to achieve overwhelming local air supremacy wherever it was required. The concept is enshrined in the *Soviet Military Encyclopedia*'s definition of "air accompaniment":

> Air accompaniment began to be employed during the Great Patriotic War as the final phase of air support when troops advanced deep within enemy defences. It usually took the form of sorties by Frontal Aviation sub-units, chiefly ground attack aircraft, either scheduled or called in from the command post. In crucial periods of battle (when troops were overcoming defensive lines at operational depth, warding off enemy counter-attacks, overcoming water obstacles from the march, etc.) successively alternating ground attack aircraft sub-units were employed continuously over the battlefield for a prescribed time (1–2 hours or more). Planning and control of air units participating in air accompaniment were accomplished centrally as a rule by the command and staff of the front and the numbered air force. The practice was to attach air formations to combined-arms field forces (formations) and sometimes to place them under operational subordination to the commander of the combined-arms field force (formation).[6]

The modern operational manoeuvre group (OMG) with its attendant air power, identified by a prominent Western defence analyst in 1982,[7] has its roots in the Operational Mobile Group of Operation Bagration, and the accompanying 153,545 aircraft sorties, in June, July and August 1944. The battlefield of the 1980s and 1990s would clearly be different from that of 1944 in many respects, not least the presence of nuclear weapons. But there is a continuity of doctrine underlying Frontal Aviation which has occasionally been obscured not because of change but because of different Soviet military priorities.

The air power of an operational manoeuvre group would include large numbers of the formidable Hind assault helicopter, armed with rockets and anti-tank missiles.

The eclipse of Frontal Aviation

With the deterioration in the closing years of the Second World War of relations between the USSR and the West, the factors influencing Soviet military policy began to change. By 1945 the German armed forces had been destroyed, the Red armies had established a *cordon sanitaire* across Eastern Europe, and the bulk of the Western armies and air forces had been demobilised. At this point Stalin saw a need to rearrange his military priorities, especially those associated with air power. The central Marxist-Leninist tenet of the inevitability of conflict between capitalism and socialism suggested that the single threat to the motherland came from long-range nuclear weapon-carrying bombers. The memories of the German attack in 1941 were still fresh, and bore out his own emphasis on surprise as an important principle of war. Consequently he directed Soviet military expenditure into air defence against Western attack and on long-range offensive weapons with which in turn to threaten North America. Among the many new aircraft which entered service between 1945 and 1956 only one, the twin-engined Il-28, was expressly designed for offensive support. The MiG-9, MiG-15 and Yak-15 were all designed primarily as interceptors rather than fighter/ground attack aircraft. A later Western intelligence estimate of the MiG-15 observed that it "was not well suited for the ground attack mission . . . [but] well suited for its primary mission, day interception against bomber aircraft . . ."[8]

Some Western analysts see the emphasis on fighters in this period as lending weight to their arguments that Soviet defence policy has in fact been driven by defensive fears rather than aggressive intent.[9] But air superiority was then and still remains intrinsic to Soviet combined-arms doctrine. There was little on the ground to oppose any Soviet move westwards between 1945 and 1950, and hence far less need to replace the Il-2 Shturmovik and its Il-10 successor. Moreover, there is evidence to suggest that Stalin himself opposed the replacement of the La-11 by jet aircraft:

When discussing the production of the heavily armed La-11 designed for ground attack in 1947 with Lavochkin, Stalin displayed a distinct preference for the proven piston-engined fighter as opposed to the unknown factor of Mikoyan's MiG-9. When Lavochkin recommended the production of his competitor, Stalin is reported to have said: "The La-11 is an aircraft in which all the defects have been eliminated, there is a pilot who can fly it and a mechanic to look after it. But what is the MiG? A heap of metal. . . ."[10]

The jet fighter on the other hand could contest air superiority either over the ground forces or over the homeland. Emphasis on air defence highlighted the fact that the Red armies were no longer likely to be the sole instrument of decision in any future war. Stalin was therefore compelled to give much greater priority to defensive and offensive air operations independent of ground forces.

Moscow's view of the shape of potential battle began to change again as NATO, faced with Soviet numerical superiority on the ground, began to introduce tactical nuclear weapons into Western Europe after 1953. They presented two threats. First, nuclear attack would devastate any Soviet forces massed for a traditional offensive. Second, even in the 1950s, they threatened an escalation which could extend the risks of a central European adventure back to the Soviet homeland. Nuclear missiles, nuclear-capable aircraft, and their associated command and control and storage areas therefore became targets of the highest priority in what became a modified form of aerial preparation for ground force attack. The definition of aerial preparation in the *Soviet Military Encyclopedia* includes the following:

Aerial preparation involves making simultaneous or consecutive strikes by frontal (tactical) aviation units and formations against objectives located at tactical and close operational depth. Such objectives can include those which cannot be destroyed by missiles and artillery, those capable of changing location just before strikes are made against them, and those requiring powerful aviation ammunition for their destruction.

The Sukhoi Su-7 underwent a radical redesign before emerging as the Su-17, a type much better suited to the demands of battlefield operations. (*Novosti*)

Long-range (strategic) aviation can also take part in aerial preparation. Nuclear strike resources, aircraft at the nearest airfields, control posts, tanks and artillery in areas of concentration and in fire positions, strong-points, centres of resistance, and water crossings are destroyed primarily by aviation during aerial preparation.[11]

This concept is clearly derived from the operational procedures in use in 1944. With the inclusion of "nuclear strike resources" among the targets, it has remained a fundamental role of the Soviet Air Forces in Western Europe for 20 years and probably contains one clue to the 1983 reorganisation. In the 1950s, however, such a reorganisation would have been pointless because the aircraft necessary to make it work were not even on the drawing boards. Indeed, during the 1950s production of manned aircraft may have dropped sharply at one stage, while those that did enter service with Frontal Aviation were ill equipped to carry out this formation's

offensive roles. In his memoirs Khrushchev maintained that missiles were given priority over aircraft, and the effects have been variously quantified in the West.[12] It also seems that the Il-10s were not replaced one for one. Yet even if they had been, both the MiG-21 and the Su-7 Fitter-A, which entered squadron service in the late 1950s, had very limited range and payload and were ill suited to the aerial preparation, close support and accompaniment roles. Nor did reconnaissance receive much better provision.

The demands of creating offensive support jet aircraft may have been beyond the capabilities of Soviet designers at this stage, or perhaps the relative stagnation was due to Khrushchev's preference for nuclear weaponry following hard upon Stalin's anti-jet prejudices. Whatever the reason, in the 1950s and 1960s Frontal Aviation would have been hard pressed to discharge all its offensive responsibilities. Paradoxically, while the aircraft production figures reflected Khrushchev's lack of interest in conventional forces, research and development work on several new combat aircraft must have begun at this time. The result was the appearance later in the 1960s of the MiG-23/27 fighter-bomber series, the virtual redesign of the Su-7 as the variable-

geometry, longer-range Su-17, V/STOL prototypes, and a new family of helicopters designed for offensive support. These third-generation aircraft could not have been envisaged, designed, tested and produced in the four years after Khrushchev's fall, nor, as some commentators have alleged, as a reaction to the Soviet conventional weakness revealed by the Cuba crisis. Khrushchev's demise would however have removed any check on their entry into service. It is probable that NATO's 1967 adoption of flexible response, with its implications of an ability to defend at varying conventional and nuclear levels, spurred the re-equipment of Frontal Aviation. But the Soviet aircraft procurement and development process is so protracted that it is incorrect to describe the programme as a response to NATO activity. More convincing is the proposition that despite Khrushchev's predilections the increasingly broad-based Soviet aviation industry had developed the capacity to produce aircraft much more suited to the offensive combined-arms doctrine, which had not been substantially affected by the arrival of nuclear weapons on the battlefield.

An unclassified CIA report in 1978[13] stated that

A combination of increased power and variable geometry meant that the Su-17 could carry twice as much 30% farther than the Su-7, and halved the required take-off run.

spending on the Soviet Air Forces grew at more than three times the rate for defence spending as a whole between 1969 and 1973, and that a very large proportion of SAF funds was allocated to Frontal Aviation between 1967 and 1977. As a result, by 1980 some 80% of the aircraft in Frontal Aviation had been built after 1969 and offered the greatly increased range and performance described elsewhere in these pages. At the same time, as explained in Chapter 2, a large part of the traditional responsibility of the Air Forces for short-range air defence of ground forces had been assumed by large numbers of surface-to-air missile systems, while longer-range offensive air power was supplied by the Su-24 Fencer and Tu-26 Backfire. The Soviet Air Forces could therefore provide short-range air support by means of helicopters or fixed-wing aircraft, air defence with a combination of interceptors and ground-based systems, and deeper accompaniment or aerial preparation from units of Frontal and Long Range Aviation. After a decade in which offensive and defensive capability had

The Sukhoi Su-24 Fencer-C is slightly smaller than the F-111 but shares its Western equivalent's all-weather capability.

increased greatly, there were thus good grounds for considering a reorganisation on the scale of those of 1941 or 1942.

The reorganisation of Frontal Aviation

As suggested in Chapter 2, the reorganisation of the air defence forces was probably prompted to some degree by the threat presented by air and ground-launched cruise missiles and the modernised B-52 force. The origins of the redistribution of offensive assets can be more readily identified. Marshal Ogarkov, then Soviet Chief of Staff, declared in July 1981: "It is not the front but the larger form of military operations – a strategic operation in the theatre of military operations (TVDs) – which should be regarded as the basic operation in a possible future war." In 1942 such an observation would have been irrelevant to the Soviet Air Forces because there

were no aircraft of any significance with the range to operate across an entire theatre. By 1980, however, both Fencer and Backfire, as well as the older medium and heavy bombers, could support ground forces several hundred miles from their bases or, conversely, operate well ahead of any deeply penetrating ground force. Moreover, there were enough of them to support more than one axis of advance. Nor could the divisional and army commanders of 1942 call on regiments of Mi-8 and Mi-24 helicopters for short-range support. Before the reorganisation, however, the helicopters were distributed in such a way as to make it difficult to concentrate force where it was most needed. Nonetheless, these aircraft could provide integral support below front level as a complement to fixed-wing support under air forces commanded at TVD level. By 1984 the net result of the reorganisation was a distribution of air assets so that command was much more commensurate with the combat radius of the aircraft within it.

Fixed-wing operations

Though fixed- and rotary-wing operations, and their accompanying air cover, are complementary in Frontal Aviation, for the purposes of this analysis they will be dealt with separately. Offensive fixed-wing operations include those performed by Su-17 Fitter, MiG-27 Flogger, Su-24 Fencer, Su-25 Frogfoot and the longer-range aircraft previously controlled by Long Range Aviation. They would be supported by tactical transport aircraft, various types equipped for reconnaissance and electronic combat support, and Mi-8 and Mi-24 regiments. Soviet and Western analysts are in broad agreement on the roles that offensive air power would play in the event of a NATO/Warsaw Pact confrontation. At an international seminar held in Bonn in July 1984 US and NATO analysts suggested that

> . . . a Warsaw Pact air operation would take place on three separate fronts in Western Europe, with Pact forces attempting to clear two or three separate air corridors per front. Each corridor is intended to be an area 25–30 miles wide and 100–150 miles deep. The

The Mil Mi-8 Hip-K is the communications jamming variant of the standard assault transport helicopter. Other versions can carry heavy weapon loads.

> plans call for rendering NATO air defence missiles and aircraft virtually ineffective in each corridor, allowing nearly free movement by Warsaw Pact aircraft. Presence of the corridor would allow Pact aircraft to slip through NATO air defence belts, then spread out and attack relatively unprotected rear areas. . . . Radar and communications systems would be attacked by a combination of electronic countermeasures, chaff and physical attack . . . by a combination of standard ordnance and the Soviets' increasing inventory of [AS-12] anti-radiation missiles.[14]

Such an attack is clearly a modern version of aerial preparation, apparently designed as an independent air operation but in fact closely related to a major offensive on land. The objectives of the attack and its critical importance to the Warsaw Pact were detailed in an article in the Polish *Air Force and Air Defence Review* of December 1981:

One of the objectives of a Warsaw Pact air operation would be the disruption of the opposing command and control systems. Spearheading this electronic campaign would be types like the Yakovlev Yak-28 Brewer-E ECM variant of the now retired attack aircraft

NATO war plans envisage the deployment of powerful groupings of armed forces in the European theatre of military operations. These groupings include a considerable amount of aviation of various types as well as missiles and nuclear weapons, which even in peacetime are constantly maintained at a high level of combat readiness. . . .

The experience of the most recent wars has shown that the air forces have always substantially affected the course of the combat action of their own troops. Consequently the problems of combatting air forces have been given much attention, and deserve still more, because a breaking up or serious weakening of the enemy's air force and nuclear missile groupings leads to a fast decline of his capabilities. By ensuring supremacy in the air, it creates favourable conditions for the action of troops taking part in the operations in the TVD. . . .

The aim of an air operation intended to rout (weaken) air force and nuclear missile groupings can be attained through:

- the destruction of aircraft and aircrew on airfields;
- the destruction of enemy aircraft and aircrew in aerial battles;
- the destruction of aircraft carriers at sea and in port;
- the destruction of operational-tactical missiles;
- the disruption of the command and control system and enemy aircraft guidance systems;
- the destruction of nuclear warheads, storage sites, fuel dumps, conventional weapons and material and technical supplies;
- the destruction, blocking and mining of airfields. . . .

The operation will be conducted under one single overall command and in accordance with a single concept and plan, so as to achieve a speedy routing of air force groupings and missile resources as well as to reduce the enemy's nuclear potential. It follows from this that an air operation has a combined-arms character. . . .

Enemy air force and missile groupings should first be routed in those areas where the principal tasks of the war are being implemented, ie in the main TVDs, where the strongest groupings of ground forces and air forces are deployed. The West European TVD is one of them. Therefore it can be stated that in no other theatre will the course of the operation depend so much on the situation in the air, on the skilful use of own air force, and on the breakup of enemy air forces. This is so because he who seizes initiative in the air will dictate his conditions. . . .

The great manoeuvrability of the enemy nuclear resources and air force, and their ability to escape from strikes very quickly, make it essential to achieve surprise and to deliver rapid, powerful and simultaneous strikes with a variety of forces. . . .

An analysis of the present state of aviation and its use in war and the prospects of further development indicates that aviation is still a powerful means of combat, capable of effective counter-action against troops both in a conventional and a nuclear war. This is why it is so likely that attempts will be made from the very beginning of a war to destroy it or neutralise the air forces. The routing or weakening of the enemy air force, nuclear missile groupings and AA defence system in

the TVD will have a significant impact on the effectiveness and success of the strategic operation and will be a factor determining an earlier attainment of its objectives. Hence the break-up of such groupings is one of the main tasks implemented in the strategic operation. The implementation of such tasks within a short time frame requires an air operation and the employment of considerable manpower and other resources of various arms of service. The decisive role in the execution of this task in conventional war belongs to the air force.[15]

The logic of the Warsaw Pact author and the analysis of the Bonn correspondent are complementary. NATO forces and missiles could inflict heavy losses on Warsaw Pact forces, just as German artillery and the Luftwaffe did in the Great Patriotic War. The objectives of the aerial

A Warsaw Pact onslaught would begin with a fire offensive against opposing troop concentrations, artillery and command posts by assault helicopters and supersonic fighter-bombers like the MiG-27 Flogger-D.

preparation offensive have therefore remained much the same while increased weapon effectiveness has magnified its possible consequences. Indeed, the Bonn correspondent did not develop his analysis far enough: the air corridors and subsequent "spreading out" are not an end in themselves, but a prerequisite to a successful offensive on land. Thereafter, both aeroplanes and helicopters could provide close air support or accompaniment as circumstances demanded. Aeroplanes with longer range and heavier payload might either operate further ahead of advancing ground forces or support them from bases deeper in the rear. For example, in the Warsaw Pact's Exercise DRUZ HBA-84, held in Czechoslovakia in February 1984, an attack began with a fire offensive in which "supersonic fighter-bombers and assault helicopters concentrated fire against the adversary's troop concentrations, artillery batteries and command posts."[16] Two days previously an enemy airborne landing had been destroyed by coordinated ground and air-launched counterattacks.

But not all exercises go quite so much to plan. In 1977 one motorised infantry battalion experienced elation and depression in short order, as the correspondent for *Red Star* explained:

The motorised infantry battalion commanded by Captain G. Sidnev attacked the enemy strongpoint from the march. The offensive was successfully developed. When the sub-unit reached a depression where the defenders' fire density was especially high, fighter-bombers appeared over the battlefield. The squadron led by Sniper Pilot Major N. Voynalovich made several aimed bombing strikes against the defenders and destroyed their command and control and fire plan. The accurate strike by the combat helicopters commanded by Military Pilot First Class Major V. Bolotov served the identical purpose. Aviation's active operations considerably eased the mission of the motorised infantrymen. They succeeded in overcoming the depression without decreasing the tempo of the offensive. . . .

However, several minutes later the motorised infantrymen were confronted with a

new test. The enemy employed powerful radio interference. Senior Lieutenant G. Grevtsov, motorised infantry company commander, lost communications with headquarters. The sub-unit was late with its approach to the assigned line. The defenders immediately took advantage of this, committing their tank reserve to the resultant breach. How vital it was to receive support from combat helicopters during these decisive minutes! However, neither the combined-arms commander nor the representative from supporting aviation called for the rotary-wing aircraft.[17]

This little cameo illustrates the close co-ordination expected of but not always achieved by armour, aeroplanes and helicopters, and the significant impact of enemy electronic warfare on pre-planned operations. The author contrasts the success of the "combination of forces . . . envisioned beforehand" with the fact that "the plan did not call for" rotary-wing support and neither the combined-arms commander nor his colleague from supporting aviation had the flexibility to deviate from it. The problem was compounded by the army commander's lack of understanding of the aircraft's combat capabilities and by the air liaison officer's lack of ground combat awareness. Not surprisingly, the article concluded with a request for much closer co-operation and understanding between the two and a willingness to extemporise when circumstances demanded it.

The elimination of such misunderstandings was one of the objectives of a major Soviet exercise, code-named Berezina, in the Byelorussian Military District in 1978. Its declared purpose was "to master co-ordination among the different arms of the service".[18] Lt-Gen of the Air Force P. Bazanov subsequently described the contribution of the air operations and assured the readers of *Soviet Military Review* that co-ordination between air and ground forces had been excellent:

Personal contacts of air unit commanders with those of ground forces was a pledge of success in their operations. Exchange of experience and knowledge of each other's

The Hind assault helicopter would number fire suppression among its various battlefield roles. The latest, Hind-E, version is particularly suitable for this task, carrying a twin-barrel 30mm cannon instead of the 12.7mm machine gun of earlier variants.

combat activities helped both sides to attain better mutual understanding and to grasp the peculiarities of a concrete combat situation. All this stood the participants of the exercise in good stead.

For instance, when breaking through the defences of the Southerners' army the advance of a motorised infantry battalion of the Northerners' army was suddenly checked by fire from emplacements and a tank reserve which they had failed to detect. The offensive could have come to nothing. Through the intermediary of the spotter plane the motorised infantry headquarters asked for a group of fighter-bombers to be sent to the battlefield. Despite poor visibility this group approached the target exactly at the preset time and delivered a powerful missile attack. The fire emplacements of the Southerners were destroyed and the advance of their tanks was stopped. The Northerners were thus enabled to press home the attack.[19]

This is significant not so much for the inevitable smooth success of the home team but for its testimony to increased pre-combat association between air and ground forces, the presence of a forward air controller, and the use of close air

support to eliminate hostile armour and artillery "exactly at the preset time". Accurate time over target is a virtue regularly emphasised in Soviet accounts of close air support. Conversely, this confirms NATO's valuation of its own counter-air effort, which would be designed to at least delay and disrupt Soviet close air support.

One type of exercise regularly practised by Warsaw Pact ground forces and in which aircraft play a major part is the river crossing. Significantly, the ground forces are not normally *defending* river crossings, but rehearsing for an offensive which would bring them up against several water obstacles in Western Germany. Such a crossing was practised in Exercise DRUZ HBA-84. On February 8, 1984, "The combined forces conducted an assault crossing of a major river in the face of a strong enemy defence. Tanks, BMPs and SPGs crossed the river on their own. They attacked the enemy on the other bank, under the cover of a massive fire suppression by low-flying supersonic fighter-bombers and assault helicopters, as well as by artillery.[20]

Above Neutralisation of enemy armour would be the responsibility of units flying the Su-25 Frogfoot.

Below The An-12 Cub-B – this example is being escorted by a Norwegian F-104 – is the elint version of Antonov's turboprop transport. The Cub-C stand-off jammer is distinguished by a larger chin radome, belly-mounted jammers in "canoe" fairings, and solid tailcone.

The open press report of DRUZ HBA-84 makes no mention of reconnaissance or radio-electronic combat, but it would be unusual if neither were employed. The Foxbat-B and D reconnaissance variants, operated by several regiments in Eastern Europe and carrying a variety of photographic, infra-red and radar sensors, would supply Warsaw Pact ground and air forces with fresh target information on NATO units. Indeed, the reconnaissance Foxbats have probably proved far more valuable than the original high-level interceptor.

The Soviet Air Forces place heavy emphasis on radio-electronic combat as an ingredient of offensive operations. The mainstay of tactical EW aviation since the early 1970s has been the Yak-28 Brewer-E, carrying active and passive jamming equipment and underwing racks for chaff dispensers and anti-radiation missiles.[21] It would escort fixed-wing aircraft on air accompaniment missions, backed up by the Cub-C variant of the Antonov An-12 in the role of stand-off jammer. Brewer is now being replaced by an EW variant of the Su-24.

Helicopter operations

In his review of Exercise Berezina in 1978 Lt-Gen Bazanov referred to the contribution of combat helicopters to offensive air support, implying that their use was still being extended:

> The tactics of their use continue to be developed during daily training on the ground or in the air. . . . During the last war there were no helicopters. Appearing later as a result of the creative efforts of design engineers they have become a formidable and highly manoeuvrable weapon.[23]

By 1986 that assertion, unlike most of the remainder of the report, was a major understatement.

The designers who have had the greatest influence on Soviet and Western helicopter design respectively were both Russians. Igor Sikorsky made his impact in the USA after emi-

Soviet assault helicopter operations continue to be based on the Mil Mi-8. This is the Hip-C variant, identified by the two weapon racks mounted on the cabin sides.

grating there before the Second World War. Mikhail Mil was one of three designers who took up a 1946 challenge to produce a communications helicopter within 12 months. His Mi-1 went into production in 1949 and entered SAF service in 1951. The following year Mil began work on what was to become the Mi-4, NATO code name Hound, which could carry either 14 troops or 1,600kg of freight. About 800 Mi-1s were built, and some 3,400 Mi-4s had been delivered by 1969.[24] In 1961 the turbine-engined Mi-8 Hip was demonstrated at the Tushino air display. Although only slightly larger than Hound, it could carry 24 armed troops.[25] Since 1961 it has been progressively modified to carry a variety of machine guns, bombs, rockets and anti-tank guided missiles. In 1983 it was estimated[26] that over 7,500 were in civilian and military service. By 1984 it was the primary assault helicopter in Soviet armies and military districts.

Developed at the same time as the Mi-8 was the Mi-2 Hoplite, designed as a turbine-powered replacement for the Mi-1. Uniquely, series production of Hoplite was undertaken by the Polish Government from 1964 onwards. Subsequently some 2,000 have entered SAF service as utility helicopters, carrying up to eight troops or anti-tank missiles. It is also used for reconnaissance, infiltration and training.

These Mi-2 Hoplites were photographed at a Soviet base in East Germany.

In 1971 a very different and altogether more formidable kind of helicopter left the drawing board. Its predecessors, the essentially passenger-carrying Hips, Hoplites and Hounds, had been converted into attack helicopters by the strapping on of air-to-ground weapons. The Hind was intended from the outset to be a kind of flying tank. Some sources allege that its design was influenced by AH-1G HueyCobra operations in Vietnam, while others trace its ancestry to the Il-2 Shturmovik.[27] Certainly there does seem to have been some ambiguity in its origins because it is not purely an attack helicopter, being able also to carry eight armed troops. In 1974 a Czechoslovak source observed that it was ''armed to clean up an area and unload a dozen troops there''.[28]

Development of Hind was accompanied by debate in the Soviet military press. In 1970 it was observed: ''A substantial shortcoming of armed helicopters is admitted to be their vulnerability to the fire of the enemy's ground weapons. . . . To reduce [their vulnerability] intensive work is being conducted in armouring their vulnerable places. . . .''[29] Since then, however, as Hind has evolved into a formidable attack helicopter, Soviet writings have concentrated upon its utility in combined-arms operations rather than expressing doubts about its effectiveness. By 1984 over 800 Hinds were believed to be in service with the Soviet Air Forces,[30] the vast majority under Army control although manned entirely by Air Force aircrew.

Above Starting out as a troop-carrier capable of suppressing opposition in the landing zone, Hind has evolved into an increasingly heavily armed attack helicopter.

Below The Hip-E variant of the Mi-8 is standard equipment with Soviet Army support forces. It is armed with four Swatter anti-tank missiles and two triple stores racks capable of carrying a total of 192 unguided rockets.

After the 1983 reorganisation they became part of "army aviation," which in practice meant that army commanders were allocated their own attack helicopters. For example, each of the five ground armies of the Group of Soviet Forces Germany had 60 helicopters: two squadrons of Hind-D/E and one of Hip-E. A further flight of six Hinds was allocated to each divisional commander.[31] It seems that this part of the reorganisation was intended to enhance the integration of the combined-arms offensive by reducing close support and accompaniment response times and by locating a senior air adviser with the ground force commander. This move has two other implications. First, such dispersal of short-range air assets is all very well if it can be confidently expected that they will be in the right place at the right time and will not have to be diverted to concentrate force in a different part of the theatre. If the organisation expects to be able to dictate the critical areas of combat such confidence would be well placed. Second, such assets can only be confidently dispersed when the high command believes that each front or army can be well provided for in all circumstances without having to draw on the assets of flanking armies. By 1983 the Soviet High Command was confident enough on both counts to allocate the helicopters to individual armies.

Helicopters in support of the main offensive

Over the last two decades Soviet ground forces have been extensively modernised and reinforced to fit them for high-speed, concentrated offensives spearheaded by tanks, armoured personnel carriers and artillery. "The Warsaw Pact image of the future battlefield is no longer one characterised by static lines but one which will coalesce into a deep belt of minor battles with major combats developing on several axes," asserted a pre-eminent British analyst in 1984.[32] One might argue that the Russians have not envisaged static lines since the massive offensive of 1943, but the analysis of the current Soviet view is well founded. The "theatre of operations" (TVD) concept mentioned by Marshal

Ogarkov in 1981 was explained later that year by a Polish naval writer who related it to the experiences of the Second World War:

> A theatre of military operations constitutes, generally speaking, a part of a theatre of war. . . .
> . . . the dimensions of a theatre of military operations should be determined by the need to create suitable conditions
> (1) for the concentration and development of the necessary forces and,
> (2) for continuous functioning of the rear and of the lines of communication.
> During the Second World War the width of land theatres of military operations amounted to 300–600km and their depth to 800–1,000km; contemporary theatres of military operations can have much greater dimensions. . . .
> . . . the depth of theatres of military operations nowadays depends substantially on the character of the operations, and especially on their depth. Contemporary offensive operations are characterised by a great capacity to penetrate into the enemy operational groupings; and by manoeuvrability and a high rate of action. It is these very characteristics which are amongst the most important factors determining the depth of contemporary theatres of military operations. . . .
> . . . the main theatres of military operations are those areas in which, due to the political, geographical, economic or operational strategic situation and in relation to the international balance of forces, the main strategic groupings of the combatants are in action.[33]

Within the TVD the helicopter would give close air support to the main ground forces, supplementing artillery and concentrating firepower in the manner observed in Exercise DRUZ HBA 84 in Czechoslovakia, either against enemy defensive strongpoints or to check his counterattacks. In such offensives the attack helicopter could overfly "accidents of terrain," operate over territory made impassable to ground forces by weather or contamination, and be used against many targets other than tanks. Training in the combined use of assault and attack helicopters

Soviet attack helicopters would overfly "accidents of terrain" – rivers, flooded areas, mountains – to extend the area of influence of the advancing ground forces. This is the initial variant of the Mi-24, Hind-A.

had been developing for several years before Exercise DRUZ HBA 84. One such exercise was reported in *Red Star* in 1978. A motorised rifle battalion was tasked with the seizure of a bridgehead on a river bank and the support of the main-force river crossing. The enemy anti-aircraft defences at the river were attacked by Hinds and the banks then immediately secured by riflemen lifted forward by a squadron of Hips; the main force then advanced.[34]

Helicopter operations are believed by some analysts to be of particular importance to the activities of the operational manoeuvre groups, formations of at least divisional strength and designed for rapid penetration of NATO defences along more than one axis from the first days of a Warsaw Pact offensive.[35] A detailed exposition of the combined-arms relationships within the OMGs was given in a Polish source in February 1982:

> The common feature of the operational activities of marching [manoeuvre] groups and raiding detachments is that they act detached from their own main forces and penetrate deep into the enemy rear to operate for a limited period; consequently they perform tasks at a considerable distance from the main forces, although in close co-ordination with them and always to their advantage. These troops are intended mainly for destroying groupings of nuclear missiles, command posts, radio-electronic means of combat and AA defence weapons. They are also used to prevent the withdrawal of enemy troops; to delay the advance of his reserves from the depth; to paralyse his system of logistics; to capture major important areas and objectives; and to hold these till the approach of their own main forces. . . . an analysis of the operating conditions of operational man-oeuvre groups and raiding detachments indicates that they will be regularly exposed to offensive countermeasures by enemy ground forces and also to strikes by his fighter-bomber aviation and close support helicopters. In addition, in operating, as they often do, a considerable distance away from their own main forces they must maintain – if need be – their ability to keep replenishing their material resources, to reinforce their combat establishment with fresh manpower or

equipment, and also to evacuate casualties. Moreover, they should be in possession of full and up-to-date information about the activities of enemy troops, and especially about the likely targets of enemy attacks. . . .

. . . The air echelon of these forces should consist of assault and multi-purpose helicopters (including some equipped with special signals apparatus and adapted to commanding troops from the air). With such helicopters, based and operating directly with the formation of the fighting troops, away from the main forces, it is possible to implement a number of fire and special tasks. It also facilitates a swift reaction to any changes in the combat situation and the gradual adjustment of tasks according to the pace of these changes. Furthermore it reduces the time needed to carry out tasks set in response to requests from the battlefield, and also makes it possible to concentrate aviation assets on the implementation of the most important tasks in a given tactical situation. In these conditions helicopters, owing to their flying and combat characteristics, are capable of providing a systematic surveillance of gaps, open flanks and the rear of troops; of attacking from ambushes in circumstances which place the enemy under the greatest disadvantage; and even of engaging small groups of enemy forces which have penetrated into the attacking formation. Operating in this way, helicopters can increase the combat potential of the raiding and manoeuvring forces, and consequently increase the pace of the offensive of the main ground forces.[36]

In this unusually sober analysis of the risks of OMG operations the Polish writer assumes that the groups would be fighting under conditions of Warsaw Pact local air supremacy, although that does not tally with his concern about NATO fighter-bomber and armed helicopter counterattacks. Nevertheless, even assuming friendly skies, he still expects ''a sizeable loss rate among helicopters,'' presumably from ground fire. This clearly suggests that he for one is not convinced of Hind's invincibility. And that is not the only penalty for deploying helicopters well forward with the ground forces. They require an integral

Above Soviet tactical transport helicopters would be used to land forces to oppose enemy units which had succeeded in penetrating the attacking formation. Here a squad disembarks from a Hip-C.

Right The replenishment of an OMG could be handled in part by the impressive Soviet heavy-lift helicopter force. This is an Mi-26 Halo. (*Air Portraits*)

ground support team which is unlikely to match the mobility of the tracked armoured vehicles and will therefore inhibit the activities of the OMG itself. It is not always easy to locate suitable terrain for a helicopter base and, once located, it must be protected from both air and ground attack. Finally, heavy firepower implies a need for regular large-scale replenishment, resulting in additional air supply to the OMG and further logistic complexities.

If on the other hand helicopters were to operate from bases in the main force area, so avoiding the penalties of forward deployment, ''the action of aviation of the ground forces [helicopters] in such conditions is hindered and sometimes rendered altogether impossible by the fact that the operational manoeuvre groups and raiding detachments may operate at distances exceeding the maximum combat ranges of helicopters. In addition, helicopters may suffer considerable losses from ground anti-air defence during their repeated flights between their operational area

and their bases in the first echelon of the main forces. This concept of using helicopters in support of troops engaged in raiding and manoeuvring activities can only be employed, therefore, when these troops are operating at short distances away from the main forces and when there is a very considerable suppression of the enemy anti-air defence and troops in general."[37]

The analyst's solution is a rather unconvincing compromise combining operations from main bases with replenishment from the OMG, which thus continues to be burdened with the impedimenta of the helicopters while losing the rapid response resulting from integral operations. But, perhaps mindful of some of the interests involved in the debate, he concludes that "it would be rash to prejudge a priori the acceptance or rejection of any variant of the use of such aviation in support of these troops. The choice should be made, as usual, in the light of the operational-tactical situation."[38]

One of Hind's functions in battle would be the escort and support of *desant* forces operating ahead of the main thrust.

Finally he summarises the traditional accompaniment contribution of fixed-wing aviation, distinguishing between "aviation of the ground forces" and "the air force". Aircraft, as opposed to helicopters, would provide air cover, detection and destruction of forces capable of counterattacking OMGs, and air supply. Other tasks, such as direct support, tactical reconnaissance and provision of cover for *desant*s, are to be shared with helicopters. A *desant* is an attack by airborne forces on specific targets ahead of the main force attack, or perhaps even ahead of an OMG thrust. The attack might be of company strength, as in an exercise over hilly wooded country described in *Red Star* in November 1983.[39] The assault force was placed by helicopter in the enemy's rear area and despite a heated battle succeeded in locating and destroying the enemy's command and control post. It was then joined by the battalion's main forces and the

whole formation was airlifted by helicopters, not back to their own lines but to the battle area to take the enemy's main force in the rear. As they joined combat they were given supporting fire from combat helicopters. Needless to say, the exercise was an unqualified success and a masterpiece of combined operations. But despite the artificiality of the scenario and the unrealistic assumption of complete air supremacy, the value of "vertical envelopment" in fluid combat conditions is self-evident.

The study concludes: "The air force can provide the most effective support and protection for operational manoeuvre groups and raiding detachments acting away from the main forces." But the overall question of aviation's contribution is still far from resolved: "However, air force operations in support of these troops are subject to restriction; many practical exercises and theoretical studies are required to work out the best ways of employing the air force to the benefit of these troops."[40]

It is tempting to draw too many conclusions from one article in one journal written by a relatively junior officer. Nevertheless, Major

Michalak's study illustrates the wide gap which can exist between military theory and the often unco-operative facts of battle. Forward deployment of any aircraft during ground combat, however self-contained, is a time-consuming business. It is difficult to co-ordinate with fast-moving ground forces – as General Guderian and the Luftwaffe in France, and General von Bock in Russia, both came to learn. Helicopters, even the Hind, are vulnerable both in the air and on the ground when compelled to stay close to hostile forces. Not for nothing do Warsaw Pact writers emphasise the need for cover "on the flanks". Sweeping offensives on separate axes mean that well disciplined defenders are left with very stretched-out targets and relatively small areas of enemy territory to traverse to deal with them; hence the particular vulnerability of improvised helicopter replenishment areas.

There may however be a clue in the debate exposed by Major Michalak – assuming that there is a debate, and not simply one uncertain Polish major – to the potential use of the Su-25 Frogfoot in the European theatre. It would have the range to support the OMGs from the main force area. Its additional speed, manoeuvrability, firepower and armour might make it a valuable addition to ground force aviation and a complement to both Hind and the MiG-23/27 and Su-17 fighter-bomber units, provided that tactical air supremacy has been achieved.

Reconnaissance

Not all Warsaw Pact studies of helicopter operations are as thoughtful as that of Major Michalak. One regular writer on helicopter operations described the "increasing role" of rotary-wing aircraft in providing the all-arms commander with essential information on the enemy and associated terrain. The following list of tasks suggests not only that the helicopter must be indispensable for reconnaissance but also that the Warsaw Pact must use most of its several thousand machines in that role:

At the present time the most typical combat reconnaissance missions carried out with the use of helicopters are: obtaining information on the enemy manpower and matériel used in different kinds of fighting, including nuclear weapons, the air defences of formations, artillery, control posts; disclosing the enemy grouping, ascertaining the layout and engineering organisation of defence lines and zones, the location and activities of the reserves, particularly armoured subunits and units; examining the condition of ground

Complementing Soviet helicopters in the battle zone would be the Su-25 Frogfoot, capable of carrying large loads of ordnance and surviving in the face of intense air defences.

communications and the nature of the terrain in the directions of the friendly and enemy actions; revealing contamination areas and zones, road blocks and flooded areas; carrying out target designation and fire adjustment.

During an offensive helicopter reconnaissance is effected primarily in the interests of subunits acting in the direction of the main blow, its purpose being to obtain the information necessary for the commander to take a timely decision in order to secure the required rate of advance and to fulfil the combat mission in the assigned time.

During the breakthrough of enemy defences reconnaissance helicopters establish the direction of counterattacks by the enemy reserve, favourable directions of advance and lines for committing friendly

second echelons and reserves to action. In the event of an airborne landing, reconnaissance helicopters collect data on the conditions of helicopter flight and landing on the designated grounds, on the enemy AA defences along the flight routes and in the landing area, on the location and nature of anti-landing obstacles, and the location and nature of combat actions of subunits detailed to fight invasion forces.

In crossing water barriers, reconnaissance helicopters obtain information on the nature of the river, its depth, speed of the current and type of bed and banks. They also select favourable approaches to crossing areas, establish departure lines and zones, composition of enemy groupings, nature of actions and presence of defensive installations on the near and far banks. When advance parties are sent out, helicopters select the most favourable routes of movement, detect obstacles on the route, establish the degree of passability of broken-country sectors, availability, loca-

Among the types used in the helicopter reconnaissance role by the Warsaw Pact is the Mi-2 Hoplite. (*Tass*)

tion and condition of bridges and other important tactical installations and engineer constructions. Simultaneously with route reconnaissance helicopters reconnoitre the enemy before the front line and on the flanks, disclose obstacles and routes for bypassing them, and also enemy-free sectors of the terrain.

In anticipation of a meeting engagement, and when pursuing the enemy or withdrawing, reconnaissance is assigned the following missions: to disclose quickly the concept of the enemy's actions, choose the most rational direction of the main effort, favourable deployment lines for march security elements and for the main forces, artillery fire positions and location of control posts. In fulfilling these missions, helicopters carry out efficient reconnaissance of the enemy on the flanks and in the gaps between units acting in different directions and isolated from the main forces, and also before their front line and in the rear.

Being capable of examining vast areas in a short time, helicopters quickly disclose various obstacles, eg road blocks, anti-tank ditches and dragon's teeth, and even minefields if provided with the necessary equipment.

In defence, helicopter reconnaissance is carried out for uninterrupted observation of the enemy's actions and to disclose changes in the composition of his manpower and equipment. When the enemy units begin advancing for the attack, reconnaissance helicopters are used to disclose positions and lines on which enemy nuclear and conventional weapons and first-echelon subunits are deployed, and to designate targets to friendly fire weapons, including combat helicopters. Much attention is given to determining the take-off time, flight routes, composition and landing areas of enemy landing forces and the actions of his combat helicopters.[41]

Nowhere in the article is there any mention of the limitations or practical problems of the kind described by Major Michalak. Yet it may be in such detailed exposition of possible roles that the Warsaw Pact's imaginative and comprehensive use of helicopters has its origins. They are also used as aerial command and relay posts, for communications and radar jamming, for minelaying, for laying smokescreens, for chemical and nuclear radiation monitoring, and for forward air control in addition to their main functions of close air support and tactical air mobility.[42] Later marks of Hind have been fitted with 30mm cannon which may be designed for use against other helicopters. Certainly the single-minded exponent of the helicopter as a reconnaissance vehicle quoted above also envisages it in air-to-air combat:

Just as tanks have always been the most effective weapon against tanks, helicopters are the most efficacious means of fighting helicopters. Use of helicopters by both warring sides will inevitably lead to clashes between them. Like tank battles of the past wars, a future war between well equipped armies is bound to involve helicopter battle. . . .

. . . Proceeding from the character of a modern combined-arms battle, helicopter

Even the formidable Hind has proved vulnerable to comparatively light ground fire when carrying external loads. This impression shows one Hind, escorted by a second, spraying a chemical agent. (*Department of Defence*)

battles, and also fighting between helicopters and airplanes, are most likely to take place during escort of attacking land forces by helicopters, carrying out missions to destroy control points, nuclear attack weapons, helicopters on the ground, and other objectives.

In all these cases combat helicopters may fulfil missions to destroy aerial targets, co-operating either with the land forces or with each other.

If combat helicopters are used to destroy similar enemy machines, they can operate from ambushes by waiting under cover for an enemy air raid in order to take off and make surprise missile launchings. More often than not such tactics will be used in a defensive battle, while offensive operations will call for more resolute and active actions.[43]

The author of this article also gives an insight into yet another kind of Soviet rotary-wing development:

Research is being carried out to develop machines possessing still higher manoeuvrability and survivability, capable of fulfilling combat missions in complicated weather conditions both by day and by night, quickly transmitting exact data on the enemy, landing reconnaissance and sabotage parties and subsequently evacuating them. It is intended to provide new helicopters with highly sensitive reconnaissance instruments, infra-red lateral and front view stations, computers and efficient radio facilities for detecting a target and warning of its approach. To extend the depth of air reconnaissance, new helicopters are envisaged carrying a side-looking radar. Work is also being carried out to develop single-seat collapsible helicopters for use as light air scouts. One version is said to weigh 118kg (maximum take-off weight is 250kg), and to have a range of nearly 400km and a cruising speed of about 140km/hr. A few dozen armed scouts, each provided with such a machine, can be airlifted to a designated area by a troop-carrying helicopter and return to base independently after fulfilling their missions.[44]

Aircraft effectiveness in offensive operations

General Belov's reference above to improved all-weather effectiveness and reduced vulnerability highlights two major current limitations on Warsaw Pact helicopter operations. Others mentioned in the Soviet press have included a poor level of crew training; lack of pilot initiative; vulnerability of assault helicopters to light ground fire, especially when carrying external loads of bombs and rockets; insufficient helicopters to fulfil the demands of operational doctrine (hardly surprising in view of the extent of General Belov's vision); problems of crew training and fatigue as a result of the low flying necessary to evade NATO air defences; accidents with high-tension cables; and airspace management difficulties in a heavy AA environment.[45]

Some of these factors also affect fixed-wing aircraft operations. Fixed-wing aircrew appear to move directly from flying and general weapons training to their operational squadrons, unlike their RAF counterparts, for example, who pass through an operational conversion unit before reaching their squadrons as fully operational pilots needing only the polish of experience. Articles in the Soviet press suggest that operational conversion can be a rather chancy business, heavily dependent on the quality of squadron leadership. For example, in the Far Eastern Military District:

In leading subunits, preparations for the reception of young pilots are usually made long before they arrive. The lieutenants are acquainted with the combat traditions of the unit. Experienced instructors study the requirements of the guidance documents with them and discuss the particular features of the aircraft which is to be mastered. A methodological council then refines the pilot training programme. This preparation permits young fliers to begin combat training immediately and instills a businesslike attitude in them.[46]

Both instructor pilots and their young charges are checked by the unit's methods council, which clearly has the support of the commanding general:

The practice of discussing the results of the first three to five flying shifts in the methodological council merits approval. By this time the individual traits of the young pilots and the methodological successes and errors of their instructors are clearly determined. It is time to correct the actions of the flight commanders and to specify the number of flights by exercise type, taking into account the individual traits of the pilots. The recommendations of the methodological council must be effective and well-founded. The methods of analysis used by the methodological council (headed by officer V. Feoktistov) are instructive. The council thoroughly accounts for the lieutenants' mistakes at different stages of the flight. Then a table is compiled showing which mistakes are repeated most frequently, in which flight, and what tendency is developing. Young pilots are often invited to a meeting of the methodological council. Their engineering training permits the lieutenants to fully analyse their actions during the flight and to find the causes for failure.[47]

But such individual care, attention and encouragement is not practised in every squadron:

. . . By the appointed time, the lieutenants had completed the combat training plan and their socialist obligations. However, Lieutenant N. Syrbu failed. Yet it would seem that he had the makings for success and becoming a rated specialist along with his comrades.

However, the professional training of the young officer was delayed because he was suspended from flying for a long time. It is a harsh punishment to sit on the ground when your comrades are flying. Only an officer's gross infraction of the flying rules makes it necessary for the commander to temporarily remove his subordinate from the sky. It was hardly necessary to take such severe measures in the case of Lieutenant Syrbu since his only fault was incorrect use of the brakes while taxiing.

Unjustifiably harsh punishments are unfortunately sometimes substituted for painstaking individual work with young officers. Naturally, this does not contribute to quality execution of flying missions and socialist obligations.

The pilot's "socialist obligations" must be discharged in a corresponding spirit of socialist competition:

> It is no secret that young officers take socialist competition to heart and actively participate in it. A young person feels the need to compete in skill and studies more strongly. In collectives where there are many young people, the shoots of innovation sprout more often. . . .[49]

But some of the younger pilots seem to need rather more encouragement than they used to:

> . . . Nevertheless, in some subunits the flame of competition is barely glimmering. Frequently the reason for this is that young officers don't take part in the competition. Their names, naturally, are included in the list of competitors but they are not to be seen among the victors. Why? Because young pilots do not always measure up to the aces where skill is concerned. This is especially true of recent school graduates.[50]

Seven years after the above was written, methods councils were still being credited, in the European theatre at least, with a major influence on the acquisition of combat skills by new squadron pilots. The training of rookie pilots was still a time-consuming business but there were now hints of a search for economies in both time and material. The extent of the training required is,

because of the lack of OCUs, far greater than in comparable NATO squadrons. Indeed, one example suggests that even more basic flying skills have sometimes to be taught on the operational squadron:

> After acquiring skills in flying in elements and flights, pilots begin working on mutual fire support and tactical co-ordination. During this period the lead pilots work on learning skills to control their groups in the air. Tactics become more complex with each new exercise and a variety of strike delivery methods are rehearsed at a particular gunnery range.[51]

Thereafter the pilot begins to take part in combined-arms exercises with ground units and helicopters. In this one four fighter-bombers are tasked to destroy an aggressor's tactical missile site:

> . . . And now a haze obscured the horizon and seemed to dissolve the taiga-covered hills. Lt-Col Tyumin decided to proceed to the target area in open formation. On the final leg each pilot would make an independent search for the target. Following the second target pass, the next element would head for the target. The bomb bursts would indicate target location.
>
> The fighter-bombers took off on schedule. They passed the descent point. The aircraft proceeded at minimum altitude. Hilltops flashed under their wings and orientation was getting more difficult, but there were no deviations from the ground track. Radio silence was maintained.
>
> Avoiding threat areas, the element approached the reference point. The conspicuous curve in the rail line and the village flashed by. They reached the forward line of troops. The next instant Tyumin saw smoke on the ground, marking the forward edge of the battle area. He glanced at his stopwatch – right on schedule. The motorised riflemen were also operating with precision.
>
> Getting his bearings, the flight leader swung to the right, and the fighter-bombers were soon over a lake. The canal lay ahead. The pilots looked the ground over closely.

The bend in the canal. A turn and they should be at the target in 30 seconds.

The aircraft proceeded to climb. They now had to spot the missiles, and the sooner they did so, the more accurate the strike would be. Seconds counted. What helps a pilot most at a time like this? Intuition, experience, knowledge, skill? All these factors together! Years of work and practice compressed into a few seconds result in a lightning-swift, sure strike. The pilot invests so much work and effort on the ground just for this moment.

A tricky precipice. A road led away from it through the taiga. To the right was a ravine with gently sloping sides. According to intelligence, the missile position was somewhere here. Lt-Col Tyumin glanced left. Against the background of the taiga, he spotted a thicket of small trees at the foot of a hill, and missile launchers at the edge of the trees. The experienced pilot needed only a few seconds to choose the optimum manoeuvre. He abruptly swung his aircraft and went into a dive. He sighted on the command post. . . . Making a correction, the pilot then hit the release button. As soon as the flight leader disengaged, Maj V. Moskalevich attacked the launchers. Flame and smoke shot skyward. Tyumin's element swung back around and made a second pass.

By this time the element led by Maj A. Rogozhkin had arrived. He and Capt V. Avramenko bombed the missile launchers and finished them off. Mission accomplished.

Returning across the forward line of troops, the pilots saw the motorised riflemen launch the assault.[52]

That this exercise was "successful" was due in part to the no doubt exemplary leadership of Lt-Col Tyumin but also to the fact that there was no disruption of a meticulously prepared plan, that the attack was almost certainly carried out over very familiar terrain against a range target, that there was no unsporting air defence taking advantage of a shallow dive, and that there was no need to contest air superiority. Nevertheless, it would introduce the young offensive support pilot to the kind of mission he would be expected

to discharge in a real conflict in Central Europe. But what it did not do was to call for any in-flight modification to plan or any other initiative on the part of the aircrew. There are of course good operational reasons why rigid adherence to the pre-flight plan would make a lot of sense under many circumstances. Co-ordinated timing with the ground forces, integration with other rotary or fixed-wing aircraft, the need to traverse fields of artillery fire and to maintain a specified height, track and time to ensure safe progress through friendly air defences: all these factors would curb any tendency towards an individual approach. Yet if the human pilot has one attribute which cannot be duplicated by a machine it is his ability to respond to the unexpected.

For over a decade "initiative" has been encouraged and praised in the Soviet aviation press to an extent quite unthinkable in the West, where the fighter/ground attack pilot is frequently the epitome of cheerful individuality. But, as in the Great Patriotic War, it still seems to require a great deal of effort to nurture the same qualities in the Soviet pilot. In 1983, as the Soviet Air Forces were preparing for the annual Day of the Air Fleet on August 21, a very explicit leading article appeared in *Red Star*:

In modern air combat with its rapidly changing situation, in a situation where very powerful fire power is deployed, pilots must have excellent flying skills, a high degree of knowledge of the capabilities of their aircraft, its weapon systems and their employment; also of the strength and weaknesses of the enemy and the effective use of tactics against him.

But in some units there are commanding officers who think that it is enough for their pilots to be able to fly well, to fire and bomb to a high standard on the range under practice conditions. They think that the rest will follow – the skill to employ good tactics and to act boldly and with initiative under operational conditions. Most commanders, of course, do ensure that this knowledge is acquired by proceeding from the simple to the difficult in stages, not always operating under simple conditions and situations. Pilots should have a wide knowledge of the tactics of all branches of the Armed Forces with whom they have to co-operate. There must be no simplification, no weakness or complacency allowed. Crews must be encouraged to act – without looking over their shoulder for advice, no whispered words or fixed pattern of behaviour.[53]

It cannot be any coincidence that as the Warsaw Pact ground forces have developed the ability to mount highly mobile, deep-striking offensives, and the traditional post-war application of closely controlled, thoroughly preplanned offensive air support has proved insufficiently flexible to match it, so exhortations to individual aircrew initiative have become more numerous. But it remains to be seen whether articles in *Red Star* are enough to overcome habits bred by the political system and fostered by two generations of military requirements, and indeed still demanded to a certain extent by the complexities of battlefield airspace management.

Engineering support

Complex, large-scale air operations in a combined-arms offensive place heavy demands on groundcrew as well as pilots. Warsaw Pact offensive support aircrew generally fly fewer hours per month than their Western counterparts. There may be several good tactical reasons for this, but it is also likely that ground engineering support may sometimes prove unequal to the task. Occasional articles in the Soviet military magazines allude to such problems, and point a message which would be unnecessary in NATO air forces. In 1981, for example, there was reference to the need for extra planning during the intensive flying phase of a reconnaissance squadron exercise. Senior Lieutenant Technical Service A. Zverev was held up as an example because he

. . . realised that the work would be intense because there would not be enough specialists. According to the exercise plan a rather large number of aircraft sorties was envisaged with only a minimum amount of time between sorties. Some thought had to be given to this.

The officer approached the solution to pending problems in a businesslike manner, just as guidance documents require. First of all, he modelled in detail the actions of the engineer-technical personnel in fuelling the aircraft. There was one conclusion: in order to prevent delays the fuelling had to be set up by using the combined method, that is, from the centralised network and using the fuel trucks. Zverev spoke with each aircraft technician about how this would be done.

Detailed instructions were received by the flight technical maintenance chiefs and by the group chiefs concerning the positioning of the aviation specialists, the setting up of coordination, and what was to be done in the event of problems. Moreover, alternative plans of action were worked out to handle a change in the situation or the number of flights, and also inputs such as the contamination of the airfield, the evacuation of equipment from a strike area, and so forth.[54]

Why, one wonders, should it be necessary to publicise activities by the "deputy squadron commander for aviation engineer service" which in the West are a basic responsibility of the squadron or wing engineering officers. The answer presumably is that in fact not all officers of the Russian Technical Service discharge their duties in such an exemplary manner. Nor are the shortcomings found only among the officers: in the same article the engineering officer author draws attention to the dangers of slipshod, unchecked line maintenance and a tendency to ignore some of the directions in "the book":

Practice indicates that many mistakes occur because of negligence. It happens that a technician or a mechanic completes his assigned work, but does not take the trouble to check the condition in which he is leaving his work area. Such forgetfulness is particularly dangerous when working in the cockpit. . . .

It's essential to follow precisely the guidance documents on both major and minor matters. Unfortunately, certain aviation specialists feel that insignificant omissions do not cause any harm. The facts given again affirm that this is not the case.[55]

Even now the Soviet Union cannot match the West's depth and breadth of civilian technical expertise, and so has a correspondingly smaller pool from which to recruit engineering officers and other ranks. Various incentives have been offered to Soviet technical conscripts to induce them to extend their service, including "instant" promotion to senior NCO and warrant officer, but this seems to have led simply to warrant officers carrying out basic maintenance. Nor apparently do groundcrew receive "special to type" training before being turned loose on unfamiliar aircraft. When working at a main base a technical officer will presumably use the manuals to acquaint himself with the aircraft equipping the wing or regiment. When the aircraft are deployed forward or away to auxiliary fields, however, a certain amount of flexibility may be called for when basic equipment is not available. On one such occasion a warrant officer with 15 years' service had cause to chide a colleague who apparently lacked the awareness of even a humble Western flight line mechanic:

> The man in the adjacent parking space, Warrant Officer V. Skugarev, had begun to wipe the plexiglass using a plain rag. I cautioned him, saying that was how a canopy loses its transparency. You need flannel that has been laundered and passed through a magnetic filter, otherwise you end up with scratches. And when a canopy is out of commission, then the aircraft might as well be out of commission also.
>
> At the beginning of my service career I frequently found myself without the necessary materials. Now I always come prepared. These are little things – a bunch of rags, a roll of safety wire, a spare steel or rubber washer – but sometimes they determine the success of the endeavour. And this simple spare parts kit can be placed in a bag and kept ready with only periodic attention needed for replacing items. Flight Technician Senior Lieutenant V. Boyko advised us to do this.[56]

On dispersed operations the warrant officer is responsible for checking all aspects of the airframe, including landing gear, flaps, tyres, etc; fuel transfer equipment and filters; cockpit instruments; and fuel and oxygen replenish-

ment. In addition he "keeps a close eye on the work of specialists from the servicing groups";[57] these include the armourers, who are apparently working away from their own supervisor. This, argues the warrant officer, has a beneficial effect:

> Work under these conditions forces a technician to know the techniques and procedures for monitoring all airborne systems and weapons, to keep track of everything that is done on his aircraft by other specialists, and make sure safety procedures are followed, and also to maintain records accurately. A pilot should begin his flight fully confident that everything that was supposed to be done has been done.[58]

Since that confident note was struck in 1978, Soviet aircraft and their equipment have grown progressively more complicated as, like their Western counterparts, they have been influenced by the microprocessor revolution. Quite apart from the capacity of aircrew to adapt to the more complex demands of closely coordinated deep-ranging operations, the ability of groundcrew to service and supervise increasingly sophisticated equipment may well be critical to mounting and sustaining operational "surges" at both main and auxiliary bases.

For example, modern aircraft serviceability is increasingly monitored by electronic test equipment, whether integral to the airframe itself or on the ground in maintenance units. Such systems complement visual observation and verbal reports in yielding measurements of airframe and engine life and routine defect identification. The demands on the Soviet Air Force Aviation Engineering Service (IAS) are consequently much greater:

> Now as never before, IAS personnel are required to have a thorough knowledge of technical specifications of onboard recorders and ground data-processing facilities, and of the rules for their operation, interpretation, and analysis of recorded parameters.[59]

Named IAS engineers are congratulated for their "endeavour and persistence," but much remains to be done – or at least it did in 1978, when the IAS general wrote in *Aviation and Cosmonautics*:

91

This Mi-26 demonstrator pilot is likely to be well versed in the type's systems, but can his military counterpart rely on service ground crew? (*Tass*)

It is not everywhere, however, that concern is shown for effective use of objective monitoring equipment. There are still cases where aircraft are allowed to take off without a thorough analysis of the working capacity of equipment based upon recordings by objective monitoring equipment on the previous flight. Some units have not set up strict supervision over fulfilment of aircraft flying modes prescribed by the programmes, while important data are sent off late to higher echelons and in violation of established requirements. . . .

. . . We must decisively eliminate the present shortcomings and raise the level of competence of technical personnel.[60]

But exactly what levels of competence are required? The same author goes on to give an example which would make any RAF junior tradesman smile with incredulity:

For example, in checking the panel of one of the radars, the operator must perform more than one set of ten switchings in a strict sequence. This is why it is now so important for

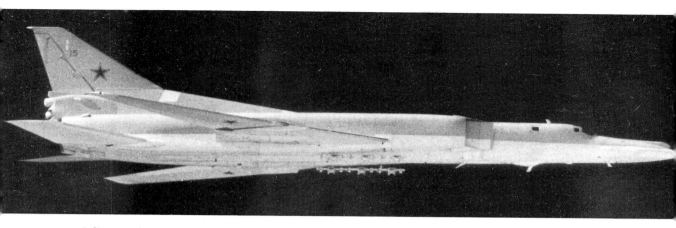

specialists to have high qualifications, to be exceptionally industrious, and to take a creative approach to maintaining aviation equipment and monitoring gear.[61]

One article by one officer does not amount to a wholesale condemnation of SAF ground electronic tradesmen, but the above example suggests that the level of technical ability among Soviet groundcrew has been well below that of their Western counterparts. Moreover, servicing of the kind described above would probably be carried out by an SNCO or warrant officer if not by the engineering officer himself, which must raise doubts about the competence of even these grades.

How well would SAF groundcrew cope if called on to keep the Fencers, Fulcrums, Flankers and the rest serviceable in the face of aircrew flying rates of seven hours a day rather than the current estimated 7–10hr per month? It seems that, as with operational conversion of aircrew, much of the responsibility lies with the squadrons or regiments themselves. In 1981 the Hind regiment named after Lenin was reported to have received an award "for success in combat training and for selfless military labour".[62] Despite the regular exodus of trained personnel on retirement or promotion, the regiment had maintained high standards over a long period. Much apparently was due to the quality of the engineering support it enjoyed, itself based on a comprehensive training programme. Training facilities were reported to include classrooms for the study of engines, armament and electronics, and laboratories where research into operational

Though procured in disquietingly large numbers, advanced types like Backfire achieve low rates of utilisation, possibly as a result of servicing shortcomings.

problems could be carried out and even small weapon launch simulators designed. But weaknesses and omissions in the training programmes remained, and these were rectified not, as might be expected in Western training establishments, by the OC training wing or flight but by meetings between the commander, the chief of the political department, the maintenance service chiefs, and the "Communist Party activists".

Poor technical supervision was duly noted, the regiment's methods council worked out a new plan, the experience of "advanced officers enjoying the reputation of competent methodists and skilled educators" was sought, and all were stimulated by "the competition of socialist emulation," with winners well publicised in the regimental "Museum of Combat Glory". Comparable remedial activity could be found, being carried out with varying degrees of enthusiasm, in units not only in the tactical air forces but throughout the SAF.

The Afghan experience

Evidence of SAF operational effectiveness is not easy to come by. Exercise achievements of the kind illustrated earlier are devalued by the artificiality of their settings and aircrew familiarity with range areas. But they do indicate that Warsaw Pact squadrons practise combined fixed-wing and helicopter operations, that aircrew are flying longer sorties at increasingly low levels, and that ways are being sought to encourage aircrew initiative within the limitations of battlefield airspace management. There is however a suggestion that some exercises may have witnessed rather more than the smoothly co-ordinated, utterly successful attacks so common in *Red Star* and *Aviation and Cosmonautics*.

In any European conflict the Warsaw Pact would use alternate airfields both defensively, to reduce the impact of NATO counter-air operations, and offensively, to support mobile operations on land. One cautiously worded article in a specialist military journal brings together several ideas relating to alternate fields, beginning with the heart of the matter:

> The design features of modern aircraft, the growing requirement for technical support equipment, and increased demands for the operational maintenance of airfields force new solutions to several rear service support problems.
>
> As we know, the most important indicator

Operating from the safety of bases in the Soviet Union, the Tu-16 Badger has been used for high-level strikes against targets in Afghanistan.

of an aviation technical unit's combat readiness is their ability to support highly manoeuvrable aviation operations not only from permanent, but also from alternate airfields.

> . . . At the present time, questions concerning rear services support of highly fluid aviation operations from alternate airfields are acquiring ever greater importance. These questions are constantly being worked on during the airfield logistic exercises which are held both in the winter and summer: . . .[63]

The questions include the difficulties of movement across soaked or frozen airfields and the provision of storage at various specified temperatures, dressing and drying areas for flying kit, and well organised dining facilities carefully divided between those for "flight and technician personnel" and those for "privates and sergeants". But whatever the requirement, ". . . the operational experience of leading rear services units shows that all supply problems can be solved in an outstanding manner and within established time limits".[64] What then is the level of achievement of all the other units? Rather less than "outstanding," one would guess.

Since 1979 the Soviet Air Forces have been able to indulge in "exercises" of a more realistic nature in Afghanistan, without the need to

establish alternate airfields and, with the exception of sporadic ground fire, under conditions of unchallenged air supremacy.

Offensive air support of operations against the Afghan *mujahideen* has been provided by both helicopters and fixed-wing aircraft, and since the campaign began tactics have been progressively refined. Hip helicopters are used to move troops quickly in the mountains, while Hinds, usually working in pairs, operate against guerrilla raiding parties and strongpoints. Their initial vulnerability to ground fire has apparently been reduced by widespread use of flares to decoy infra-red surface-to-air missiles, and in October 1984 an extensive eyewitness report by a British journalist[65] described increasingly low-level attacks by helicopters, MiG-21s and the most recent addition to the close support inventory, the Su-25 Frogfoot. Rockets, parachute-retarded bombs and guns were used in the face of sporadic SA-7 launches and anti-aircraft machine guns, with attacks pressed home at much lower levels than the previously reported 2,000–3,000ft. A forward air controller travelled with army convoys, and the shorter-range helicopters and MiGs appear to have been scrambled from bases inside Afghanistan. Significantly, the longer-range Su-24 Fencers and Tu-16 Badgers contributed their medium-level attacks from the security of bases across the Soviet border in Uzbekistan. Although the aircraft did not appear to carry night target-acquisition systems, target areas were illuminated either by flares dropped by An-12 transports or by searchlights mounted on Hip helicopters. The Afghan terrain is not the most congenial for night flying, and such operations indicate an increased capability not often seen in the European theatre.

There are many differences between actual combat flying in Afghanistan and what might happen in Europe, so any assessment of likely capability in the one theatre that is based on experience in the other must be heavily qualified. Some of the differences are self-evident, terrain and weather perhaps the most so. January, February and March can bring heavy snow, rain and mud in Afghanistan but for the greater part of the year the skies are clear, resulting in far easier flying conditions than in Europe. Afghan targets are generally small, elusive and scattered. With the exception of the air and ground campaign in the Panjshir Valley in spring 1983, operations have been carried out by small numbers of aircraft rather than the regiments expected to support an OMG. Similarly, the scale of opposition to air attacks bears no resemblance to that likely to be offered by NATO forces. Hit-and-run attacks by the *mujahideen* on air bases in Afghanistan itself have occasionally been destructive or disruptive, but the airfields in Uzbekistan have enjoyed immunity akin to that of USAF bases in Thailand in the Vietnam War. Conditions for groundcrew at Termez are therefore no more demanding than those on Warsaw Pact bases during exercises. Moreover, the bases on either side of the border have remained static, with no problems of redeployment and complications of mobile resupply. All operations have been mounted without any electronic interference, whether from jamming or from active, destructive electronically based countermeasures. But above all Soviet aircraft have enjoyed absolute and uncontested command of the air, a difference so fundamental as to outweigh all other factors.

On the other hand, many Russian aircrew have experienced combat: enough helicopters have been shot down to raise the training effectiveness of Afghan sorties well above that of the artificial, well flown and unopposed range exercises previously the sole staple of Soviet fliers. Until the Afghan War the SAF had to base its understanding of modern air combat on second-hand experience derived from the debacles suffered by their successive friends in the Middle East. Now Soviet Air Force commanders can experiment at first hand with close support tactics calling for tight co-ordination between ground forces and fixed and rotary-wing aircraft. Several decorations have been awarded for individual bravery and it is reasonable to assume that the helicopter crews in particular will have benefited from their exposure to fire, however limited. Techniques of rapid response and forward air control will have been tested, aircrew initiative will have been required when operating in pairs over unfamiliar terrain and probably out of touch with ground controllers. The war has also proved an interesting proving

Until Afghanistan the Soviet Air Forces had to derive their understanding of modern air combat from the experiences of the USSR's current and former clients. These Badgers were operated by the Egyptian Air Force. (*US Air Force*)

ground for the Su-25 Frogfoot. It carries heavier payloads for longer ranges than Hind, and its manoeuvrability and self-protective measures against ground fire suggest that it could in fact be a valuable addition to the firepower supporting a deep-penetrating OMG – always provided that air superiority had been won before it appeared.

The future

The evolution of Soviet offensive air support over the last two decades has not been as erratic as some observers have believed. Despite the debates over the significance of nuclear weapons, the theory of combined-arms offensives has remained basically constant since 1945. It is the technology that has changed. The increased mobility and firepower of armoured and motorised rifle divisions has been matched by the deployment of helicopters and fixed-wing aircraft in sufficient numbers and with the right

performance to recreate the preparatory fire, accompaniment and close support practised in the later offensives of the Great Patriotic War. Tactical aviation is now organised, in theory at least, to make the most of rapidly responding, shorter-range helicopters and longer-legged fixed-wing aircraft. The debate about how best to combine them may not yet be over, and there is no reason to assume that the Warsaw Pact has resolved the complex problems of battlefield airspace management. In the next decade we can expect to see improved all-weather target acquisition, better self-protection, and increasingly smart air-to-ground weapons. It is possible that the introduction of the Il-76 Mainstay AEW&C may further improve the co-ordination of tactical offensive operations as well as complicating Western counteroffensives. Whether such improvements can overcome the handicaps of uncertain engineering support, the complications arising from forward and lateral deployments, and the habits of conformity to carefully rehearsed flight plans and close control remains to be seen. But one thing is certain: if the Warsaw Pact tactical air support units ever achieved command of the air in the theatre of operations, the military balance would be tipped disastrously against NATO ground forces.

Tactical offensive operations

Notes

1 A comprehensive account of the SAF in the Second World War is given by Alexander Boyd in *The Soviet Air Force since 1918* (Macdonald and Jane's, London 1977), while an excellent distillation is given by J. T. Greenwood in *Soviet Aviation and Air Power* (ed Higham and Kipp), (Brasseys, London 1978).

2 Boyd op cit, page 144.

3 Greenwood op cit, page 119.

4 *Soviet Combined Arms, Theory and Practice*, John Erickson, College Station Papers, published by the Centre for Strategic Technology, Texas A and M University 1981.

5 Greenwood op cit, page 114.

6 As translated in *Soviet Military Concepts*, USAF 1978.

7 C. N. Donnelly, *International Defense Review*, Vol 15, No 9, 1982.

8 US Joint Chiefs of Staff 632/1, *Tactical Evaluation of the MiG-15 as an All-weather Fighter and Ground Attack Plane*, May 26, 1953.

9 See for example *Evolution of the Soviet Tactical Air Forces*, Matthew A. Evangelista, *Soviet Armed Forces Review Annual*, Vol 7, 1982–83, Academic International Press 1984.

10 Quoted from M. S. Arlazorov, *The Designers*, Moscow 1975, by Boyd op cit, page 212.

11 *Soviet Military Concepts* op cit, pages 1–2.

12 For example, R. L. Garthoff alleged that the strength of Soviet tactical aviation had declined by over 50% by the early 1960s (*Soviet Military Policy*, Faber 1966, page 120), while A. J. Alexander (*Soviet Decision Making for National Security*, Allen & Unwin 1984, page 17) suggests that in 1954–55 fighter aircraft production was reduced from 5,000 to 500 a year; this seems an extreme assessment.

13 *CIA Estimated Soviet Defence Spending, Trends and Prospects*, SR 78–10121, June 1978.

14 Seminar report in *Aviation Week and Space Technology*, July 16, 1984.

15 *The Character and Importance of Air Operations in Modern Warfare*, Col (DPL) Pilot Alexander Musial, translation No 138 by the Soviet Studies Research Centre, Sandhurst.

16 *Rude Pravo*, Prague, February 10, 1984, as quoted in *Jane's Defence Weekly*, May 5, 1984.

17 *The Lessons of Co-ordination*, Lt-Col A. Zakharenko, *Red Star*, August 5, 1977.

18 *Air Operations at the Berezina Exercise*, *Soviet Military Review* 11/1978, page 18.

19 Ibid page 19.

20 From the report in *Jane's Defence Weekly* op cit, page 685.

21 The electronic and weapon fit of Brewer-E is described in detail in *Jane's Defence Weekly*, July 14, 1984, pages 18–19.

22 Ibid.

23 *Soviet Military Review* op cit, page 19.

24 *Combat Helicopters of the Warsaw Pact*, J. W. R. Taylor, *Jane's Defence Review* No 2, 1980, page 115.

25 *Soviet Helicopters*, John Everett-Heath, Jane's 1983, page 68 et seq.

26 *Jane's All the World's Aircraft 1982–83*, quoted in Everett-Heath ibid, page 72.

27 Everett-Heath ibid, page 87.

28 Everett-Heath ibid.

29 *The Offensive*, Col A. A. Sidorenko, Military Publishing House Moscow, page 131.

30 *The Military Balance 1983–84*, IISS, page 18.

31 *Soviet Helicopter Combat Doctrine*, John Everett-Heath, *Jane's Defence Weekly*, March 3, 1984, page 333.

32 *The Soviet Helicopter on the Battlefield*, C. N. Donnelly, *International Defense Review* 5/1984, page 559.

33 *The General Concept of a Theatre of Military Operations*, Lt-Cdr Z. Binieda, *Polish Naval Review* No 12, 1981, translation No 137 by the Soviet Studies Research Centre, Sandhurst.

34 *Helicopters are carrying out a landing*, Maj G. Ivanov, *Red Star*, August 26, 1978.

35 See *The Soviet Operational Manoeuvre Group: A New Challenge for NATO*, C. N. Donnelly, *International Defense Review* Vol 15 No 9, 1982.

36 *Aviation in the Raid Manoeuvre Operations of Ground Forces*, Maj (Diploma) Wajereck Michalak, *Polish Air Force and Air Defence Review*, February 1982, translation No 139 by the Soviet Studies Research Centre, Sandhurst.

37 Michalak ibid.

38 Ibid.

39 *Motorised Riflemen attack from the Sky*, Col V. Yerashev and Maj A. Borovokov, *Red Star*, November 5, 1983, page 1.

40 Michalak op cit.

41 Maj-Gen M. Belov DSc(Military), *Soviet Military Review* 2/1980, pages 29–30.

42 Donnelly op cit, page 26.

43 Col M. Belov DSc(Military), *Soviet Military Review* 9/1979, pages 18–19.

44 Belov op cit, page 29.

45 Examples extracted from those listed by Donnelly op cit, page 566.

46 *Lieutenant's Flights*, Lt-Gen of Aviation V. Pan'kin, Commander of Aviation in the Red Banner Far Eastern Military District, *Red Star*, August 11, 1976, page 2.

47 Ibid.

48 Ibid.

49 Ibid.
50 Ibid.
51 *Supporting Land Forces*, Lt-Col
    A. Mikhailov, *Aviation and
    Cosmonautics*, September 1983.
52 Ibid.
53 *Tactical training of the air force
    pilot*, *Red Star*, August 17,
    1983, translated by Wg Cdr
    F. J. French RAF ret.
54 *There Should be Enough Film*,
    Eng Maj Reserves V. Trifonov,
    Aviation and Cosmonautics No 1
    1981, page 7.

55 Ibid.
56 *At a Field Base*, Warrant Officer
    N. Artemov, *Banner Bearer*,
    August 1978, page 12.
57 Ibid.
58 Ibid, page 13.
59 *Foremost Experience into Air
    Force Engineer Service Practice:
    Introducing Modern Control
    Methods*, Eng Col Gen V.
    Skubilin, *Aviation and
    Cosmonautics*, September 1978,
    page 26.
60 Ibid.

61 Ibid, page 27.
62 *Multiplying Combat Traditions*,
    Col V. Lebedev, *Soviet
    Military Review* No 8 1981,
    pages 24–25.
63 *At the Alternate Airfield*, Col B.
    Voroby'ev, *Rear and Supply of
    the Soviet Armed Forces*, August
    1977, pages 74–76.
64 Ibid.
65 John Gunston, *Aviation Week
    and Space Technology*, October
    29, 1984, pages 38–43.

CHAPTER 4

Maritime operations

ON August 11, 1984, the London *Jane's Defence Weekly* startled the defence world by publishing three satellite photographs of the Nikolaiev shipyard on the Black Sea. In the docks were the two sections of a nuclear-powered aircraft carrier (CVN), estimated to displace some 75,000 tons and designed to carry fixed-wing aircraft. The photographs confirmed reports which had been circulating for several months but which had been doubted by many who lacked access to such space age intelligence. And yet with hindsight the surprise was not so much the appearance of the big carrier as the fact that it had taken the Soviet Union 67 years to decide to add this formidable instrument to its already extensive maritime aviation armoury.

The Yak-38 Forger V/STOL fighter has played a central part in the Soviet evolution towards a full-fledged naval aviation capability.

With occasional exceptions, the development of Soviet naval aviation has been consistently influenced by two factors: the geography of the Soviet Union itself, and the limitations imposed upon the nation by its industrial and economic weakness in comparison with the other great powers. The Nikolaiev CVN, said to be named *Kremlin*, represents the end of a long battle by Soviet naval commanders, who have struggled since the earliest days of the Red Navy to convince the political leadership that the strength of a superpower must be projected far from the nation's frontiers.

Early developments

The Russian Naval Air Service was formed in 1913. In July 1917 the Directorate of Naval Aviation, established the previous year, assumed functional control of naval air units from the Observations and Communications Services of the Baltic and Black Sea Fleets.[1] Aircraft contributed to maritime reconnaissance and anti-shipping attacks in the Baltic and, more extensively, attacked ships and land targets and flew anti-submarine patrols in the Black Sea area. But plans for a further expansion of activities were brought to nothing by the Bolshevik Revolution and subsequent Civil War, and the Naval Air Service virtually ceased to exist. Then, with Lenin taking a personal interest, strenuous attempts were made to restore aircraft factories. Flying training, reduced because of shortages of aircraft and the bourgeois tendencies of the young aircrew, was re-established and expanded. The Petrograd School, for example, was reopened to train airmen "of proletarian origin and committed to the Revolution who were capable of quickly assimilating the fundamentals of flying".[2] In 1919 the responsibilities of Naval Aviation (NA) were defined as "air reconnaissance, the defence of vessels and shore installations against enemy air attack, and the provision of air liaison facilities between fleets and flotillas and army and front headquarters".[3]

In 1920 the Revolutionary Military Council placed naval aviation alongside all other air units under the Chief Directorate for the Workers' and Peasants' Red Air Fleet. Naval aviation units operating with the fleets remained under the operational control of C-in-C Naval Forces, however.[4] In the Civil War NA squadrons supported the Red Army with reconnaissance and ground attack in the Volga and Caspian areas, while in the north they provided air defence of the Petrograd and Kronstadt ports as well as participating in counter-revolutionary activities against mutineers at Krasnaya Gorka and Kronstadt itself. Seaplanes harassed the evacuation of White Russian forces from the Crimea, attacking trains, airfields and shipping. By the end of the Civil War in 1920 NA had flown over 2,000 sorties

and dropped a third of the total bombload of all the Red air forces in the conflict.

But for at least three more generations NA was destined to remain a poor relation in the Soviet military aviation family. Two infant unified air forces had fought over the Volga in 1919. But whereas the British Royal Air Force was independent, the Soviet naval air elements were subordinate to Army High Command and restricted by a defence policy which saw the major threat to both revolution and heartland coming overland rather than from the sea. The military lesson of the Civil War seemed to be that even a combination of the world's greatest maritime powers had not been able to overcome the might of the Red Army. When Mikhail Frunze, Commissar for War in 1925, warned that ". . . the most important type of technological force which will play a large role on the fields of future battles is the air fleet,"[5] his focus was squarely on the Red Army's battlefields. During the next decade, however, his view was increasingly challenged as the regimes in Germany and Japan became more expansionist and potentially hostile.

At that time established Soviet naval doctrine held that coastal defence and associated combined operations as practised in the Civil War continued to be the primary roles of NA. But then the *Naval Digest* began to refer to foreign military developments as a means of criticising this "white water" strategy. On one side of the debate, defending the coastal strategy, were Tukhachevsky and those admirals who argued that the German threat lay in ground forces and tactical aviation and that therefore the Baltic and Black seas should be defended by well co-ordinated land-based aviation together with mines and submarines. On the other were those, including naval academic staff and officers of the Pacific Fleet and Naval Air Force, formed in 1933, who emphasised the threat posed by Japanese carrier groups and the German intention to build two carriers of her own. They believed that the Soviet Union could afford to build battleships and carriers of sufficient quality and quantity to challenge potential enemies beyond the confines of the Black and Baltic seas. In the event, though Tukhachevsky lost both the argument and his life, the blue-water men still did not get their carrier. One theorist of Soviet naval aviation reminded readers of *Naval Digest* that carriers were themselves vulnerable to air attack from land bases when operating in small areas of water and that they made heavy demands on limited resources. While carrier development was significant, small seaplane tenders would be more relevant to Soviet military requirements.[6] Thus, as the Soviet Union moved towards the outbreak of the Second World War, the argument for carriers was lost partly because of geographical realities, partly because of limited resources, and partly because the admirals and generals of naval aviation could not agree among themselves.

In 1935 operational control of Naval Aviation was detached from the Chief Directorate of the Air Forces, and in 1939 a new Naval Air Force Directorate was created. Fighter, minelaying and torpedo-bomber regiments were expanded, though largely with discarded Red Air Force aircraft already obsolescent. In June 1941 fewer than 10% of the fighters were modern; only a quarter of the whole force were torpedo-bombers; the bombers in the Northern Fleet lacked radio and navigational aids; and the naval airfield construction programme along the Baltic and in the Caucasus was incomplete. No wonder then that Russian naval airmen suffered at Luftwaffe hands treatment similar to that received by the Red Air Force elsewhere. Naval Aviation took heavy losses in the Baltic, Ukrainian and Caucasian regions before the tide of the war began to turn after Stalingrad.

In its effect on the Soviet armed forces, including naval aviation, the Great Patriotic War has been likened to a "crucible": "As a life and death struggle testing the survival of the regime and imposing great human and material losses upon the population, it overshadowed the experiences of a generation".[7] In the southern theatre of operations against Germany, NA played an increasingly significant part from 1943 onwards. In September 1943 naval aircraft flew alongside army units in classic combined operations to provide offensive air support at Novorossiisk below an air-superiority umbrella also jointly established. As Soviet aircraft production expanded, massed attacks by as many as 100 machines were carried out against port installa-tions or German convoys in the Black Sea. The attacks were preceded by extensive air reconnaissance and launched with fighter escorts. The results led post-war theorists to emphasise the importance of offensive maritime air power in support of amphibious operations and against surface shipping. Operations in the Baltic, though not as extensive, were ultimately similar in scale and included widespread if not very effective minelaying. It is however important to remember, when considering the validity of such precedents for the 1980s, that the bulk of successful Soviet NA operations both in the West and later against the collapsing Japan were flown with almost unlimited air superiority and ultimately theatrewide command of the air.

Post-war priorities

NA's contribution to victory in the Great Patriotic War was occasionally tactically significant, but minuscule when compared with the activities of either the land forces or the Air Forces proper. The acquisition in 1945 of Eastern European territories afforded both a *cordon sanitaire* and a convenient springboard should further opportunities for expansion present themselves. The northern approaches remained hazardous for invaders, the Baltic was secured along its southern shore, and to the east was the potential ally China in place of the annihilated Japan. The major threat lay in the air and the main potential opponent was out of range of everything but long-range bombers and intercontinental ballistic missiles. But this same potential enemy possessed an instrument – the high-speed carrier task force – which could present a threat if allowed to approach within range of Soviet territory. Some Western analysts have identified Soviet plans, apparently approved by Stalin, to build 1,200 submarines, 436 major surface ships and 5,000 naval aircraft[8] as part of an anti-amphibious programme in 1945–46. A concern for defence was not however the only reason for what appears to have been Stalin's own interest in a blue-water navy:

> The conditions of modern war at sea demand the mandatory participation in the combat

operations of navies of powerful carrier forces, using them for striking devastating blows against the naval forces of the enemy as well as for the contest with his aviation. Both at sea and near one's bases these tasks can only be carried out by carrier aviation.[9]

The Khrushchev years

Stalin's death in 1953 seemed to herald the demise of the ocean-going Navy. Khrushchev himself criticised Soviet admirals as wishing to fight the next war with the weapons of the last, and in 1956 promoted a very junior captain, S. G. Gorshkov, to command the Navy. Gorshkov was a veteran of the Black Sea campaign in 1945, and it is believed that his directive from the First Secretary was to concentrate naval efforts on defence of the homeland and co-operation with the ground forces.[10] Seldom can a commander-in-chief have interpreted his master's wishes so liberally. But whatever his longer-term diversion from the specified path, Gorshkov's first actions were in keeping with Khrushchev's belief that any future war would be nuclear and the fact that by the mid-1950s the old Second World War fast carrier groups of the United States Navy had

been superseded by task forces capable of launching nuclear weapon-carrying aircraft against the Soviet homeland. NA, now known as Soviet Naval Air Force (SNAF), lost its fighters to the Air Defence of the Homeland (PVO *Strany*) in a move presumably designed to improve co-ordination of air defences in coastal regions and avoid their duplication. Less logically, a number of short-range offensive aircraft were transferred to Frontal Aviation. Finally, the long-range capability of SNAF was extended by the transfer from Long Range Aviation of many bombers considered, perhaps in the light of Khrushchev's rocket theories, to be superfluous to intercontinental requirements. A quantity of Tupolev Tu-16s were modified to carry two nuclear anti-ship cruise missiles; they were NATO code-named Badger-B. Others, designated Badger-D, were equipped to give mid-course electronic guidance to the missiles. The Badgers were followed by a number of Tupolev Tu-95 Bears and Myasishchev M-4 Bisons, used for long-range maritime reconnaissance. The rationale behind these transfers was subsequently explained in a collection of naval essays published in Moscow in 1969 but probably conceived before Khrushchev's departure the previous year:

> In the mid-1950s, as a result of the revolution in military affairs, the Central Committee of our Party determined the path of development of the Navy and also its role in the country's system of defence forces. It took the

The unique power-projection abilities of America's carrier battle groups, and the threat that they pose to Russian interests, stimulated the development of an oceangoing Soviet Navy. This is USS *Midway* with escorts and support vessels. (*US Navy*)

course for the construction of an ocean navy capable of executing strategic missions of an offensive nature. Submarines and naval aviation equipped with nuclear rocket weapons occupied the most important place in this.[11]

Between Admiral Gorshkov's appointment in 1956 and the appearance of that comment, however, several other events had occurred which were also prompting the Soviet Navy, and with it the SNAF, to move out from white water.

Air power over blue water

With the advent of the USN Polaris fleet in the early 1960s, the nuclear threat to the Soviet Union acquired another dimension. In the same period the Soviet Navy's own missile-carrying boats (SSBNs) began to deploy further away from Soviet waters. In 1956 the Suez crisis had been resolved after Anglo-French uncertainty about American support rather than as a result of Soviet interference, despite Khrushchev's belated rocket threats. In 1958 US forces had intervened in Lebanon and in 1963 the Cuban crisis had clearly exposed the Soviet lack of oceangoing conventional naval strength. It is not possible to determine exactly what led Admiral

Myasishchev M-4 Bison-B maritime reconnaissance aircraft. Large numbers of strategic bombers were transferred to the Soviet Naval Air Force in response to the development of American nuclear-capable carrier forces. (*RAF*)

Gorshkov to move so far away from his original mandate. But the desire to be able to intercept hostile submarines, to protect and communicate with Soviet boats, and to project at least a token naval presence in support of distant friends may have inclined him towards those naval officers who had quietly adhered to a belief that a major power should have the ability to operate across the world's oceans.

The fact that Soviet admirals other than Gorshkov understood the potential of carriers in regional power projection was revealed in 1969 by the First Deputy C-in-C of the Soviet Navy, Admiral of the Fleet V. A. Kasanatov:

> If we speak of the role and place of aircraft carriers in local wars and various conflicts, they appear differently. During recent years aircraft carriers repeatedly stepped forth as the main forces of the Navy in the war in Korea, during the Suez adventure and in many military conflicts in the Middle East, and now they are playing the same role in the United States' undeclared war in Vietnam.[12]

The *Moskva*-class helicopter carriers represented the Soviet Navy's first attempt to embark a significant quantity of air power. (*Royal Navy*)

Certainly the military rationale for a carrier force has been analysed by Soviet writers:

> . . . under contemporary conditions it will be necessary to call for great numbers of anti-submarine warfare (ASW) aircraft to fight enemy nuclear-powered submarines, for they will have to be sought out in the vast expanses of the world's oceans. Also, the complexity of carrying out open-ocean ASW missions will make it necessary to use aircraft in close co-operation with other ASW forces.[13]

Admiral Gorshkov himself wrote: "The under-estimation of the need to support submarine operations with aircraft and surface ships cost the German High Command dearly in the last two wars."[14]

But if you want to destroy hostile submarines, or support your own, you must know where they are: ". . . victory will belong to him who will constantly know the location of the opposing side's submarines and deploy sufficient means to defeat them."[15] In the 1950s Soviet ASW operations focused on Western submarine activity in the Baltic and other coastal waters. Subsequently the flying boats which were used in this role, culminating in 1960 in the Beriev Be-12 Mail, were gradually supplemented by shipborne helicopters. A Ka-10 Hat had carried out trial landings on the deck of the cruiser *Maxim Gorky* in the Baltic in 1950, but it was not until 1966 that the Kresta-class cruisers appeared with a hangar for a single Ka-25 Hormone, the first fully operational Soviet shipborne ASW helicopter. The following year the NATO navies found themselves confronted by *Moskva*, able to carry 18 Hormones. She was soon joined by her sister "anti-submarine cruiser," *Leningrad*, capable of ASW, submarine protection and tradi-

Above The Soviet Naval Air Force is the world's largest user of anti-submarine flying boats, operating a total of 80 Beriev Be-12s from the coastal air bases of the Northern and Black Sea fleets. (*Swedish Air Force*)

Below The Kamov Ka-25 Hormone-A has been the standard Soviet shipborne anti-submarine helicopter for the past 20 years. (*US Navy*)

Navy's own submarines. They also seem to have given the "big carrier" lobby further encouragement as SNAF began to win a significantly larger share of the Soviet military budget.

tional showing of the flag. With hindsight, *Moskva*'s practical impact on the naval balance was overestimated. Although well equipped with surface-to-air defences, she presented little threat to NATO warships and would herself have been vulnerable to both surface and air attack. But the helicopter carriers did extend Soviet ASW capabilities further out into blue waters as well as extending support to the Soviet

Current operations

During the last decade units of SNAF have been seen operating over most of the world's oceans, not just from their home bases but from airfields used with the agreement of Third World friends and from the decks of various types of oceangoing ships. Moreover, for the first time in Soviet military history the SNAF has received new

types of aircraft destined for both services at the same time as or ahead of the Soviet Air Forces. By 1978 the Deputy Chief of Staff of the Naval Air Arm was able to summarise as follows the roles handled by his aircraft:

> The anti-submarine fleet, with its variety of planes and helicopters, is capable of seeking out and destroying submarines wherever they may be. It is equipped with modern search systems and diverse strike weapons.
>
> Marine missile-carrying aircraft have a long flight range and can strike with a high degree of accuracy at sea and ground targets without leaving the umbrella of active air defence.
>
> Naval reconnaissance planes have a variety of equipment for detecting and observing underwater and surface targets, and can maintain prolonged searches for and observation of such targets at a great distance from their base in any sea or weather conditions.
>
> The present-day use of support ships means that anti-submarine helicopters can seek out and destroy various submarines and operate with success in all areas where there are Soviet ships.[16]

It is not surprising that anti-submarine operations should receive so much emphasis or that support of friendly submarine activities should not be mentioned. Militarily, if aircraft can detect

Above Principal targets for the Soviet Naval Air Force's ASW aircraft are Western ballistic missile submarines like HMS *Renown*. *(Royal Navy)*

Right Bear-F being escorted by a pair of USAF Phantoms. This example is distinguished by the magnetic anomaly detection (MAD) boom projecting from the fin tip.

hostile boats, they can be equipped to communicate with friends. Politically, the natural Soviet emphasis is on the hostile proclivities of NATO navies rather than on the greatly increasing capability of the Soviet fleets' own SSBNs. By 1984 the US Navy had 34 SSBNs and 90 attack submarines, some of which were to be fitted with cruise missiles. In addition, both Britain and France maintained SSBNs while West Germany operated 24 conventional attack submarines. In the East, China had 100 conventional boats and was developing an SSBN. The Soviet Union had 80 missile-carrying boats and a further 270 attack submarines.[17]

Whereas SNAF had extended its range in the 1960s by the acquisition of obsolescent LRA bombers, in 1973 it began to receive a special maritime version of the Tu-142 Bear, code-named Bear-F. Over the next 10 years the Bear-F was progressively re-equipped with new submarine-detection devices, including advanced sonobuoys and magnetic anomaly detectors. Its efficient turboprop engines give it an unrefuelled radius of some 3,500 miles.

Moreover, its large airframe has probably facilitated the installation of more advanced electronic equipment than could be fitted to contemporary short-range offensive support aircraft. In 1981 what was probably a Bear-F training sortie received guarded coverage in the *Soviet Military Review*:

> The exercise was in full swing when the search striking group commander received a report from one of his ships that an "enemy" submarine had been detected. But after a thorough analysis of the data and estimate of the situation it became clear that it was a false target.
>
> It is well known that the technical facilities that a modern submarine is equipped with allow it to deceive ASW teams as to target identification. If, in addition, the detected

submarine executes a cunning manoeuvre it may quite well manage to break away from pursuit. . . .

As the search area had expanded the [search group commander] divided it into two parts and decided to direct the searchers to the first sector and ask for the Air Force to help with the second. . . .

A boundless expanse of ocean lay ahead. There was not a cloud in the sky but a strong northern wind raised towering waves on the ocean surface. The airmen realised that the search would be difficult. As he left the airfield behind, the crew commander could not help recalling the warning of the duty forecast officer: weather conditions in the designated area would be complicated. And indeed the sky soon darkened, visibility deteriorated and extreme turbulence began. . . .

The crew prepared the special equipment for operation and established radio communication with the commanders of the search group ships. Then the airmen started the search, probing the ocean surface run after run. . . .

The crew commander ordered his assistant to direct the plane to a new square and himself carefully analysed the actual situation and estimated in what direction the sub was most likely to execute an escape manoeuvre. Taking into account the boundary of the ice field and a number of tactical factors, he came to the conclusion that the search should be continued in a neighbouring area. . . .

The navigator marked on the map the co-ordinates of the new search square, worked out the route and as soon as the aircraft reached the assigned line, switched on the required equipment and tuned it, cutting out interference. . . .

On the second run the navigator almost shouted: "Target, skipper!"

Continuing to watch the target, they brought the search group ships in contact with the submarine. The searchers had to "destroy" it, while the airmen were re-routed to carrying out an incidental mission: to check whether there were any surface targets in the area.[18]

Later in the same sortie, rather like their RAF equivalents in a Nimrod over the North Atlantic, the Soviet crew carried out a routine piece of surface vessel identification close to the Arctic icefield. The "plodder" was duly photographed and her details radioed back to base. Then, going perhaps a little belatedly through anti-flak manoeuvres, the Bear climbed away through the snow clouds and returned to its base, probably located somewhere in the Kola Peninsula.

Another Bear variant, the D, seems to have been employed since 1967 on long-range surface fleet location and identification as well as electronic reconnaissance and intelligence-gathering. Between 1970 and 1981 pairs of Bear-Ds made return flights from the Kola bases to Cuba.[19] Since then Bear-Ds have been deployed permanently in the Caribbean, flying electronic intelligence missions along the fringe of United States eastern airspace. Bear-D operations have also been extended to West Africa, from 1973 from Conakry in Guinea and since 1977 from Luanda in Angola. It is probable that in 1982 Bear-Ds from Luanda shadowed the British Falklands task force in the Ascension Island area. Further east, Bears have flown regularly from Da Nang and Cam Ranh Bay in Vietnam, whence they have carried out surveillance against units of the United States Seventh Fleet in the Pacific. The forward deployments, coupled with the Bear's very long unrefuelled range, have provided the Soviet Union with extensive oceanwide intelligence. US sources have also suggested that Bear-D has an anti-surface missile targeting capability.[20] In a shooting war the Bear-Ds would be very vulnerable to US Navy F-14 Tomcats, but whether they were neutralised before or after a missile attack on the US task forces would depend on the nerve of the American commanders and the rules of engagement in force at the time.

Variants of the An-12 Cub and Tu-16 Badger carry out reconnaissance over the Baltic, while

surveillance activities in the Mediterranean and in the north-west Indian Ocean include regular sorties by an ASW reconnaissance version of the Il-18 airliner, the Il-38 May. Flying from bases in South Yemen, these aircraft operate over the mouth of the Persian Gulf to track Western naval activity relating to the Iraq-Iran conflict.

In the early 1980s the offensive long-range anti-surface shipping role was still entrusted largely to the Tu-16 Badger. This type needs in-flight refuelling to extend its basic combat radius of some 1,500 miles, but it can carry stand-off missiles capable of being launched from outside the range of most naval surface-to-air missiles and would still present a sharp challenge to fighters on combat air patrol. It

could seriously threaten convoys lacking the breadth of cover provided by Phoenix-armed Tomcats. In 1983 Badger-C strike aircraft deployed for the first time to Cam Ranh Bay. Based there, and with in-flight refuelling, they have the range to threaten the USN 7th Fleet headquarters at Subic Bay in the Philippines.[21] NATO strategy in anything but the shortest of wars in Europe would depend on heavy surface reinforcement, and both convoys and their ports of destination could be on the Badger target list. On the other hand, any Badger seeking to interdict the Atlantic sea lanes would have a very uncomfortable ride through the NATO air defences across and to the east of the Iceland-Faeroes gap. Meanwhile, unless the tankers needed to support such a sortie stayed "at top of climb" back in Soviet fighter-protected airspace, they too would be vulnerable to interception. Moreover, it is probable that their major targets would remain the NATO carrier and other naval units capable of launching attacks against the Soviet Union itself.

A typical Badger-C strike/attack training sortie over the Pacific was described in *Soviet Military Review* in 1978:

> The mission for the sortie was to detect and destroy "enemy" ships.
>
> Missile-carriers soared into the morning sky and headed for the east, where the search area was located. Through breaks in the clouds the dark glassy sea was visible. Fighting ships were heading for the same area.

Above Badger-Gs taking on an American carrier battle group would have to contend with the ultra-long-range Phoenix missiles of the F-14 Tomcat (foreground) and powerful jamming from the EA-6B Prowler.

Above right Badger-G carrying a single AS-6 Kingfish long-range air-to-surface missile. (*Swedish Air Force*)

Right Wingtip-to-wingtip "buddy" refuelling by two Badgers. (*Tass*)

One of the planes was piloted by Deputy Squadron Commander Vladimir Seryogin. An experienced pilot, he was all poise and attention – not a single unnecessary motion or word. The crew formed an excellent team, needed no words to understand one another. Seen through the window was the cigar-shaped fuselage of the neighbouring aircraft, piloted by its young commander, Senior Lieutenant Vladimir Danilov. . . .

Among the remarkable features of this aircraft are high speed and load-carrying capacity and long flying range. Equipped with a powerful armament, such a missile-carrier can be used to fulfil various combat missions. It is also capable of destroying targets without entering the enemy air defence zone. . . .

The crew prepared for refuelling in the air. To carry out this responsible and complicated operation, it is necessary in a very short time to assume a position exactly under the flying tanker, adjust the speed to equal that of the tanker, catch the fuel hose nozzle with the wing and make contact. . . .

In the search area the missile carrier was piloted by instruments. The crew members concentrated on the radar screen. Soon they saw a blip appear, and locked on the target. Then came the long-awaited command: "Launch!"

The missile-carrier shook as though relieving itself from a heavy load. The missile flashed and bore down on the target, leaving a fiery trail. . . .[22]

It is likely that a real attack against a task force would be carried out by several aircraft rather than just two, with a mix of missile-carriers, tankers and reconnaissance aircraft. A rather vague and probably typographically garbled report of a larger-scale exercise appeared in the London *Sunday Times* on November 13, 1984, following one or two earlier specialist press reports of infringements of Japanese airspace by groups of SNAF aircraft. The *Sunday Times* article[23] referred

111

to a group of five Badgers, including three acting as tankers, and two Bears which flew south over the Sea of Japan. The three tankers returned northwards, presumably after refuelling their "buddies," the other two Badgers turned east into the Pacific, while the two Bears continued south, probably to one of the Vietnamese airfields.

The biggest Western maritime flutter was caused by the entry into service in 1974 of the SNAF's newest land-based acquisition, the Tu-26 Backfire. The in-flight refuelling probe originally fitted to Backfire has since been removed, ostensibly to persuade the United States that the type does not present a threat to the North American mainland. It is not known whether political expediency was in this case a cover for military ineffectiveness. Backfire was the first aircraft ever to enter naval and SAF service simultaneously, and has subsequently joined naval regiments at a rate of about 15 a year. Maximum speed is Mach 1.92 and combat radius at cruising speed over 2,000 nautical miles. The prospect of a large-scale Backfire attack either round or across the North Cape and down into the Atlantic, or straight out into the Pacific from Petropavlovsk on the Kamchatka Peninsula, prompted an extensive reconsideration of US naval defensive priorities.[24] In a Soviet

Backfire-B armed with a single AS-4 Kitchen air-to-surface missile. (*Swedish Air Force*)

Right The Soviet Naval Air Force's newest shore-based anti-submarine helicopter, the Mil Mi-14 Haze-A.

Below right The carrier *Minsk*, second of the *Kiev* class. Visible on deck are four Forger-As, a Forger-B two-seater (aligned with flight deck centreline) and a Hormone ASW helicopter. (*Tass*)

worldwide exercise in 1983 Backfires operated south of the Kurile islands for the first time,[25] while on September 23, 1984, a flight of at least 20 was intercepted by Japanese fighters 167 miles off the Japanese west coast.[26]

A greatly expanded and improved long-range offensive naval air arm has a further, strategic, value to the Soviet Union. The basing of Backfire, Badger and Bear regiments at different ends of the Soviet Union allows naval air power to be concentrated in one theatre with a speed unattainable by the surface units or submarines of the four fleets. Though any such concentration would constitute a warning of possible conflict, the long reach of SNAF has nevertheless overcome many of the geographical handicaps which have vexed Russian admirals since the time of Peter the Great. SNAF can now counter the dispersed, manoeuvrable nature of opposing task forces and convoys with the high mobility of modern aircraft. The steadily increasing range and accuracy of the SNAF's stand-off weapons means that these systems will continue to be possibly the primary threat to Western surface vessels. In peacetime, Soviet Naval Air Force

units remind the West that command of the sea is no longer the prerogative of ships or shipborne aircraft. They can also demonstrate political interest or support, as on the occasions when aircraft from Vietnamese airfields have flown over the Spratly Islands in the South China Sea, possession of which is disputed by Vietnam and China.

SNAF also retains its traditional role of shorter-range offensive operations in support of amphibious landings. In exercises in the Baltic in 1983[27] Mi-14 Haze ASW helicopters set up a defensive screen while SNAF Su-17s supported the landing forces. Such operations form part of a tradition originating in the Wrangel fighting in 1920 and were no doubt witnessed by the young Lt Gorshkov in the Black Sea operations of the Great Patriotic War.

Carrier operations

Apart from the occasional use of seaplane tenders, however, there is no comparable history of offensive operations with aircraft carriers, and Admiral Gorshkov's published attitude towards these ships seems to have been ambivalent.

In 1967 he argued in an article in *Naval Digest* that the "sun was setting" on the aircraft carrier and that its "inevitable decline" was "irreversible".[28] But it would be over-hasty to conclude that this was necessarily Gorshkov's true opinion: it would not have been the first time that a Soviet leader had denigrated a weapon system not yet developed by the USSR. Though *Moskva* was about to enter service at that time, the first keel of a *Kiev*-class carrier was still three years away from its slot in the Nikolaiev yard.

In 1976 *Kiev* herself joined the Northern Fleet after attracting a large number of Western military photographers during her maiden voyage out of the Black Sea. She was followed by *Minsk* in 1979, *Novorossiisk* in 1983 and *Baku* in 1985. *Kiev* was the Soviet Navy's first platform for fixed-wing aircraft, operating the V/STOL Yak-38 Forger as well as Ka-25 Hormone helicopters. Forger and Hormone have now been closely observed in operation over several of the world's oceans. But even now Forger's exact role remains something of a mystery, since the type has no

all-weather interception or attack capability. Assuming that the *Kiev* class is designed to contribute to combined naval operations, Forger may be intended to protect the anti-submarine Hormone-As and missile-guidance Hormone-Bs. The type would also present a limited threat in clear air to any Western maritime patrol aircraft which strayed too near its Mach 0.95 capability and IR-homing air-to-air missiles, and is capable of bombing and rocket attacks against surface targets in clear weather. Some Western authorities have suggested that Forger is equipped with "high-authority auto-stabilisation" and that "it is flown automatically at low speeds".[29] If that is the case, one Russian pilot had a doubly disturbing landing on *Kiev* on his 26th birthday in 1980.

After learning to fly in a DOSAAF flying club, Major Glushko became a fighter pilot and after several requests secured a transfer to *Kiev*. He became a display pilot and indeed was offered a posting as a test pilot, which he rejected on the grounds that "he felt that his character might not find the discipline, and particularly the self-discipline, of the work to his taste."[30] Instead he continued his service on board *Kiev*, and worked to perfect a "sliding landing technique":

> In this the approach is made with very low forward speed without actually hovering. The aircraft touches down and using the iner-

tia of the low speed quickly clears the landing area, thus allowing the next aircraft to land at once. He decided to make such a landing right opposite the control bridge. But he did not quite make it and at once corrected [to avoid] the barrier, turned slightly, [and] applied some thrust to bring him back to the point he had selected. Thinking over this effort afterwards, he was a bit ashamed – supposing there had been a gust or the aircraft had lost stability; he had throttled back too late in any event.[31]

Some days later, assigned the mission number 23, he had to get it right:

On the second sortie [of the day] he again did well and told himself he had earned the cake which with stewed rabbit is the traditional birthday fare in *Kiev*. But he still had to return to the ship and to land.

As well as Glushko there were two other aircraft airborne, but the weather was obviously worsening and OC Flying ordered aircraft to return as soon as possible to the ship. There was a frontal squall approaching which the ship could not avoid.

A Forger lifts off from the aft flight deck of *Minsk*. (*Tass*)

"23, you're clear to land."
Glushko got set on his approach path.
"23, check your speed, speed."
Glushko was slow in checking his error. The other two aircraft had landed normally. Only Glushko and the rescue helicopter were airborne. The helicopter saw the snow squall approaching and requested an immediate landing. Glushko was coming out of his turn at this moment. . . .

. . . The following are extracts from the R/T log (with some post-flight comments by Glushko interspersed):
Controller "23, what is your fuel remaining?"
23 (Major Glushko) "I have . . . remaining." (calm voice)
Controller "Understood, we will make the landing."
23 "Say again, there is interference."
Controller "You're clear to land. Start your approach."
23 "Understood."

Afterwards Glushko said that as he came out of his turn, he could not see the *Kiev*. There was only a mass of whirling snow and cloud. Soon heavy turbulence started; he was not alarmed – he was too busy coping with it. The snow and cloud removed all sense of visual orientation, there was no top or bottom to the airspace in which he was flying.
23 "Home me in."
Controller "Roger, you're on the glidepath."
23 'Turn on the deck lights."
He explained: "I asked for the lights in order to see the ship as soon as possible. The turbulence continued to throw the aircraft around and I couldn't reduce speed without risking losing control."

Meanwhile the controller and the radar operator were watching the blip of the aircraft on the screen:
Controller "Range. . . . Watch your speed."
23 "Roger."
"I was trying to reduce the speed, but the turbulence was still very strong. I still could not see the ship."
Controller "Range. . . . Reduce your speed!"
23 "I am reducing speed."
"But I only had to reduce the power and the aircraft began to go nose down and I went

below the glidepath. I had to put power back on again."

Controller "23, turn left three degrees. Why are you not reducing speed? Why are you losing height?"

23 No answer.

"The most important thing was to get the heading right. Unless I did that I could miss the ship and I hadn't enough fuel to go round again for another approach. I put the stick forward and descended. There was no time to explain on the R/T."

At 20 metres he saw the ship's wake. He did not reduce speed; his hands were too busy with the stick. He looked ahead and then suddenly saw the ship itself. In the midst of the snow and mist the *Kiev* appeared illuminated in a sort of ball of light from the deck lights. Glushko turned off from the heading of the wake, gained a little height up to cloud base and entered the ball of light. The aircraft nose came up. He reduced power but the speed reduced more slowly than the rate at which the aircraft approached the deck. The video-film has preserved the scene of this landing as seen from the flight deck. In the film, blurred with flying snow, the aircraft appeared in an unusual attitude. The nose is high, the aircraft is rocking from side to side;

it is "parachuting" down to the deck. It passes over the stern at 5–6 metres above the deck; the nose dropped and he landed, striking the deck nosewheel-first.

Controller "Brakes, brakes, 23. Shut down engines."

Glushko had already applied the brakes and heard how the locked wheels shrieked, losing bits of tread. The aircraft came to a standstill.[32]

This is an intriguing account for several reasons, not least being what it reveals of the standard of celebration food in the Soviet Navy. Glushko received the congratulations of his colleagues, but in his reflections later that evening bitterness was mixed with pride. The *Red Star* article might have been a warning against overconfidence or temporary distractions, or might simply have been seeking to encourage volunteers to become test pilots, because Major Glushko's last action on his birthday was to think again about becoming one. The extract does however clearly indicate that Forger has a roller landing capability,[33] suggests that its auto-stabilisation needs some manual assistance, and leaves no doubt about the difficulties it would have in finding anything in bad weather. Some might say that it also suggests that even a competent fighter pilot regards test flying as safer than trying to land a Forger in a snowstorm.

If Major Glushko did become a test pilot, and if he sorted out his overconfidence and errors, he

Forger-A about to land on board *Kiev*. Compared with Royal Navy and US Marine Corps techniques, Forger landings are a lengthy affair, calling for a long, straight-in approach from dead astern. (*US Navy*)

might by 1985 have been contemplating the possibility of flying conventional fighters on to a carrier. It is likely that the decision to build the CVN at Nikolaiev had been taken by 1980, though only after a great deal of well publicised debate within the naval staff.

At first the debate, no doubt influenced by Khrushchev's opinions, focused on the intrinsic value of carriers. Admiral Gorshkov's 1967 view reflected several expressed during the previous decade by Marshals Zhukov, Eremenko and Sokolovskii, among others. But in 1969 Rear-Admiral K. A. Stalbo was confident enough to disagree strongly with his commander-in-chief in no less an outlet than a major textbook designed for use in Soviet naval academies:

> During World War II aviation and particularly carrier aviation played a role that was equal in importance to that played by submarines in combat operations. . . . The use of carrier aviation practically eliminated from combat operations battles involving artillery-torpedo groupings of surface forces. They were replaced by carrier forces.

> The appearance of carrier aviation enabled a country to pose an air threat almost anywhere in the world. At the same time, groupings of surface forces, covered by carrier aviation, could operate within range of the

Three Forger-As deck-parked on board the carrier *Minsk*. The nearest aircraft carries a 23mm cannon pod on its starboard outer stores pylon. (*Tass*)

enemy's shore-based aviation and along his shores. This, in turn, prompted the development of assault landing operations.

> Thus, aviation came into being as an independent arm of forces, possessing great striking power and high manoeuvrability.[34]

Though Rear-Admiral Stalbo went on to become Vice-Admiral Stalbo, Gorshkov, in his now famous eleven essays in the 1972 *Naval Digest* on "Navies in War and Peace," made no mention of carriers at all. His silence can be variously interpreted, but the facts are that during the following decade the debate in Soviet naval journals moved away from the need for carriers and towards a discussion of what size such ships should be. It is probable, as argued by one leading United States analyst, that Gorshkov's original views were submerged in the overall strategic debate. At this time Soviet military thinkers were beginning to doubt whether a war in the nuclear age would necessarily be short, and might instead call for some degree of command of the sea and of the air above it.[35] It followed that if surface ships were to have an ocean-going role, they must be provided with

Though the naval hierarchy continues to debate the value of large nuclear-powered carriers like USS *Dwight D. Eisenhower*, the Soviet Navy is to acquire at least one CVN of its own. (*Wright & Logan*)

integral air defence. Abandoning the cover of historical reflection, Admiral Stalbo continued his vigorous espousal of CVNs in 1978 with an article in *Naval Digest* which claimed that they could screen friendly SSBNs, counter opposing SSBNs, contribute to amphibious operations, protect sea lanes and show the flag. He disagreed with those who had championed the smaller, *Kiev*-type ship with the argument that CVNs were

> . . . more cost-effective. Even though they are more expensive than conventionally powered aircraft carriers, they are considerably more effective. . . . [Moreover,] the cost of building and maintaining a conventional carrier over its 25-year service life is higher than the cost of a nuclear carrier over the same period.[36]

Carriers of more than 80,000 tons, he went on, could provide far better all-weather air cover and were less vulnerable than the smaller types. It would, however, seem that rank does not inhibit Soviet admirals: 12 months later the chief editor of *Naval Digest*, Rear-Admiral Pushkin, took exception to the fact that Stalbo had dismissed the vulnerability of large carriers to submarine and air attack in a couple of sentences.[37] In

Pushkin's view the large carriers were at least as vulnerable as the others and, significantly in the light of the traditional Soviet carrier debates, they were too expensive.

The debate rumbled on, with some writers reverting to the traditional device of citing "foreign analysts" as a means of disguising their commitment to an officially unpopular line. Indeed, one Soviet observer of the lessons of the Falklands War was not above constructing some "foreign analysis" of his own. In November 1983 a lengthy article in *Naval Digest*, largely attributed to foreign analysts, touched on many aspects of the South Atlantic campaign, in the process clearly indicating what at least one faction in the Soviet Navy believes to be essential features of modern sea warfare.[38] After reporting in detail on his major topic – electronic countermeasures – the author repeatedly refers to various weaknesses in British naval air operations, including the lack of adequate air cover at the time of the loss of HMS *Sheffield*, the lack of long-range airborne target-acquisition radars, and incompatibility between various electronics systems. But then come various odd paragraphs which do not follow his previous drift, though they do probably carry messages for the Soviet naval staff:

> The conflict confirmed still another factor of no little importance in the armed struggle at sea that had been manifested back during World War II: the participation of land-based

aviation in inflicting strikes on naval targets. In connection with this, precise co-ordination between air force and navy units, and also in training aircrew personnel, is necessary.[39]

Can this perhaps be a reminder not to overlook the continued importance of Badger, Backfire and the rest? Both sides suffered from the lack of conventional aircraft carriers: ''. . . the British Navy's lack of long-range fighter-interceptors, which did not allow effective interception of enemy aircraft in the 640km zone between the continent and the Malvinas. . . .,'' while the failure of the Argentinian pilots was due in part to ''the lack not only of reconnaissance and inter-ceptor aircraft, but also of staging bases (aircraft carriers, in particular) which could increase the range of aircraft operations. . . .''[40]

The article's conclusions were also attributed to ''foreign military specialists'':

The necessity to win air supremacy and to maintain it for a long time at both the operational and the tactical levels becomes a problem which if not solved does not allow success in combat operations to be counted on. In preparing for operations in an area far from their bases, the British command prob-ably considered this factor; however, they clearly underestimated the enemy and did not achieve a dominant position in the air.

Early warning of an air threat acquires spe-cial significance. In the opinion of most West-ern military theoreticians, this task should be resolved primarily by aerospace and elec-tronic surveillance. The use of radar picket ships for this purpose without air cover is only partially justified.

American specialists believe that the great losses of surface ships from Argentine air strikes was caused by the British lack of carrier-based aircraft for long-range radar detection and aircraft command and control, like the US Navy's Hawkeye.[41]

And lest there be any doubts about the compara-tive value of aircraft like the Harrier and Forger:

Vertical take-off aircraft, as the foreign press reports, demonstrated relatively high tactical qualities in combat with enemy attack aircraft in the close-in air-defence zone, but there are no grounds for overestimating their combat capabilities. The enemy flew mainly bomber missions, with full combat loads and at maximum range.[42]

Up to this point the author could probably produce an authoritative Western source for his views, but he attributes to ''British specialists'' the steps which must be taken to increase the effectiveness of the carrier strike group. These include

The Grumman E-2C Hawkeye gives the US Navy unparalleled airborne early warning cover and command and control facilities. (*US Navy*)

. . . equip[ping] carrier strike groups with long-range highly manoeuvrable interceptors for conducting formation air battle, which should prevent enemy aircraft from penetrating the first line of defence during mass raids (the use of the Sea Harrier V/STOL for short-range air defence has confirmed its effectiveness only in performing this mission).[43]

This sentiment may indeed lie in the hearts if not the mouths of British admirals, but it is more directly attributable to the interests of the author, following in the steps of Admiral Stalbo, than to any ''British specialist'' analysing measures within the compass of a British government.

By 1984 it looked as if Admiral Stalbo had won the day. The only doubts about the CVN under construction at Nikolaiev were whether her size was in the order of 65,000 tons, as forecast by the United States Government,[44] or closer to the 75,000 suggested by analysts of the Jane's photographic scoop of August 1984.[45] The same article reported that flight tests using a simulated angled deck with arrester wires had been taking place at an airfield in the Black Sea area for ''three to four years,'' and that *Kremlin* could be expected to begin sea trials in 1988–89.

Minsk and her sisters have taught the Soviet Navy much about V/STOL aviation at sea. In the late 1980s the new CVN *Kremlin* will bring with her the even sterner demands of conventional naval aircraft. (*Tass*)

There is no doubt that she will add substantially to Soviet maritime air capability, but history suggests that in war she would operate according to Soviet traditions of combined operations rather than as the pivotal weapon system, as in a USN task force. She would extend Soviet anti-SSBN operations; cover friendly SSBNs; present a localised threat to opposing surface shipping; and facilitate Soviet amphibious operations and complicate Western planning of similar activities within her sailing radius. Peacetime activities will include the showing of a formidable flag in Third World ports. But, as the evolution of Soviet maritime aviation since 1945 illustrates, the presence of one CVN on the Nikolaiev slipway does not necessarily guarantee that several others will follow. The evolution of the threat and of political objectives, and the outcome of clashes of will within the naval hierarchy, will determine how many sister ships take to the oceans.

By 1985 SNAF had matched the expansion of the Soviet surface and submarine fleets. It was perhaps not yet ready to offer a serious challenge to Western naval supremacy, but it could certainly threaten NATO reinforcement strategy, increase the vulnerability of Western surface forces, extend protection to and communication with friendly SSBNs, monitor Western naval forces far beyond Soviet frontiers, and make regular gestures of friendship or interest for the benefit of countries well beyond the reach of the Red Army.

Notes

1 *Soviet Naval Aviation 1917–20*, an unpublished paper written in 1979 by Alexander Boyd, to whom I am indebted for details of the earliest Soviet maritime air operations, translated from various Soviet sources published between 1923 and 1969.

2 Ibid.

3 Ibid.

4 Order No 447/78, March 25, 1920, quoted by Boyd ibid.

5 Quoted in *The Development of Naval Aviation, 1908–1975*, Jacob W. Kipp, in *Soviet Aviation and Air Power, A Historical View*, ed Higham and Kipp, Brassey's, page 145.

6 Quoted in Kipp ibid, pages 147–148.

7 Kipp ibid, page 157.

8 For example, G. E. Lindsay and Michael McGuire, quoted in *Soviet Navy ASW Aviation*, Dr Milan Vego, *Navy International*, June 1984, page 373.

9 Unreferenced extract from *Military Thought* "shortly after the end of World War II," quoted by Norman Polmar in *Stronger Sealegs For Soviet Air Power* in *Air Enthusiast/International*, June 1974, page 272.

10 For example, Polmar ibid.

11 *Istoriia voenno-morakogo iskusstva*, S. E. Zakharov *et al*, quoted in Kipp op cit, page 158.

12 Quoted in Polmar op cit, page 277.

13 *Combat Actions of Aviation Against Submarines*, Lt-Col Y. A. Bryukhanov, *Naval Digest*, June 1966, quoted by Vego op cit, page 377.

14 *Navies in War and Peace*, S. G. Gorshkov, *US Naval Institute Proceedings*, November 1974.

15 V. Efremenko, *Naval Digest* No 10 1970, quoted in Kipp op cit, page 160.

16 *Soviet Naval Air Arm*, Maj-Gen of Aviation N. Vishensky, Deputy Chief of Staff, USSR Naval Air Arm, *Air Defence Herald*, 1978.

17 All figures taken from *The Military Balance*, International Institute for Strategic Studies, London, 1984.

18 *Search*, Capt 2nd Rank N. Pavlov, *Soviet Military Review* 11/1981.

19 Details of Bear reconnaissance activities were summarised in *Jane's Defence Weekly*, May 12, 1984, pages 727–728.

20 Ibid.

21 Statement by USN Rear-Admiral J. L. Butts to House Armed Services Committee. Reported in *Jane's Defence Weekly*, March 17, 1984, page 394.

22 *Lightning Over The Sea*, Maj N. Yorzh, *Soviet Military Review*, February 1978, page 31.

23 *Sunday Times*, November 24, 1984, page 6, report by David Watts from Tokyo.

24 See for example the paper by W. D. O'Neill, *Backfire: Long Shadow of the Sealanes*, United States Naval Institute Proceedings, March 1977, pages 27–35.

25 Butts op cit.

26 *Aviation Week and Space Technology*, October 8, 1984.

27 Butts op cit.

28 *Naval Digest*, February 1967, pages 9–21, quoted by Lt K. Lynch USNR in *Their Seabased Aviation*, United States Naval Institute Proceedings, October 1982, page 46.

29 For example, the uncredited article *In Soviet Service, The Yakovlev 36MP*, *Air International*, January 1979.

30 *Shipboard Pilot*, A. Tkachev, *Red Star*, May 31, 1980, translated by Wg Cdr F. J. French RAF ret.

31 Ibid.

32 Ibid.

33 Experiments of the kind practised by Major Glushko may have been taken further. In August 1984 *Flight International* suggested that Forger had been observed making short take-offs and landings, "previously thought to be extremely difficult if not impossible." *Flight* also suggested that such capability indicated "a very high-authority automatic stabilisation and flight control system". *Flight International*, August 25, 1984, page 169.

34 *A History of the Art of Naval Warfare*, Rear-Admiral K. A. Stalbo, Moscow 1969.

35 *Aircraft Carrier Development in Soviet Naval Theory*, C. C. Petersen, *Naval War College Review*, Jan-Feb 1984, pages 4–13.

36 *Aircraft Carriers of the Post War Period*, Vice-Admiral K. A. Stalbo, *Naval Digest*, June 1978.

37 *American and Japanese Submarine Warfare against Aircraft Carriers in World War II*, Rear-Admiral A. Pushkin, *Naval Digest*, September 1979.

38 *Electronic Warfare During the British/Argentine Conflict*, Capt B. Rodionov, *Naval Digest*, January 1983.

39 Ibid.

40 Ibid.

41 Ibid.

42 Ibid.

43 Ibid.

44 *Soviet Military Power*, 1984, page 63.

45 *Jane's Defence Weekly*, August 11, 1984, page 171.

CHAPTER 5

Long Range Aviation

"LONG Range Aviation" is the translation of
Dal'naya Aviatsiya (DA), the name given to that
part of the Soviet Air Forces responsible for
medium and long-range bombing between 1946
and its most recent reorganisation at the beginning of the 1980s. It is therefore neither an up-
to-date nor a comprehensive title, but it covers
the years in which the Soviet bomber force
emerged as "long-range, missile-equipped"[1]
and is the most convenient way to categorise
those offensive aircraft which were not previously under the command of Frontal Aviation
and are not now commanded within military
districts.

Just as the Soviets' ideas of air supremacy

Bear-H, a new-production version of Tupolev's four-turboprop
strategic bomber, is capable of carrying cruise missiles
underwing.

include a uniquely Russian strain, so their view
of strategic bombardment, while resembling
those of the USAF's Strategic Air Command and
the erstwhile RAF Bomber Command, has been
influenced by specifically Soviet circumstances.
In the United Kingdom it was strategic bombing,
together with air defence of the UK and air operations in the residue of empire, that prompted
the emergence of a Royal Air Force independent
of the army and navy. In the United States the
strategic bombardment role of the United States

123

Army Air Corps laid the foundations for its emergence as the United States Air Force. Both countries, secure from attack by sea and land, could distinguish quite clearly between operations in support of surface forces and those directed at the industrial heart of an enemy. In the Soviet Union, just as air defence of the homeland became inseparable from tactical air defence in the First World War, the Civil War and the Second World War, so for the greater part of its history long-range air bombardment has been associated with operations on land, and for much of the time has been a poor relation.

This was not necessarily so, however. After the First World War, and again after the Second World War, there were strong influences at work to encourage the construction of a Soviet strategic bomber force designed to attack not just an enemy's military rear areas but, in the manner of SAC and Bomber Command, to take the war directly to the enemy's industrial and political heart. Indeed, by 1985 there were signs that this could become a practical proposition for DA, reconstructed in 1980 as the "Aviation Armies of the Soviet Union" (AASU)[2]. Western analysts have occasionally belittled Soviet bomber development, emphasising its insignificant contribution in the Second World War, its limited evolution since 1945, and its uneven record of technical success by comparison with the Western effort. It can however be argued that in view of the military, political, economic and technological factors influencing Soviet military aviation since the First World War the very survival of DA, let alone its significant strengthening over the last decade, is no mean feat.

Though AASU currently remains the Cinderella of the Soviet Air Forces, it is certainly a formidable member of the Soviet military household and there are several reasons why it is unlikely to be sent back below stairs in the foreseeable future.

Potential and eclipse: 1914–1940

Soviet accounts of the nation's early military aviation combine genuine pride in Russian achievement with efforts to ascribe it entirely to Marxist-Leninist inspiration. The only official history of "Heavy Aviation" is an example of this kind of writing:

> It was not by chance that the world's first heavy aircraft took off from Russian soil. Moreover, this event would have taken place much sooner if the reactionary autocratic regime had not retarded the progress of native scientific thought, and if the powers that be in Russia had not deferred to foreign authorities, curbing the talents of their own nation.[3]

The aircraft was the four-engined *Le Grand*, prototype of the Il'ya Muromets reconnaissance bomber, designed by Igor Sikorsky and built at the Russo-Baltic railway waggon factory. In February 1915 the first Muromets squadron – "The Flotilla of Flying Ships" – began operations against German troops and military targets from its base at Yablonny airfield near Warsaw. During the next two years the Flotilla flew 300 sorties against seaplane bases, ammunition dumps, railway junctions and other targets. In ensuing campaigns in the Civil War and against Poland the Muromets was developed until with a crew of five it could carry 320lb of bombs to a ceiling of 9,000ft over a combat radius of approximately 100km.

Inevitably, Lenin is credited with a personal interest in the heavy bomber – which was just as well, because Sikorsky and many other Russian aviation pioneers fled the turmoil of the Revolution, leaving the infant service denuded of much of its real talent and inspiration. Nevertheless, a Heavy Aviation Section was included in the Aeronautical Department of the Main Administration of the Air Fleet in 1920, and in the following year a three-year plan envisaged the construction of 30 additional bombardment units of six bombers each, together with "long-range reconnaissance subunits and special-purpose detachments made up of four-engined aircraft".[4] In August 1922 the 10th Congress of the Russian Communist Party directed that priority be given to the development of heavy aircraft. Lenin's interest apparently extended down to the smallest detail:

> He personally participated in a discussion on feeding Muromets aircrews, and signed a

Between 70 and 80 examples of the Il'ya Muromets heavy bomber were built during the First World War. They operated successfully in that conflict and the ensuing Civil War. (*Sikorsky*)

resolution by the Council of Labour and Defence which stated that "aircrew personnel of the Il'ya Muromets division must be fed according to the standards and in the manner prescribed by Order No 1765 (1920) of the Revolutionary Military Council of the Republic, whereas all other personnel of the division at the front and in the rear must be fed by the front Food and Ration Committee and the rear area Food and Ration Committee, respectively".[5]

One wonders whether the father of the USAF's Strategic Air Command, General Curtis LeMay, and a famous C-in-C of RAF Bomber Command, Air Chief Marshal Sir Kenneth Cross, were aware of the example they were following when they also instituted special rations for their aircrew.

Flying training for the heavy bomber squadrons was carried out at the Higher Aviation School for Aerial Combat and Bombing at Serpukhov, which some 40 years later was to become one of four academies training officers for the Strategic Rocket Troops. In 1923, however, the Muromets were withdrawn from service and the Soviet Government was forced to look to foreign designs. The official Soviet history would have the world believe that in the event indigenous Russian skills made collaboration with the grasping capitalists unnecessary:

Our young aviation needed new aircraft. Accordingly, consideration was given in 1924 to a bid by a British firm for the design and manufacture of a modern heavy bomber for the VVS. However, the Englishmen imposed patently unacceptable conditions, namely, 500,000 roubles in gold, and a year and a half for the design work alone. The Soviet Government declined the tendered foreign "services". The order for the new aircraft was placed with the Central Aerohydrodynamics Institute for the attention of a collective headed by A. N. Tupolev. The Soviet designers, airframe engineers, and working-level enthusiasts completed the assignment in record time. They designed and built the bomber in nine months, at a cost of just 40 per cent of the sum bid by the British firm.[6]

It is perhaps a pity that the British Government and Rolls-Royce were not similarly mercenary in

1946, when they presented the Soviets with Nene and Derwent jet engines.

In fact, Russian military aviation between the wars depended very heavily on foreign expertise and example. British de Havilland DH.9 and DH.9A bombers – some captured during the Civil War, some bought – were flown and adapted for Soviet use. But the most significant foreign influence resulted from the secret Russo-German agreement covering production of German military aircraft at Fili near Moscow and the establishment of a flying training base at Lipetsk in central Russia. Most new German aircraft of the time, including the Dornier DoP four-engined heavy bomber and the Junkers all-metal trimotor K30, were tested at Lipetsk. Their lines were clearly discernible in Tupolev's early ANT series, in the TB-1, the first Soviet twin-engined all-metal bomber, and, most obviously in the four-engined TB-3.[7]

Two examples of the use of the TB-3 by Stalin foreshadowed DA's more recent activities. First, he ordered the appearance of eight examples of the ANT-6, the original version of the bomber, in the May Day flypast of 1932, less than five months after the first production model had been delivered to the VVS for acceptance trials. Thereafter, massed formations of TB-3s made an impressive contribution to the annual event, drawing the attention of the world to the supposed military might, and indeed heavy bomber pre-eminence, of the USSR. Also in 1932, three senior officers were sent to the headquarters of the Special Far Eastern Army Air Force to advise on the preparation of bases and servicing facilities for heavy bombers. In the following year the first three TB-3 brigades were allocated to the Far East, indicating over very long range the serious interest being taken by the USSR in Japanese encroachment in Manchuria. The Japanese response of improving their air defences in the region suggests that the gesture did not go unnoticed.

Meanwhile, as the expanding bomber force was paraded before the world, much thought was being given to its use in war. Little is known about the actual extent of the influence of foreign air power theorists on VVS thinking between the wars. Guilio Douhet's thoughts on the role of strategic air bombardment were not translated

Production of the Tupolev TB-3 four-engined bomber ran to a total of 818 between 1931 and 1938. The type saw action in Manchuria against the Japanese and in the Winter War with Finland.

into Russian until 1935, but when they were they carried an introduction by V. V. Khripin, a fact perhaps of greater significance than the translation itself. Khripin had joined the Bolsheviks after flying with the Imperial Air Force, and reached senior command by 1919. But, perhaps because of his questionable bourgeois origins or indeed his ideas about air power, he did not win any of the highest positions in the infant VVS. He did however write regularly in Soviet military journals on air warfare, emphasising the essential need for an independent air arm. There is no reason to suppose that such ideas would be any more popular with army commanders in Russia than they were in Britain or the USA. In fact they would probably have been even more divisive in a country which had hitherto seen no reason to distinguish between strategic and tactical air power in either offence or defence, which was still desperately short of industrial resources, and in which the army was still very close to the political revolution which it had supported and defended.

Khripin was however not alone in his thinking about modern warfare. Among those sharing his views were Mikhail Tukhachevsky, who became Director of Red Army Ordnance, Yakov Alksnis, who became head of VVS, and A. I. Egorov, who became Chief of Red Army Staff; all were promoted in 1931. Tukhachevsky had argued for the development of airborne forces, long-range air bombardment and the use of chemical warfare to deny to the enemy areas needed for troop concentrations, preparation, resupply and reinforcement. Alksnis shared Tukhachevsky's views on long-range aerial bombardment and encouraged the study of foreign technical and military literature. Egorov's thoughts on shifting the fight beyond the battlefront were embodied in the "Provisional Directives for the Organisation of Battle in Depth," published by the Soviet General Staff in 1933:

> . . . In the event of an attack on the USSR by a capitalist power or coalition . . . the task of our air forces is to strike at the roots of mobilisation and at the concentration of enemy armies, and to destroy the economic-industrial life of whole regions, primarily those of military significance.[8]

In 1936 the Special Purpose Air Arm (AON) was created. Directly subordinate to the Defence Secretariat, it was commanded by Khripin. The AON comprised all the VVS heavy bombers and long-range transports, together with supporting fighters and shorter-range fighter-bombers. At the time this must have seemed extremely close to an independent air force, even though Khripin was nominally outranked by Alksnis. Moreover, in an age when air defences worldwide were being challenged by innovations in offensive air power, the industrial heartlands of Germany and Japan – both potentially hostile and both just within TB-3 range – must have seemed attractive targets for the AON. Thus, less than three years from the outbreak of the Second World War, Russia had the ideas, the developing equipment, a surprising degree of inter-service agreement, the embryonic organ-

isation and a politico-strategic rationale for producing a fully fledged long-range bomber force. Yet by 1940 the whole scheme lay in discredited tatters.

Some of the reasons for the eclipse are clear, some more speculative. Most obvious was the execution of all the protagonists of independent air power: Tukhachevsky, Egorov, Khripin, Alksnis and the professor of air tactics at the Frunze Military Academy, General A. Lapchinsky. All were victims of Stalin's purge in 1937 and 1938 of the higher ranks of the Soviet armed forces. There may well have been a strong fear of guilt by association among the survivors, and no one stepped forward to take up their ideas. Even Tupolev, the pre-eminent designer of heavy military aircraft, was despatched to Siberia. The chief aeronautical scientist at the Central Institute of Aerodynamics and Hydrodynamics was replaced by a politically reliable but scientifically unimpressive nonentity. One designer, Kalinin, was accused of sabotage and executed when an experimental aircraft crashed during a test flight, killing four Party members. Yet aircraft production expanded rapidly during the period of the Third Five-Year Plan, beginning in 1938, to an estimated 700–750 machines per month by 1940.[9] Of these, however, very few were heavy bombers. The TB-3 was obsolete by 1939, and its putative successors, the TB-7 and Pe-8, never went into large-scale production.

While aircraft production had expanded, quality had not kept pace. Soviet medium-range bombers in particular suffered heavily at the hands of the German Messerschmitt Bf 109s in Spain, though this experience seems to have prompted the Russians to improve their fighters rather than their bombers. Moreover, as the contemporary British government also decided, four single-engined aircraft were more attractive than one four-engined bomber, particularly when bombsights and long-range navigation aids were still at a very early stage in their development.

Some writers have suggested that the increased mechanisation of agriculture and the creation of *Osoaviakhim*, a voluntary organisation dedicated to training young people in military skills, greatly increased the "mechanical literacy" among the people. Even so, the enormous increase in aircraft production in the 1930s must have stretched human and industrial resources to the utmost, and the subsequent problems with the technical training of ground crews must have been severe. There must have been lively debate about the allocation of resources: to air supremacy, to tactical offensive support in shturmovik style, to strategic bombing? Shorn of the imaginative leadership of Tukhachevsky and his like, the Soviet generals must have reverted to the safe and orthodox and given priority to air power in combined-arms operations, a doctrine with reputable roots in the Revolution.

Much has changed in the 50 years since that first rapid eclipse, but political inhibition, technological limitations, and questions of resource allocation still have a bearing on Soviet long-range aviation. On the other hand, Tukhachevsky, Khripin, Egorov and Lapchinsky seem to have prevailed posthumously: their writings were rehabilitated and published by the Soviet Government in 1965,[10] and there is much in common between the roles allocated to AASU in 1985 and those hoped for from AON in 1935.

Myth and reality 1941–1954

In the foreword to *Long Range, Missile Equipped*, Marshal of Aviation Agal'tsov explains: "The reader is made familiar with the important role played by long-range bomber formations during the principal operation of the Great Patriotic War. . . . The facts cited in this book testify to the great contribution made by ADD toward destroying Hitler's air force on the ground and winning air superiority for the VVS."[11] Later the author himself refers to "200,000 sorties, ie 6% of the VVS total, during the Great Patriotic War . . . 40% in support of ground forces . . . 30% against enemy rail communications. . . ."[12]

Long Range, Missile Equipped, liberally illustrated with cameos of heroism by bomber aircrew, was written by a deputy chief of the Soviet Air Force Political Directorate for "those of our young people who intend to dedicate themselves to service in the Air Force."[13] Though intended to promote contemporary Long Range Aviation by references to its deeds in the Second World War, it makes an already dubious case

Designed with open crew positions, as shown here, the TB-3 eventually featured nose and dorsal turrets. Defensive armament totalled ten 7.62mm machine guns

worse by falling into apparent historical inaccuracies. A six per cent share would not normally be regarded as significant, and the contribution of Soviet bombers to victory is no exception. The obsolete TB-3s of the Tukhachevsky era were shot out of the skies in daylight by Bf 109s in the summer and autumn of 1941. While admitting to heavy losses in the opening months of the war, the author omits to record that the bombing impact on the advancing German forces was negligible. By day the bombers were destroyed, by night their lack of navigational and bombing aids made them not only ineffective but also susceptible to further losses through navigational error. Attacks on Konigsberg and other East Prussian targets failed disastrously, apparently prompting the suicide of one of Long Range Bomber Aviation's commanders, Lt-Gen Kopets. Very soon afterwards, in March 1942,

Stalin extracted the remaining long-range bombers, together with the heavy transports, from tactical aviation and DBA and redeployed them into a new organisation, the *Aviatsiia Dal'nego Deistviaa* (ADD), or Long Range Air Force. There seems to be no first-hand explanation for the reorganisation, but such a decision could only have been taken by Stalin himself. It may have been an attempt to centralise command of longer-range assets to avoid the penny-packet operations, and associated lack of impact, of the early months of the war. Or it may have been, as one contemporary airman believed[14], due to the fact that Stalin wanted an air arm directly subordinate to himself which could be used as a strategic reserve. Or he may have wished to launch attacks on targets in Germany itself in a traditional strategic bomber manner. If so, Stalin appears not to have had much grasp of the nature of such operations, as revealed by this 1944 assessment from the head of the US military mission to Moscow: ". . . it was plainly evident that neither he nor any of his military advisers had any conception of the specialised technique required to ensure target coverage, formation control or defence against hostile forces."[15] Vasil'yev implies that the aim was in fact to enhance central control and strategic direction of both operational support and strategic missions.[16] If this is the case, the same kind of thinking was to re-emerge in the reorganisation of the heavy bombers in the early 1980s.

In the event, the achievements of ADD were minuscule compared with those of 8th Air Force or Bomber Command, and its main concern continued to be support of the ground battle. Raids seldom involved more than 75 aircraft, even though ADD ultimately disposed of 1,500 machines in 50 regiments. It remained hampered by lack of navigation and night bombing aids. On the credit side, night harassment attacks contributed to the breakdown of German air reinforcement in the Battle of Stalingrad, and air superiority during the Kuban campaign was greatly facilitated by large-scale attacks on Luftwaffe-held airfields in the Crimea. Flown as transports, Soviet bombers dropped supplies to partisans behind the German lines and to Tito's forces in Yugoslavia. Later in the war the Luftwaffe was sufficiently concerned about night attacks to establish a night fighter organisation behind the battlefronts in eastern Europe.

Only one new bomber, the Tu-2, saw extensive squadron service during the war. ADD's "heavy" bombers – the Tu-2, Pe-2 and Il-4 – were all twin-engined. A "strategic" attack was as often as not one carried out in the immediate rear of the enemy. This is explained in part by the fact that there was little incentive to revise the priorities of Russian aircraft production. After the Casablanca agreements of 1942 the German heartland became the target for American and British round-the-clock strategic bombardment, and it made far more sense for Russian industrial resources to be allocated to fighters and fighter-bombers. It is therefore accurate but misleading to suggest that the Soviet air forces were deficient in heavy bombers in the Western sense; the truth is that they simply did not need them. By using ADD regiments virtually as an extension of the air armies, the Soviet High Command was able to concentrate great force wherever it was required.

In November 1944 ADD was retitled the 18th Air Army and nominally integrated with the VVS. In fact it remained directly under the Soviet High Command, available for allocation as circumstances dictated. For example, in March 1945 800 bombers from the 18th Air Army were allocated to support Zhukov's campaign against Berlin, supplementing the 7,000 aircraft in the tactical air armies of the First Byelorussian Front. Significantly in the light of subsequent Soviet air power concepts, Zhukov's offensive was to be preceded by a massed strike by the 18th Air Army aircraft, followed immediately by shorter-range bombers and fighter-bombers.

The concentration of Soviet bombers on ground support rather than long-range bombardment led some post-war Western analysts to conclude that Russia either lacked an air strategy altogether, or moved from an "extemporised, opportunistic, a fill the gap strategy . . . [to] . . . the utilisation of manned 'flying artillery' to support its ground armies."[17] More accurately, there was no "independent" Soviet air strategy, rather a consistent and ultimately relentless use of air power to provide a third dimension to combined-arms warfare on a scale unknown in the West or the Pacific. In such a context, the existence of a "real" long-range bomber force was irrelevant to the central Soviet objective in the Great Patriotic War: the defeat and expulsion of the Wehrmacht from Russian soil. And yet in April 1944 Stalin asked the United States for more than 500 four-engined B-24 Liberators and B-17 Flying Fortresses under Lease-Lend. He is also reported to have asked a number of "very intelligent questions about United States long-range bombers"[18] at the Teheran Conference the previous year.

One can only speculate about Stalin's reasons for these enquiries. He would have realised that the much longer range and heavier bomb load of the American aircraft could have been used not only against Germany but also to enhance the current operations of ADD. He could have seen them as giving a much needed technological boost to his own aviation industry, or he could even then have been thinking of the time when temporary allies would once more be ideological enemies. Neither the B-24 nor the B-17 could have attacked the USA from Russia, though both designs were susceptible to further development. Within 12 months, however, the question was rendered academic when three USAAF B-29s force-landed and a fourth crash-landed in Siberia after operations against Japan. Tupolev was charged with copying the B-29 airframe and the engine designer Shvetsov with reproducing the Wright Whirlwind engine. By March 1945, less than a year later, the several thousand parts of the B-29, at the time the world's most advanced military aircraft, had been copied, assembled, flown and actually put into production. There is little need to speculate about Stalin's motives in forcing ahead with the Tu-4, as the copy was labelled. He knew about Western atomic weapon developments; he could have had no doubts about the power base of any future anti-Russian coalition; and if he did entertain ideas of world domination by Soviet communism, there was only one country strong enough to stand in his way. To counter the long-range threat of USAAF B-29s he ordered the production of over 1,000 Tu-4s. The Tu-4 could have reached North America on a one-way mission, and after 1949 the USSR began to make atomic bombs for airborne delivery.

And so in the latter 1940s a resurgence of

Soviet long-range bomber strength seemed imminent for the first time since the heady days of Lapchinsky, Khripin and the rest. In 1946 the bomber regiments were again reconstituted, this time to form the *Dal'naya Aviatsiya* (DA) or Long Range Aviation (LRA), a title by which Soviet strategic aviation was to be known for the next 35 years. This time there was political support at the highest level, a clearly defined motive, the promise of an appropriate weapon, and, as the Tu-4 entered service in increasing numbers, a growth in the technical and operating expertise for which there had been no demand during the Second World War. Though the vulnerability of the B-29 to the MiG-15 over Korea may later have dampened Stalin's enthusiasm, Tupolev went on to produce a Tu-4 derivative with a projected range of over 6,000 miles which flew as the Tu-85 in 1950. Redesigned with swept wings and turboprop engines, it entered production as the Tu-95 Bear in 1955.

In the same period the development of a 19,000lb static thrust turbojet engine, the Mikulin AM-3, might have encouraged Stalin to drive his aircraft designers to meet the standard set by the United States' B-47 jet-engined bomber, which entered squadron service in 1951, and the prototype B-52, which flew in April 1952. Tupolev produced the twin-engined medium-range Tu-16 Badger, but is reported to have

The Bear strategic bomber, still in production as the Bear-H cruise missile-carrier, was preceded by the Tupolev Tu-4 copy of the American Boeing B-29. (*US Navy*)

Development of the Tu-16 Badger may have been stimulated by the emergence of the USAF's B-47.

believed that the high fuel consumption of the AM-3 made it unsuitable for installation in an intercontinental bomber.[19] But the Myasishchev bureau went ahead with a four-engined bomber designed for a 16,000km range. Designated M-4 (NATO code name Bison), it took part with the Tu-16 in the 1954 May Day flypast over Red Square. At the time Bison was believed to have a slightly shorter range than but a similar bomb load to the early B-52,[20] and was regarded, with the Tu-95 Bear, as a direct threat to North America. Some observers,[21] in arguing that

Stalin's preoccupations were with Europe, have failed to take into account the time lapse between military planning and execution. In the mid-1950s some two dozen airfields were built as bomber bases in the Arctic Circle and Northern Russia from Murmansk to Eastern Siberia and supported by a special air transport organisation. In-flight refuelling, particularly of the Tu-16 Badger, was given much greater emphasis from 1957, which led to speculation about "one-way" attacks on the USA. Bison, Bear and Badger could have carried the thermonuclear weapon

The outwardly impressive but ultimately disappointing Bison. This is a Bison-C, a maritime reconnaissance variant distinguished by its more pointed nose profile.

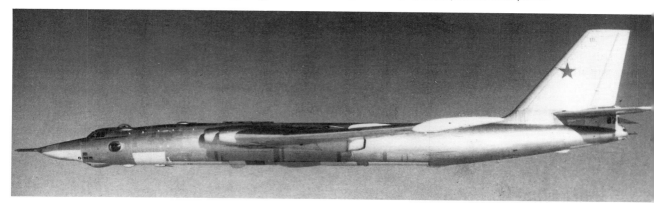

developed by the Soviet Union after 1953.

In sum, before he died in 1953 Stalin could have looked forward confidently to having an intercontinental bomber force equipped with nuclear weapons and threatening the USA from forward air bases. This vision was shared by influential opinion in the United States. The end of US strategic air power superiority was foreseen; Bison was reported to be invulnerable to US interceptors because of its height and speed capability, and the USSR was expected to produce some 600–700 of the type.[22] Yet just three years later, in 1957, the limitations on Bear's speed and Bison's range and numbers were apparent. It had become clear that the most serious threat to the United States, if not to Western Europe, would come from the intercontinental ballistic missile (ICBM), not the manned bomber. It later became fashionable to denigrate both the Russian bomber programme and those who had overestimated its capability. Thirty years later, the capability and potential of the Soviet bomber force are again contentious issues. The exaggerated hopes and fears of the 1950s may therefore be worth close examination, now with the benefit of hindsight.

Potential and eclipse 1955–1970

The fact that Soviet long-range aviation did not in the event pose the threat expected of it in 1954 was due partly to the limitations of contemporary Soviet technology and partly to a Western misunderstanding of Soviet air power doctrine. But primarily responsible was a major shift in the Soviet Union's assessment of the usefulness of the manned bomber as the main weapon in an intercontinental nuclear war.

Tupolev's misgivings about the capacity of Soviet jet engines were first substantiated by the poor performance of the M-4 Bison. Khrushchev is not an impartial observer, but his account of the accident-strewn development of the aircraft and its subsequent failure to come anywhere near its specification has not been disputed. Of its supersonic successors, the Tu-22 Blinder was produced in only limited numbers, while a further delta-wing design by Myasishchev, the M-50 Bounder, which caused a flutter when displayed at Tushino in 1961, never entered regimental service.

Western fears stemmed in part from expectations in the United States that Soviet theories of strategic air power were much closer to those of the USAF than in fact they were. In 1955, for example, a distinguished and influential USAF reserve general explained the origins and emergence of post-war Soviet long-range air power, arguing that ". . . bomber aircraft are needed [now] both to support ground forces and to carry out independent strategic operations. . . . It is hard to see how the Soviets could have failed to conclude that the development of a strong and genuinely global air capability must

Tupolev Tu-22 Blinder, one of the Soviet Union's two premature attempts to produce a supersonic strategic bomber.

The Myasishchev M-50 Bounder was less of a success than Blinder, failing even to enter regimental service.

had exaggerated the contribution of Soviet long-range air power to victory, long before General Vasil'yev's hagiography of 1972. From 1946 onwards the role of strategic bombing had been given greater prominence in the writings of some senior Soviet officers. For example, Douhet's ideas were resurrected in the Air Force journal *Herald of the Air Fleet* in 1946:

> . . . it has now become an indisputable fact that along with operational-tactical aviation, the main task of which consists of direct support to the operations of ground troops, there must also exist strategic aviation. It would appear that contemporary air forces are capable of deciding not only tactical, but also operational and strategic tasks, which no arm other than aviation can fulfil.
>
> Concerning the form of future war the following thoughts suggest themselves: in future engagements the place of application of the main force will be not so much the front as the rear of the enemy.[25]

In the same year the deputy commander of Long Range Aviation attested to the value of strategic aviation in forcing an enemy to divert large forces away from the front to strengthen his air defence system.[26] But the subtle implications of such statements, compared with the previous, far more sweeping assessment of the role of strategic aviation, were not always picked up in the USA. There was undoubtedly a keen Soviet interest in strategic air power – but only within the traditional context of Soviet all-arms doctrine. References to "independent" air power were much less common than criticism of USAF bombardment theories – hyperbolic exaggeration of the role and significance of strategic aviation"[27] – and reaffirmation of traditional doctrine. Soviet writers of the time may well have been deliberately denigrating strategic air power at a time when LRA was in no position to retaliate in kind, but they were also consistent in stressing its "supplementary" function. This was expressed in *Military Thought* in 1949:

> Soviet military science considers that the outcome of war under contemporary conditions is decided on the field of battle by means of the annihilation of the armed forces of the

become the highest-priority objective of their military preparations."[23] In the following year General Nathan Twining returned from a visit to Moscow and stressed the threat to United States air power:

> Of late there has been a wealth of visible evidence that the mightiest of all potential aggressors is determined to surpass the technology in general of the United States, and our air power in particular. I needed no trip to Moscow to convince me of this. . . .
>
> The evidence can be seen in the form of big jet bombers and swift jet fighters which wing their way in ever increasing numbers through Soviet skies. The evidence can be heard in reports of atomic explosions originating deep within the Soviet land mass. . . .[24]

Western observers had noted the many articles in Soviet military journals since 1945 which enemy, and that one of the most important tasks of aviation is active assistance to the ground and naval forces in all forms of their combat activity. This definition of the fundamental mission of aviation is not contradicted by the need to employ part of its forces to strike the deep rear of the enemy, on his military-industrial targets, but our military science does not consider such blows an end in themselves, but only a helpful means of creating favourable conditions for the success of the combat operations of the ground and naval forces.[28]

Underlying such thinking was an assumption that future wars would still be decided on the battlefield, regardless of the destructive power of nuclear weapons. In this respect there seems to be a discrepancy between what Soviet military theorists believed and what Stalin was seeking. A well publicised Soviet defector to the West left his readers in no doubt. He reported Stalin as saying in 1947 that possession of a transatlantic missile ". . . would make it easier to talk with the gentleman shopkeeper Harry Truman, and keep him pinned down where we want him."[29] But then in 1949 the manned bomber must have seemed a better prospect for delivering a nuclear weapon to New York than did an ICBM based on captured German drawings and test data.

Even when the impact of nuclear weapons on warfare in general and aviation in particular was acknowledged after 1954, the emphasis in Soviet writing remained at first on the "supplementary" rather than the "independent" function, though ". . . the relative weight of aviation in the composition of the armed forces [had] grown significantly in the postwar period".[30] These analyses revealed not only the essential difference between the LRA and USAF concepts of strategic bombardment, but also a major theme in the evolution of thinking about nuclear warfare in general. To the Soviet Union nuclear weapons belonged within traditional combined-arms strategies, and so were destined for targets whose destruction would directly or indirectly affect the central battle: military-industrial complexes, communications and longer-range military forces. It is thus reasonable to assume that from the early 1950s SAC bases

and nuclear-armed US Navy units were high-priority targets for LRA. But, in the traditions of Western strategic air power, SAC saw attacks on military intallations as secondary to the main objective of destroying the enemy's warmaking potential. SAC's primary role was summarised in 1949 by the then Secretary of the United States Air Force, quoting General Omar Bradley: "At the instant of aggression, the United States must fling the full force of its strategic bombing offensive against the enemy's heartland . . . to destroy, at the very outset of hostilities, the enemy's means of making and supporting an attack against this nation and its allies."[31] These contrasting air power concepts are paralleled by the two sides' opposing notions on the use of nuclear weapons: Soviet war-fighting, Western deterrence based on massive retaliation against the enemy heartland. The Soviet Union insisted that LRA was a supplement to its war-fighting strategy rather than an irreplaceable element in it, and as a result pursued an increasingly flexible weapons procurement policy.

Despite technical limitations and the "supplementary" strategic concept, the impetus of Soviet bomber development, based on aircraft such as the M-50 Bounder, could well have been maintained had Khrushchev so wished. In the event, he decided that increasing reliance would be placed on long-range surface-to-surface missiles for the delivery of Soviet nuclear weapons. He was probably influenced by the internal debate on nuclear strategy which emerged after Stalin's death, by improvements in Soviet missile technology in the 1950s, by his own views on bomber vulnerability, and perhaps even by the fact that the Malenkov-Kaganovich opposition to him may have been associated with the bomber protagonists. In 1947 Malenkov had been an advocate of the manned bomber, capable of flying "across oceans," rather than "outmoded . . . flying bombs . . . good for 400 kilometres and no more."[32] But by the mid-1950s missile development had reached the point where the ICBM offered greater promise than the manned bomber. Khrushchev subsequently claimed the credit for the switch in emphasis, listing range limitations, vulnerability, persistent obsolescence, and cost and geographical disadvantages as the reasons. Nor was this view

unique to Khrushchev. As early as 1955 the Commander-in-Chief of the Soviet Air Forces himself, Air Chief Marshal Zhigarev, had forecast to his own staff the demise of the manned bomber:

> . . . strategic long-range bombers are expensive to build, man and maintain and they need to be housed in large airfields where they are vulnerable to air attack, they tie up large numbers of maintenance personnel and need great supplies of fuel. Missiles can be built more easily and cheaply, do not need such a complicated supply and servicing organisation, and are easily concealable and so are less vulnerable.[33]

The first generation of long-range Soviet bombers had proved disappointing and the psychological impact of the ICBM tests in 1956 and the launch of Sputnik in 1957 was very obvious. Debates in the Soviet military, not evident under Stalin, were encouraged to the point where in 1958 a series of General Staff seminars was held to examine "problems of military art and a future war," the results of which were subsequently published in the form of articles in *Military Thought* beginning in 1960. Oleg Penkovsky, who had passed news of the seminars to the West, explained them in some detail, stressing their focus on nuclear war-fighting and the emphasis given to a speedy conclusion: "A decision in favour of one side depends on readiness and ability to finish the war in the shortest possible time."[34] The reappraisal of nuclear war-

It was little wonder that the hulking Bounder, seen here with an escorting MiG-21, sent Western analysts racing for their slide rules.

fighting culminated in the appearance in 1962 of the collected writings known as *Military Strategy* and edited by Marshal Sokolovsky, in which the relative roles of rocket forces, long-range aviation and ground forces were stated unambiguously. No longer should nuclear weapons simply "pave the way to the front":

> Since the war, great advances have been made in the development of the means for armed combat. There have appeared nuclear and thermonuclear weapons with colossal destructive and striking power, and strategic rockets with unlimited range as the basic means for delivering nuclear warheads to a target. A new branch, the strategic rocket forces, has appeared in our armed forces; it will solve the main problems of modern warfare if an aggressor dares to disturb the peaceful building of Communism in our country. The scope of warfare is expanding; it now encompasses the entire territory of the countries in the opposite camp, and not simply the theatres of military operation as in the past.
>
> The targets in a modern war will be the enemy's nuclear weapons, his economy, his system of government and military control, and also his army groups and his navy in the theatres of military operation. The main objectives, therefore, will be outside the

combat theatres, deep within enemy territory. The defeat of strategic weapons, the disorganisation of the enemy rear, and also the defeat of main groups of forces in land theatres are to be accomplished by powerful strategic means: strategic rocket troops and partly by the long-range air command. They will fulfil their tasks by nuclear-missile strikes, according to the plans of the Supreme Command, to attain victory over the enemy in the interest of the entire armed conflict and in the interest of a rapid defeat of the enemy countries as a whole. It will not be necessary for the strategic rocket troops to attack with the ground forces. They are not a means of support for the ground forces.[35]

In December 1959, between the holding of the seminars and the publication of the doctrine, Khrushchev had created the military instrument to support it: the Strategic Rocket Forces, under the command of Artillery Marshal M. I. Nedelin. Since then the SRF have always been regarded as the primary service. By associating the new organisation with the influential artillery arm of the ground forces, Khrushchev probably strengthened army support for his "revolution" in military affairs. Soon afterwards the Serpukhov Higher Aviation School, together with schools at Kharkov, Perm and Rostov, stopped training bomber crews and began preparing the Strategic Rocket Force's future officers. "Revolution" there might have been, but the primary respon-

sibility for nuclear war-fighting would lie for some years to come with artillery officers whose careers prospects had suddenly been greatly improved. Conversely, the role of the remaining LRA bombers, including the large force of Tu-16 Badgers, was ill-defined and aircrew careers proportionately uncertain.

Long-range bomber development did not however stop completely. By 1961 it was obvious that Soviet missile development had not proceeded at the pace implied by Khrushchev and expected in the West, even after some research and production capacity had been switched from bombers to missiles. Soviet bombers were observed carrying air-launched guided missiles to extend their strike range and give them a stand-off capability. Production of Badger continued into the 1960s, and a limited number of Blinders entered regimental service. Badgers joined the Naval Air Forces, and LRA aircraft participated increasingly in naval anti-shipping exercises. But the evaporation of the intercontinental manned bomber threat to the West resulted in decisions not to replace 1950s-vintage interceptors, the USAF's F-102 and F-106 and the RAF's Lightning.

So, for the second time in 50 years, the Soviet Union had deliberately elected not to give a leading role to the long-range bomber when most of the evidence seemed to point in that direction. On this occasion, however, the decision was taken after a great deal of debate, under the influence of rapidly evolving strategic circumstances, and in the light of apparent technological disadvantages – not as a result of irrational and despotic behaviour, as had happened 20 years before. Moreover, this time the options

The limited range of the Tu-22 Blinder must have influenced the decision to reduce Soviet dependence on strategic bombers.

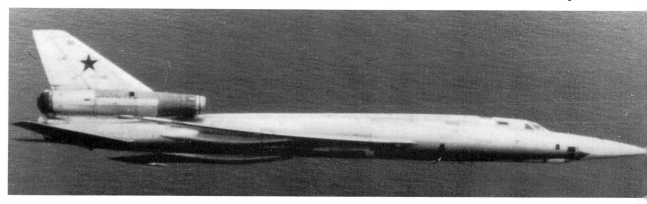

had not been excluded: shortly after Blinder production ceased in the early 1960s, its successor must have been moving on to the drawing board. Despite Khrushchev's strictures against it, the long-range manned bomber was therefore to re-emerge as a formidable military and diplomatic instrument in the hands of his successor. The process probably owed something to the removal of the discredited leader and a little to bureaucratic inertia. But changes in the strategic environment and technological advances were principally responsible for the manned bomber's reinstatement in SAF service.

Resurgence 1970–1985

Disenchantment among the military over his defence policies was probably among the factors contributing to Khrushchev's downfall. His proposals to reduce conventional forces, the fiasco over Cuba, the inability of the Soviet forces to prevent Western intervention in the Middle East and the MacNamara exposition of a more flexible war-fighting posture for the West must have called into question Khrushchev's heavy dependence on nuclear missiles. While lip service was paid to the primacy of the SRF at the Gagarin Military Academy, the Russian equivalent of the United States Air War College, air power doctrine was at the same time being assiduously fostered. In 1967 Academy commandant Marshal S. A. Krasovskiy wrote a wide-ranging treatise on air power in the nuclear age in the journal *Military Thought*. He emphasised the increase in spatial scope and the greater importance of the factors of time and speed in bringing conflict to a rapid conclusion. Soviet military thinkers seem at that time to have been agreed that the USSR could not prevail against the superior economic and technological strength of the West in a protracted war, a view which was probably maintained into the 1980s.

In the late 1960s even "the slightest delay in operations [would] have a negative effect on achievement of the goals of armed conflict . . . ." Krasovskiy was not however prepared to concede that missiles alone could bring victory:

Nuclear weapons constitute a very important means of destruction. They will be used above all by the Strategic Rocket Forces. The course and outcome of an armed conflict depends on the success of operations of this service of the armed forces.

However, aircraft also have an important role in the actions and combat operations of the ground troops and the navy. Moreover, aircraft are able to carry out a number of missions more effectively than other services of the armed forces. For example, through highly accurate rocket or bomb strikes, they can put out of operation very important fixed targets without destroying the entire objective, and they can also successfully suppress many mobile and highly manoeuvrable targets.[36]

He went on to list most of the traditional roles of air power, laying particular emphasis on missions to destroy the means of enemy nuclear attack, especially the "mobile facilities, the number of which now, as is known, has increased by several times."[37] The scenario was a European rather than an intercontinental war. Badger, Bison and Bear, equipped with either stand-off missiles or free-fall bombs, could reach most parts of any European theatre, even if North America was beyond them.

In 1984 the role of long-range aircraft was defined in the *Soviet Military Encyclopedia*:

Long-range aircraft are a component of the Soviet Air Forces designed to strike against military installations deep in the enemy's rear and continental and ocean [sea] theatres and to carry out operational and strategic aerial reconnaissance. The armoury includes all-weather strategic and long-range missile-carrying aircraft and bombers. The strike systems comprise various types of airborne missiles and bombs including those with nuclear charges.[38]

The context suggests that "continental theatre" means either the European peninsula or the eastern Asian land mass and their surrounding waters, rather than North America. Certainly the latter remains out of effective range of the Soviet bomber force, while the whole of Europe and large areas of China have become vulnerable to a new generation of Soviet aircraft and missiles.

In 1969 reports of a new Soviet manned bomber, variable-geometry in design and allegedly possessing intercontinental potential, began to circulate in the West. A prototype was seen at the Tupolev plant in Kazan in July 1970, together with what appeared to be a major extension to the factory itself. The aircraft was originally designated Tu-26, NATO code name Backfire, and began to enter regimental service simultaneously with both the LRA and SNAF in the early 1970s. It carried an in-flight refuelling probe and was believed to have the range to reach North America. But Soviet statements insisted that the aircraft had a range of only 1,375 miles, that it was not designed for intercontinental strategic operations, and that it was intended for use in Europe, Asia and the surrounding areas.[39] Nevertheless, Backfire played a prominent and controversial role in the SALT negotiations and, in the absence of supporting evidence, the Soviet assurances were treated with scepticism. In fact Backfire assumed a significance out of all proportion to its actual capability. Much was made of the apparent removal of its in-flight refuelling probe as a gesture of reassurance. As more data became available, however, its true nature as an important addition to the SAF's theatre capability became clear.

Although at first the Tu-26 Backfire did indeed suffer a range shortfall, subsequent variants are probably capable of much more than the 1,375 miles claimed by Soviet negotiators.

During the late 1970s the possibility of a non-nuclear phase in a European war began to be acknowledged in Soviet writing. Under such circumstances the need to locate and destroy NATO's theatre nuclear resources would be even more pressing. Success in this would present Western leaders, faced with Warsaw Pact conventional superiority, with a difficult dilemma: acceptance of conventional defeat, or a move to a potentially catastrophic intercontinental nuclear strike. Even without forcing such a traumatic choice, Backfire operations could present a serious threat to NATO's conventional strategy, which depends on heavy, rapid reinforcement of in-position ground and air forces in the first days of any conflict. Harbours, airfields, railheads and associated installations in Western Europe and Britain would offer extremely lucrative targets to the Soviet "medium" bomber force. Disruption or denial of reinforcement would have a rapid and serious impact on NATO's war-fighting capability.

Given the traditional Soviet emphasis on the link between battlefield activity and the use of air power against targets in the enemy's rear, the primary role of Backfire, Blinder and Badger seems obvious. Moreover, if there is a logical connection between Soviet doctrine, likely European scenarios and Backfire's capabilities, the type's performance is "limited" only if it is seen as a potential threat to the USA. Placed in the context of Soviet preoccupation with Europe, and to a certain extent with China, Backfire becomes a practical weapon system entirely in

harmony with current doctrine. It is therefore Backfire's visible contribution to the theatre balance of power, rather than its putative threat to North America, which principally concerns the European analyst.

Since its entry into regimental service in 1974, Backfire's performance has been progressively improved by airframe modifications, uprated engines, new stand-off missiles such as the AS-4 Kitchen, and improved ECM self-protection equipment. Its full capability is examined in detail elsewhere in these pages, but its true range certainly exceeds the 1,375 miles attributed to Backfire-A by the Soviet Union, while falling short of that needed to present a realistic threat to the USA.

The most recent Soviet bomber to be identified has no such range limitation. In 1979 a new four-engined bomber, quite different from an earlier aircraft said to be similar to the Tu-144 Charger supersonic transport, was reported to

This Backfire-B, armed with an AS-4 Kitchen long-range air-to-surface missile, is being shadowed by a Swedish Draken fighter. (*Swedish Air Force*)

be under development. Two years later the newcomer was seen at the Ramenskoye test centre near Moscow. It was parked near two Tu-144s, permitting Western analysts to draw conclusions about its size and hence its capabilities. Apparently powered by four engines, resembling those fitted to the Tu-144, and similar in configuration to but larger than the USAF's B-1A, it looked like a quantum step forward beyond Backfire. Code-named Blackjack, it seemed to be able to carry either free-fall bombs or air-launched cruise missiles – perhaps the AS-15 or a new, 3,200km-range supersonic missile known as the BL-10.[40] Even allowing for the relative inferiority of Soviet on-board electronics, still to a certain extent more bulky than comparable Western systems, it looked capable of carrying a great deal of self-screening and other ECM equipment. It did not appear to incorporate stealth technology, but its low-level capability, range and speed, and its possible stand-off weaponry, suggested a formidable strategic weapon system. By 1985 Blackjack, in conjunction with Backfire, had prompted an extensive re-evaluation and reconstruction of North American air defences. How does the SAF itself see its newest bomber?

Should the 1985–86 arms talks give rise to new limits on strategic missiles, Blackjack, like Backfire before it, could become a significant and flexible intercontinental weapon system. The long-range deployment of USAF B-52s, as in recent exercises with the Egyptian Air Force, cannot have gone unnoticed in Moscow. The manned bomber, unlike the ICBM, can be visibly brought to a higher state of readiness, a traditional diplomatic signal. A regiment of Blackjacks could be moved swiftly from the European to the East Asian theatre or even, provided further facilities were established, to foreign bases such as Cam Ranh Bay in Vietnam. Long range offers not only a long reach but also the capability to approach nearer targets from unexpected directions. To appreciate the significance of extended low-level endurance one has only to reflect on the likely outcome of the Battle of Britain if Germany had possessed bomber squadrons capable of flying beyond British radar range across Central France to attack South-east England from the west at low level.

But as recently as the winter of 1985 there had been no published evidence that Blackjack was anything more than another Soviet prototype, and nothing to suggest that it would in fact ever achieve regimental status. Indeed, one could ask why Blackjack was allowed to appear so conveniently for Western intelligence at Ramenskoye. The many previous Soviet revelations of bomber strength which in the event fell far short of pessimistic Western forecasts must inspire caution. Nor should the failure of the Tu-144 itself be overlooked. The much heralded "equivalent" of Concorde was relegated to short-haul internal routes before being withdrawn from Aeroflot service altogether. If Blackjack is fitted with Kuznetsov engines similar to those of Charger, much will have had to be done to give it a realistic intercontinental supersonic capability. Nonethe-

less, the type cannot be ignored by Western air forces. If it does enter regimental service it will represent a significant threat to both Western Europe and North America. Its greatest strength could well be the use of its extended range to reach unexpected points from which to launch either cruise or supersonic missiles. It could operate in the manner envisaged 80 years ago by H. G. Wells when he observed that in the air there were no streets, no designated highways by which an aircraft had to approach a specific point. He should perhaps have added "provided it has the range and endurance to approach from any point of the compass". Blackjack could do just that against many targets in Eurasia and North America, and would greatly reinforce Backfire in operations against a variety of land and sea targets.

Blackjack is not the only actual or potential manned threat to the North American mainland. A further variant of the well proven Tu-95, the Bear-H entered regimental service with the SAF in about 1984. Bear-H, the first new model of the type to be introduced for over a decade, is equipped to carry a long-range cruise missile, likely to be the 1,000–2,000-mile range AS-15. Thus armed, Bear-H could threaten targets in most of the interior of the USA while standing off beyond US airspace. The Soviet Union has presumably used its reconnaissance satellites to create the database necessary for cruise missile targeting, and while AS-15 may lack the miniaturised sophistication of the USAF's ALCM or the Tomahawk GLCM, it undoubtedly represents a stiff challenge to North American air defences. For one thing, it means that some form of anti-missile defence system will have to be created.

Perhaps it was only to be expected that the example of the B-52/ALCM system should be swiftly copied but – compared with the publicity given to Blackjack – Bear-H's appearance on the strategic scene was almost surreptitious. It is however probably cheaper and certainly much more immediate in its impact.

It is easy to dwell on the significance of Backfire, Bear-H and Blackjack to the exclusion of one other Soviet bomber which, though lacking intercontinental significance has had a major impact on the European and Far Eastern air

power balance. Reports of an aircraft resembling but smaller than the USAF F-111 began to circulate in the West at the end of the 1960s. The Su-24 Fencer entered squadron service in 1974 but, in contrast with Backfire and Blackjack, the Soviet Union took great care to prevent Western appraisal of it until 1979, when a regiment briefly deployed to a base in East Germany. There are now more than 700 Fencers in service in Eastern Europe and several military districts in the USSR itself. From its bases in East Germany Fencer could carry out conventional or nuclear attacks on most of NATO's European rear area. It is credited with terrain-avoidance radar, all-weather capability, and both free-fall or stand-off weapons. In Western parlance it is a tactical fighter-bomber, but the Soviet Union could use it either in direct support of a ground offensive or, with the longer-legged Badgers, Backfires, Bisons and Bears, more deeply.

Further evidence of Soviet awareness of the potential of the manned bomber was yielded by the major SAF reorganisation which appears to have taken place in 1981. Previously LRA had been organised in three groups, each comprising regiments of heavy and medium bombers and associated tankers and ECM aircraft. In 1981 five Air Armies of the Soviet Union (AASU) were formed. Under SAF command in peacetime, AASU could apparently be controlled directly by the Supreme High Command in war. The change coincided with a statement by the then Chief of Staff, Marshal Ogarkov:

Bear-H and its AS-15 cruise missiles permit the Soviet Air Forces to threaten the US heartland from the comparative safety of international airspace.

It is not the front but the larger form of military operations – the strategic operation in the theatre of military operations – which should be regarded as the basic operation in a possible future war.[41]

Two armies, with headquarters at Leignica in Poland and Vinnitsa in the Ukraine, are equipped with Fencers and assigned to the Central and Soviet Western European theatres respectively. A third, at Irkutsk, comprises all the light and medium bombers in the Far Eastern theatre. A fourth, at Smolensk, has Badgers, Blinders and Backfires for assignment to either eastern or western areas. The fifth, with its headquarters at Moscow, controls all heavy bombers with a potential strategic role.[42] The reorganisation provides for assignment and control of the bombers according to their range, and should permit the degree of centralised direction advocated by air power theorists since the earliest days of long-range offensive air power. If deterrence should fail, compelling NATO to resort to flexible response, the Soviet bomber armies could be used either in the conventional phase or to supplement a missile-launched nuclear attack. In either case the reorganisation provides for much greater flexibility and concentration of force. By reducing duplication it also probably permits

Soviet ECM support types include Badger-J, distinguished by its underfuselage "canoe" radome. Badger-Js are mixed in with missile-carrying Badger-G formations to provide jamming cover. (*Swedish Air Force*)

most cost-effective use of specialist staff officers at the air army headquarters.

But as with all the other branches of the Soviet Air Forces, AASU needs far more than reorganisation and new aircraft if it is to achieve its full potential. Regrettably, there is much less open-source information on Soviet bomber operations than on offensive air support, air defence or even maritime operations. AASU aircraft regularly fly with SNAF units on maritime operations, either in the direct strike/attack role or for in-flight refuelling, ELINT or ECM support. There is therefore a degree of co-operation, which presupposes regular joint training, between crews

of AASU and SNAF, an example that some Western air forces might do well to follow.[43]

Even assuming that only a proportion of AASU activity comes to the attention of Western observers, flying hours per crew per month do seem to be below Western levels. One shred of evidence, albeit over a decade old, occurred in a typically heroic description in *Soviet Military Review* of a regimental exercise against an "enemy" airfield involving a flight of "several hours". "The difficulties of the mission had been discussed at a Party meeting held in the squadron several days before." The article was headed by a photo depicting two Badgers, and the author referred to "the roar of the jet turbines". The mission culminated in a formation low-level attack on the airfield with free-fall bombs. It was naturally successful, "ploughing the runway with bomb explosions, destroying aircraft in parking places, fuel and lubricants and ammunition depots."[44] Leaving aside the hyperbole of the author, who had obviously been affected by the nausea induced by vibration, engine noise, uncomfortable temperatures and increased pulse rate, his observation about crew preparation for the flight may still be significant 10 years later:

> Care is taken in the squadron to ensure that everyone has his meal and goes to bed at the right time and necessarily goes in for some sport. Incidentally, *on the days preceding flights* [not italics in the original] even films shown in the Officers' House are selected so as to develop an elated mood in the viewers.[44]

If, as seems to be the case, offensive support sorties can last many hours, it is possible that several days' preparation may also still be the norm, despite a recent suggestion that "flights lasting many hours are now everyday work for our airmen of the long range air force."[45] On the other hand, while flying hours per month may not be plentiful, a build-up of experience on type over many years should produce a degree of expertise. Occasionally, however, the accumulation of years can be accompanied by a decline in competence. One such example was considered significant enough to be published in detail in *Red Star* in 1983. "A rocket-carrying supersonic aircraft" undershot while landing, struck an obstacle and broke off its starboard undercarriage leg. The pilot, 53-year-old Lt-Col Victor Scherbin, had been repeatedly warned by both the tower and his navigator that he was too low. He had served 31 years on the unit and achieved Sniper Pilot rating. But he had also developed several weaknesses which had not been brought to the attention of his superiors by the CO of the regiment, also a lieutenant-colonel but with much less seniority. The sour comment of Scherbin's navigator as he walked away from the badly bent aircraft will strike a chord among navigators the world over: "And they call him a sniper!" But as usual in such cases, the object was not simply to pillory one ageing pilot:

> Indeed not long ago there had been a meeting on the causes of accidents in the Air Force's military soviet where it had been pointed out that there had been an increase in the number of incidents which could cause accidents and that these had been made by the command flying staff – the most experienced, the first-class category pilots and navigators. Frequently those who are under instruction pay more attention to the finer points of the instructions and points of flying discipline, [and] prepare themselves better for flying exercises than those who are responsible for their training. . . . With age the speed of reaction slows down, as do the abilities to appreciate and evaluate a situation. The older aircrew should keep a close watch on their state of physical fitness and health and be frank with the medical officer. Further, they should assess themselves objectively.[46]

This illustration contains two points of particular interest: SAF aircrew are retained on one type for lengthy periods unless they have been selected for higher military training and further advancement; and long years on type do not necessarily make up for infrequent flying and inadequate supervision.

Operational training for the long-range regiments is, as elsewhere in the SAF, provided on the regiment itself. The squadron commander may be responsible for devising new tactics and for their subsequent dissemination to other units; there is little evidence to suggest that ideas flow from units such as the RAF's Central Tactics and Trials Organisation and operational conversion units. Inevitably, this can produce uneven results, to the extent that in 1983 it was considered necessary to publicise the example of one bomber squadron commander, Lt-Col Anatoliy Maksimovich Kurilets. He set a personal example by analysing his own errors during an in-flight refuelling sortie, and was a model training commander. In his squadron

> . . . there is also much concern for the dissemination of advanced experience. Let's say that new tactics are used in firing a missile. The squadron commander, together with the political worker and Party bureau secretary, immediately arrange for a demonstration, analysis, and exchange of experience with other crews. And this is beneficial. Officer I. Pelipenko's aircrew, for example, delivered a

precise missile strike against an "enemy" target during the next tactical flight exercise by employing experience gained by his comrades-in-arms.

The work experience of this vanguard squadron commander has been synthesised and adopted in other units. Anatoliy Maksimovich has spoken on numerous occasions at Party committee meetings, Party meetings, and job-related conferences, and has shared his ideas on improving the training methods of crew and detachment commanders. His suggestions in essence consist of making the monitoring of aviator training continuous, effective, and extremely demanding.

Other communist leaders can learn much from this commander whose squadron has earned excellent ratings.[47]

The message for the "other communist leaders" is explicit: by no means all of them match the paragon Kurilets.

A great deal of groundcrew training – apparently far more than the continuation training associated with Western air forces – also takes place on the regiment. Several Soviet articles have emphasised the need for increasing levels of technical competence among groundcrew as a result of the growing complexity of modern aircraft. In some cases courses of instruction are organised at "higher military-education institutions" to cover "new and especially complex specimens of aviation and equipment"; in others, "qualified teachers and specialists" visit the regiments. But according to a former Deputy Commander in Chief of the Air Force for Combat Training:

A large role in further developing and improving the training facility belongs to innovators in the units. Thus, in the military collective headed by officer B. Kononenko, via the efforts of efficiency experts, classrooms are equipped with working test benches and models which provide visual aids in studying the special features of a working principle and the principles of operation of the more complicated units and systems on the aircraft. They make it possible for flying personnel to develop skills in the use of armament, equipment, and radar naviga-

tional devices, and for technical personnel to master the sequence for carrying out operations during an efficiency check of the units and systems. One should note that such a training facility as was created in this collective can confidently be called exemplary. . . . At the same time isolated military collectives still exist where the necessary attention is not accorded to the development of a training facility. Sometimes in technical classrooms one can see test benches, charts and posters which do not contribute to a thorough understanding of the physical processes taking place in one or another assembly or subassembly or to a clarification of the interdependence of their physical properties and quantitative parameters, showing operating time in various modes. At times visual training aids do not reflect changes made or modifications, and as a result, the special features of equipment use. Methods for instrument monitoring of the status of components and sub-assemblies are poorly described. There are no posters devoted to the characteristic equipment malfunctions occurring as a result of misuse or to methods of detecting and eliminating these discrepancies. There are not enough visual aids to instruct checking and adjustment, tuning, and dismantling and assembly operations. Although rarely, all the same it happens that essentially good classrooms which have been equipped with enthusiasm, simulators, ranges, and other elements of the training facility are used episodically and not effectively enough.

The task of commanders, political workers, technical personnel, and Party organisations consists in making the training facility in all units a model in content that is universally and completely used to further improve the technical and practical skills of the personnel.[48]

As always, the key to success was "socialist competition".

Besides uneven training achievement and unsatisfactory supervision there is one other significant threat to SAF unit efficiency. The endemic Russian addiction to alcohol seems to permeate all ranks and branches of the SAF.

Frequent articles in military publications refer to "the battle against drunkenness" and the "seductive serpent". Named culprits are always said to be exceptions, but the following concluding observations from a medical officer suggest that the problem may be more widespread:

> One should not overlook the fact that combat readiness of the regiments where these officers served has experienced a decline to a certain degree, and the money invested by the state in training these airmen has been lost.

Pilots form one of the leading detachments of Soviet military cadres. The great majority is made up of educated, cultured people and highly qualified specialists. They know and correctly understand the significance of strict adherence to preflight procedures for their professional longevity, for the combat readiness of aviation units and sub-units, and for

Bear-G escorted by a US Navy F-14 Tomcat fighter. The Soviet strategic bomber force is once again obliging the West to take its anti-aircraft defences seriously. (*US Navy*)

flight safety. But unfortunately one still encounters sad exceptions to this general rule. And as long as they exist, we must not remain indifferent to what is going on around us, to the fact that alcohol is an enemy against which we must fight with all our might.[49]

The future

Assessments of the current effectiveness and future potential of Soviet long-range aviation are apt to vary widely. If one chooses to emphasise widespread alcoholism, inconsistent training standards, the demands on both aircrew and groundcrew from increasingly complex equipment, and apparently deep-rooted difficulties in producing a truly intercontinental bomber, it is possible to argue that Western fears may be exaggerated. Certainly it is unlikely that problems arising in Western air forces from the combined impact of advanced electronics, automated systems, complex engines and variable-geometry aircraft are going to be any easier to resolve in the Soviet Union. The burdens of a largely conscript groundcrew, even one drawn from the better qualified among a rapidly expanding number of high school technical graduates, will continue to weigh heavily on the regiments for some time yet, especially when the pay and conditions of service for all ranks below warrant officer are not conducive to re-enlistment. But in long-range aviation, as elsewhere in the SAF, quantity has a quality all of its own. There is a harmony in Soviet doctrine, training, equipment and organisation which fits them particulary well for a short, intensive war with either conventional or nuclear weapons. The Soviet Union has fully grasped the traditional air power tenets of flexibility, concentration of force and centralised control without committing itself to Douhetian theories of "independence," which on occasion in the West have actually militated against flexibility.

By 1985 the re-emergence of the LRA, latterly in the form of the AASU, had forced a massive diversion of Western resources into all forms of air defence, something unthinkable only 25 years previously. Blackjack aside, the medium and heavy bombers posed a serious threat to the installations of NATO and China, and to the reinforcements essential to their respective strategies. Should Blackjack or any other intercontinental bomber enter regimental service armed with either cruise or supersonic stand-off missiles, North America would face a grave additional threat which in times of tension would offer the Soviet Union far more options than do ICBMs. The Soviet Union would possess a new, very valuable bargaining chip in arms control negotiations, and her ability to exert military influence swiftly well beyond her frontiers would be greatly enhanced. The Russians may therefore finally decide that a truly intercontinental bomber force is as essential to a world superpower as is the possession of an ocean-going aircraft carrier task force. If so, they will have no hesitation in allocating the resources necessary to achieve it.

Notes

1 *Long Range, Missile Equipped* is the title of a short hagiography of Soviet bomber aviation written by Maj-Gen B. A. Vasil'yev, Moscow 1972.

2 *Major Reorganisation of the Soviet Air Forces*, Mark L. Urban, *International Defense Review*, June 1983, page 756.

3 Vasil'yev op cit, page 6.

4 Ibid page 13.

5 Ibid page 14.

6 Ibid page 16.

7 See Boyd, *The Soviet Air Force Since 1918*, for a comprehensive analysis of the impact of German design practice on Soviet aircraft construction in this period.

8 Quoted in *Shturmovik*, unpublished manuscript by Alexander Boyd, 1980.

9 *The Civil War to the Second World War*, G. Schatunowski, in *The Soviet Air and Rocket Forces*, Asher Lee (ed), Weidenfeld and Nicolson, London 1959.

10 *Questions of Strategy and Operational Art in Soviet Military Works 1917–40*, Soviet Ministry of Defence 1965.

11 Vasil'yev op cit, page 2.

12 Ibid page 64.

13 Ibid page vii.

14 Air Chief Marshal Sir Philip Joubert de la Ferté in Asher Lee op cit.

15 *The Strange Alliance*, Maj-Gen J. R. Deane, quoted in Asher Lee ibid, page 86.

16 Vasil'yev op cit, page 36.

17 *Soviet Air Strategy in the Second World War*, Hanson Baldwin, quoted in Asher Lee op cit, page 85.

18 Quoted without direct reference in *History of Soviet Air Power*, Robert Kilmarx, Faber, London, page 320, but attributed to General Arnold by R. L. Garthoff in Emme (see Note 23), page 531. Arnold

distinguished between "intelligent questions" and lack of knowledge about strategic bombing.

19 Eg unpublished manuscript, Alexander Boyd, 1982; N. S. Khrushchev, *The Last Testament*, Deutsch, London, page 39.

20 *Long Range Air Attack*, Air Chief Marshal Sir Philip Joubert de la Ferté, page 110, in *The Soviet Air and Rocket Forces*, Asher Lee (ed), Weidenfeld and Nicolson, London 1958.

21 Eg *Soviet Power and Europe 1945–1970*, T. W. Wolfe, page 41.

22 For a number of similar sources see Kilmarx op cit, pages 253–254.

23 *The Foundations of Soviet Air Power: A Historical and Managerial Interpretation*, R. D. Potts, in *The Impact of Air Power*, Emme, Van Nostrand 1959, page 522.

24 Quoted in Emme ibid, page 512.

25 Quoted in *Air Power and Soviet Strategy*, R. L. Garthoff, in Emme ibid, pages 527–528.

26 Marshal of Aviation Skripko, *Red Star*, August 11, 1946.

27 Quoted by Garthoff in Emme op cit, page 528.

28 Col-Gen of Aviation Nikitin, February 1949, quoted by Garthoff in Emme ibid, page 529.

29 *Stalin Means War*, G. A. Tokaev, Weidenfeld and Nicolson, London 1951, page 115.

30 Chief Marshal of Aviation P. Zhigarev quoted in Garthoff op cit, page 536.

31 *Our Air Force Policy*, W. S. Symington, Secretary of the USAF, at Maxwell AFB, June 17, 1949, quoted in Emme op cit, page 630.

32 G. A. Tokaev op cit, page 104.

33 Quoted in Asher Lee op cit,

pages 10–11.

34 *The Penkovsky Papers*, Collins, London, pages 167–170.

35 *Military Strategy*, Marshal V. D. Sokolovsky, Pall Mall, London, page 280.

36 *Military Thought*, Marshal S. A. Krasovskiy, No 3, March 1967.

37 Ibid.

38 Quoted by N. Sautin in *Flight to Coordinate 'N'*, *Izvestia*, January 26, 1984.

39 Quoted in *Soviet Bombers, A Growing Threat*, Bonner Day, *Air Force Magazine*, November 1978, page 85.

40 For a very comprehensive speculative analysis of Blackjack see *Blackjack, The Biggest Bomber By Far*, Bill Sweetman, *International Defense Review* 5/1984, pages 549–552.

41 Ogarkov in *Kommunist* journal, July 1981, quoted by Mark L. Urban in *International Defense Review* 6/1982, page 756.

42 Urban ibid.

43 *Aviation and Cosmonautics* of September 1981 carried a photo spread of a Tu-16 unit suggesting that it trained in bomb and missile attacks against both land and maritime targets.

44 Lt-Col V. Divakov, *Soviet Military Review*, December 1974, pages 36–37.

45 Sautin, op cit.

46 *Red Star*, July 10, 1983.

47 *Hold Yourself Strictly Responsible*, Lt-Col N. Stupner, *Aviation and Cosmonautics*, March 1983.

48 *Enhancing the Training of Aviators*, Col-Gen of Aviation P. Kirsanov, *Equipment and Armaments*, August 1976.

49 *The Illness Attacked Gradually*, Lt-Col of Medical Services A. Pleshan, *Aviation and Cosmonautics*, December 12, 1978, page 43.

CHAPTER 6

Transport operations

The An-124 Condor, largest aircraft in the world and flagship of the Soviet strategic air transport force. (*Brian M. Service*)

IN WESTERN air forces it is not uncommon to hear cheerfully disparaging remarks about "truckies" or "trash haulers". They are usually directed by fighter or bomber pilots at transport aircrew. Even after 75 years of powered military flight, a surprising number of observers equate "air power" with offensive operations or the defensive riposte. But there is more to air power than the direct application of military force by attacking targets in the air or on the ground; it can be used to distribute military force too. This function, carried out by transport aircraft has, however, remained unfashionable in the West. There may be two reasons for this. First, the glamorous image of air combat in both world wars and the perennial perception of the fighter pilot as defender, avenger and all-round super-

man, tend to influence any assessment of aircrew worth, even among professionals. The second influence condemning the "truckie" to the second division is the air force view of long-range offensive operations as being synonymous with "independence," while such ancillary roles as transport and air support seemed to suggest subordination to the army. As air forces sought to establish their position in Western defence policy formulation and procurement, they seem to have perceived only two alternatives: independence of the armies and navies, or subordination to them. The third relationship –

149

"complementary to" has seldom been pursued or encouraged.

In the Soviet Union the transport pilot, if not wholly a second-class citizen, certainly does not enjoy the very high status, nor the subsequent pension, of his fast-jet contemporary. Military Transport Aviation itself lacks the glamour of the "long-range missile-equipped" units and the "defenders of the motherland's skies". So much so that in 1979 *Pravda* was constrained to comment on it:

> Military Transport Aviation has no combat heroes like Pokryshkin and Kozhedubov; it did not participate in bombing Berlin, nor did it shoot down the fascist vultures. Can this be the reason why very little is written about its pilots? Can this be why songs and poems are

The Soviet transport pilot: hardworking and under-appreciated. This is the captain of a crew that set a world closed-circuit speed record with a 30,000kg payload in the Antonov An-22. (*Tass*)

not composed about them? I am sure that this oversight will be corrected because in the VTA, as is the case throughout aviation, heroic individuals and genuinely hardworking airmen are serving.[1]

On the other hand, military air transport operations have frequently been given great emphasis in Soviet military doctrine, and never more so than in the current decade, when not only are they an essential ingredient in all-arms war-fighting strategy, but they are increasingly being used as a long-range instrument of peacetime foreign policy.

Military transport operations are primarily the responsibility of the 750 or so fixed-wing aircraft of the branch of the Soviet Air Force known as *Voyenno-transportnaya aviatsiya* (VTA), or Military Transport Aviation. Soviet civil aviation, in the form of the national flag carrier Aeroflot, is widely regarded as a regular reserve to VTA and, under the command of a Soviet air marshal, regularly provides some of its 1,600 heavier aircraft for military exercises, the twice-yearly roulement of conscripts to and from Eastern Europe, and other trooping flights. A further significant contribution to tactical air mobility comes from the Soviet helicopter regiments, many of which are under Army command and quite separate from the VTA organisation. Finally, the SNAF and SAF also control their own medium and light transport regiments for specialist air support activities.

Early organisation and operations

In the Revolution of 1919, the crucible for most Soviet fighting forces, there was little scope for transport operations. Scarcity of aircraft and their small load-carrying capacity meant that they could not be diverted from offensive support and air defence. During the next decade, however, the development of specialist cargo-carrying aircraft seems to have been encouraged for both civilian and military reasons. In his relatively short period of influence Trotsky sought to develop military and civil aviation in close co-operation, encouraging the design of aircraft usable in both environments and instituting administrative ties between the two. The Soviet-German connection was also an influence at this time.

In 1921 a jointly owned Russo-German airline, Deruluft, began operations between Moscow and Konigsberg, continuing until 1937. The Junkers F.13 metal monoplane was produced at the Filii plant from 1922 onwards, and entered both military and civilian service. Trotsky's view of civilian and military aviation requirements was endorsed in 1921 by the inauguration of a ten-year plan by the Council of Labour and Defence. There was a general awareness of value of aviation in a very large country encumbered with a mainly medieval road system and completely inadequate railways. By the end of 1922 a national network of air routes was being studied and the Inspectorate of Civil Aviation, subordinate to the military, had been created. In 1923 the forerunner of Aeroflot, Dobrolyot, began passenger services in Southern Russia. The same year Trotsky sought to enhance national awareness of both civilian and military aviation by creating the Friends of the Air Fleet. Workers were encouraged to donate to funds for the purchase of aircraft; air displays, exhibitions, slogans – "Proletariat! Take To the Air" – formed part of a nationwide campaign to inculcate air-mindedness among the people. There was however no agreement at this stage on military operations, primarily because of disagreement between Trotsky, who was not convinced of the future desirability of an offensive war, and Frunze and Tukhachevsky, who both believed that the offensive must dominate Soviet military doctrine. But after Trotsky's death and until the decimation of the High Command in 1936–37, military air transport operations became steadily more significant.

From 1922 Andrei Tupolev designed a series of transports culminating in December 1930 in the ANT-6 variant of the TB-3 bomber. Meanwhile, three Junkers-Gorbunov JUG-1 bomber/transports had airlifted a reconnaissance party of 15 men in the campaign to subdue the Basmachi in Turkestan.[2] In military exercises in the Moscow military district on August 2, 1930, 12 paratroops were dropped over Voronezh with their small arms and ammunition. That date is now the official birthday of the Soviet Airborne Forces. In the following year the airborne experiment was followed up on June 1 by the formation of a squadron of converted TB-1s and P-5s to develop air-landing operations. June 1 is now the official birthday of VTA. The entry into service of the ANT-6 meant that artillery and light armoured vehicles could be airlifted, and many more paratroops dropped. In 1936 3,000 troops were dropped in the Byelorussian District exercises. At this time the Soviet Union led the world in the development of airborne forces.

Operations 1939–45

The newly formed units were soon in action. In 1939 an "air-landing brigade" fought against the Japanese at Khalkin-Gol in Outer Mongolia. In the same year parachute brigades were lifted by 170 TB-3 bombers during the occupation of Bessarabia and dropped unopposed to secure towns, airfields and other installations. In June 1940 the Airborne Forces were centralised under the direct control of the High Command. Thereafter they were used in a variety of operations throughout the war. A total of 6,000 paratroops were dropped near Orel in October 1941 to check Guderian's Panzer group. In the counteroffensives near Moscow in December smaller units were dropped to impede the German withdrawal. A force of 200 paratroops was dropped to secure an airfield to allow for forward air landings by other forces. At the end of January 1942 2,300 troops were dropped in the Vyazma operation, followed by a further 7,000 two weeks later. In September 1943 4,500 paratroops were dropped in 296 transport sorties in an operation to secure a bridgehead across the River Dnieper. At the outset of the Manchurian campaign in 1945, 20 airborne assault teams were dropped to disrupt Japanese command and control, sabotage installations and generally create as much havoc as possible before the major Soviet overland offensive.

But these raw figures fall well short of portraying the reality. Almost without exception, airborne operations were carried out at night to reduce the vulnerability to interception of lumbering, virtually defenceless transports. There were never enough aircraft to carry the designated number of troops: in the Dnieper operation 30% of the troops and 50% of their supplies never got off the ground.[3] Navigation was frequently inaccurate, troops were scattered over wide areas, communications were haphazard, shortage of fuel and delays in refuelling disrupted drop-zone timetables, drops were dislocated by the need to avoid German AA fire, and information on German defences was inaccurate. All in all, with the possible exception of the Manchurian operations against a demoralised and weakened enemy, Soviet airborne oper-

Tupolev G-2s – TB-3s converted to carry up to 30 paratroops at a time – demonstrate their mass-drop capability during the Second World War. (*Tass*)

ations in the Second World War did not live up to their pre-war promise – so much so that Stalin converted eight airborne corps into rifle divisions in 1942.

Airborne resupply and reinforcement on the other hand frequently made a valuable contribution to the land offensives, especially after air superiority had been won. Throughout, civilian aircraft and ADD bombers were used as troop and supply transports. Immediately after the German invasion in June 1941 the Civil Air Fleet was mobilised and some 50% of the aircraft

The contribution to Soviet victory of the transport forces in general and the airborne troops in particular is summarised in Sokolovsky's *Military Strategy* of 1962. In 34 pages of summary and acknowledgement of the value of all branches of the services, transport operations receive just five lines:

> A weak aspect of the Soviet Air Force was the absence of a special transport command, although one was formed during the war. This had a negative effect on the use of airborne troops, as well as on the organisation of the air supply of rapidly advancing forces, especially in the closing stages of strategic operations.[5]

The significance of that weakness had already been explained:

> Our prewar theory devoted an important place to the use of airborne troops in connection with the problems of deep penetration and fast operation. Airborne troops were regarded as an instrument of the higher command and were designated to solve tactical problems in enemy rear areas and for continuous action throughout the entire depth of enemy defence. However, these correct theoretical concepts were not supported by the necessary material foundation, since the practical application of airborne troops was limited by the insufficient development of air transport.[6]

Post-war eclipse

There is little evidence to suggest that in the years immediately after the Second World War Stalin gave much priority to military transport. He concentrated production on air defence, long-range bombers and nuclear weapons. The centralisation of airborne assets in 1946 was not accompanied by the kind of accelerated development programme which produced the MiG series of fighters or the early Tupolev and Ilyushin bombers. It was not until 1962 that an eminent commentator, Sokolovsky, felt able to advocate once more the importance of airborne

deployed as units in military fronts.[4] In 1942 they were formally incorporated into the VVS. Several thousand troops were ferried from Moscow to Stalingrad in November 1942, while airlift replaced ground reinforcement routes when the latter were made impassable by bad weather. In the later stages of the war air drops or landings of reinforcements, fuel and ammunition enhanced the mobility of armoured formations and sustained units which had outrun conventional overland resupply. Captured enemy airfields were swiftly prepared to receive Soviet transports so that the reinforcement capability could be pushed still further forward. Finally, in the closing months of the war the provision of supplies to partisans operating behind German lines was extended to anti-German forces in Poland, Czechoslovakia and Yugoslavia.

operations, though even he was sceptical about the resupply of an offensive:

> In the future, air transport (using planes that do not require permanent airfields) may become a very effective and mobile means of delivery. For the time being, the role of aircraft in delivering supplies is limited, since their carrying capacity is inadequate and they require complicated airfield equipment and escorts during flight.[7]

No new transports of any significance entered VTA service until 10 years after the end of the Great Patriotic War. By 1955 the most prestigious transport aircraft available to fly Khrushchev's delegation to the Geneva summit was still only the twin-engined Il-14. The comparison with contemporary four-engined Western aircraft was embarrassing to the Soviet Premier,[8] while the Il-14's troop-carrying capacity was little more than that of the wartime DC-3 built under licence from the USA.

It is probable that Khrushchev gave greater encouragement to transport designs than to other types of military aircraft. His ambivalence in relation to the bomber has already been noted, and he shared Trotsky's view of the dual role of aviation in the service of Mother Russia. He made disparaging remarks about the earlier helicopter designs but wished it to be remembered that

> . . . during my discussions with Comrade Mil, I always insisted that new designs should be adequate not only for transporting military personnel but for civilian use as well. I told him to concentrate on building helicopters for peaceful purposes. A helicopter can be used in peacetime to lift pipes and lay pipelines; it can be used as a flying combine harvester or as a flying streetcar. We established helicopter routes in the Crimea and the Caucasus to carry passengers between Simferopol and Yalta and other cities.[9]

Khrushchev took particular pride in being associated with the Il-62 and the Tu-114, both, significantly, products of design bureaux that had hitherto concentrated on bombers in the post-war era. At the same time the role of military transport aviation was being reconsidered in

the major strategic debates encouraged after Stalin's death in response to the questions posed by nuclear weapons. The focus was on the direct influence of nuclear weapons themselves, but it seems to have been quickly agreed that airlift would be required.

Modern doctrine and modern transports

Sokolovsky advocated the use of airlift to resupply offensive forces over the great areas of combat envisaged for a nuclear war. Yet despite the weight of presumably authoritative opinion in his book, it received direct criticism in a review in *Red Star* of September 22, 1962. General Kurochkin commented:

> Prominent military functionaries of our Party

and state like M. V. Frunze, B. M. Shaposhnikov, and M. N. Tukhachevsky made a tremendous contribution to the theory of strategy. The well-known military theoreticians A. A. Svechin, A. A. Neznamov, V. K. Triandafillov and E. A. Shilovsky also exerted a definite influence on the development of military and strategic thought in the Soviet Army. . . . In developing the questions of Soviet military strategy, the authors of the book should, without fail, have approached these people. The work would have been richer and it would have promoted

Left Ilyushin Il-12s drop paratroops during a public display at Moscow's Tushino airfield in 1954.

Below Soviet paratroops carry out the traditional "sit-down" before boarding an An-12 Cub transport aircraft. (*Tass*)

the correction of the conditions existing in the period of the cult of personality when all that was new and advanced in military theory was ascribed to Stalin alone.[10]

The resentment of Stalin displayed above was due to more than mere sycophancy to the Khrushchev regime. There is little doubt that Stalin had dominated what passed for strategic thinking in the later years of his life, and this must have irked the military professionals. Of greater relevance is the glowing tribute to Frunze, Shaposhnikov and especially Tukhachevsky. These three generals had been strong advocates of the offensive, with Tukhachevsky in particular emphasising the importance of airborne forces. During the 1960s a coherent body of doctrine about air mobility emerged, moving from concepts of air mobility in nuclear war to the role of air transport support in deep offensive operations. In 1960 the first four-engined long-range Soviet transport entered service with VTA. This was the An-12 Cub, capable of lifting 90 troops or 44,000lb of freight over a range of 2,000 miles. Five years later the prototype An-22 Cock was offering a lift of 99,000lb over 6,800 miles.

A collection of writings by pre-war strategists issued in 1965 by the Soviet Ministry of Defence included three hitherto unpublished chapters of a book prepared by Tukhachevsky in the early 1930s. The emphasis in the selection was on offensive, deep-penetrating, all-arms operations, with an important role being allocated to airborne forces:

> . . . The enemy rear can be paralysed and the dislocation of enemy forces in depth achieved by airborne assaults in the areas between corps, army and frontal reserves. The seizure and destruction of railways and roads can, even with modest forces, easily create very deep zones of obstruction on which the enemy would be obliged to expend a great deal of time in reoccupation and restoration. . . .
>
> The strength of airborne detachments is not merely that of each one in isolation, but also and predominantly that they will operate where the enemy is known to be inferior to them so that they can freely attack military

trains, destroy rail and road bridges, disrupt communications and lay delayed-action charges, etc. If to this we add the possibility of using permanent contaminating substances, then their significance becomes even more apparent. . . .

> If we take any European country and its civil air fleet then it becomes obvious that any one of them could, in several flights, inundate its enemy's rear with airborne detachments – and using the example already given of assault detachments in combat with entrained infantry divisions, it can clearly be seen how dangerous this is for the enemy rear, either immediately behind the front line or in depth. . . .
>
> The air force will maintain contact with the assault detachments and supply them with ammunition. The troops of such detachments should, in this context, be trained in the use of enemy weapons to enable them to use weapons and ammunition seized in the enemy rear.[11]

The roots of current Soviet doctrine are obvious in the above quotation: paralysis and dislocation in rear areas, local superiority, "contaminating substances" – Tukhachevsky was aware of the significance of chemical warfare but could not have foreseen the future impact of contamination by radio-activity – the use of civil aircraft, and the need for resupply by air.

These ideas were updated the following year (1966) in a widely publicised article in *Military Thought*:

> The equipping of the Armed Forces with nuclear weapons constituted a basis for military-theoretical thought to decide on the necessity of using airborne troops more broadly in military operations. . . .
>
> Essential changes in the development of theory and practice of the use of airborne troops were determined by the appearance of new aircraft with greater speed, range, and load capacity, as well as by the more modern airborne landing equipment.
>
> Because nuclear weapons constitute the chief means of destroying the enemy, the main aspect of cooperation now becomes coordination of the forces of airborne troops

Above This civil-registered An-12 is part of a 200-strong fleet nominally operated by Aeroflot but available for military duties at very short notice.

Below The An-12 Cub is still a Soviet Air Force standard tactical transport. (*Tass*)

with nuclear strikes, troops attacking from the front (in operations in a coastal area, with the navy and amphibious landing forces), and also with the forces which protect the airborne landing from enemy action.[12]

Lest there be any remaining doubts, the com-

mandant of the Gagarin Academy used the same journal in the following year to summarise the tasks of transport aviation in a nuclear environment:

In conditions of a nuclear war, aircraft will be the most mobile force in implementing com-

157

plete support to the troops, and above all to groups which have broken out into the operational depth of the enemy or which find themselves for some reason isolated from the main forces. They are capable of delivering to them quickly everything necessary to carry out combat operations and also to evacuate the wounded and sick. Aircraft [fixed- and rotary-wing] will be most broadly used in carrying out these missions.

The use of military-transport aviation in support of combat aviation increases the manoeuvring capabilities of the latter and permits the constant supply of air units with ammunition, fuel, and other material means.[13]

The advent of nuclear weapons threatened to change the very nature of war; mercifully it has not yet done so. On the other hand, a much less dramatic invention has had a very great influence on the waging of war. Limited Soviet experiments with helicopters and autogyros had taken place before Tukhachevsky's execution,

but he had not been aware of their potential. By 1967 the Mi-8 Hip, capable of carrying 24 troops, was in service and the Mi-24 Hind was on the drawing board. The use of the helicopter for tactical air mobility and casualty evacuation had been well demonstrated in various Western colonial and counter-insurgency campaigns as well as increasingly by the United States in Southeast Asia. But rotary-wing aircraft also promised to be particularly useful within Russian offensive operations:

> The creation of the helicopter has increased the possibilities for landing troops from the personnel of regular ground troops who have not been trained in airborne landing. And this, in turn, has helped to resolve certain serious problems. When landing by parachute, the troops were greatly dispersed after their landing and their combat efficiency remained low for a certain period of time, but troops delivered to the landing region in helicopters are ready to go into combat immediately.[14]

By 1971 occasional references to the possibility of a non-nuclear phase in a major war had begun to appear in the Soviet military press. The textbook *Military History*, issued for use in military

The ability of the Mi-26 Halo to carry light armoured vehicles makes it invaluable to air-mobile forces.

This ASU-85 self-propelled anti-tank gun has just been delivered by An-12 Cub to an airfield newly occupied by a Guards airborne division during Exercise Dvina. (*Tass*)

academies, concluded with a summary of the major features of contemporary military operations. The emphasis was still on a nuclear environment, marked by tactical nuclear strikes, highly mobile attacks, and novel forms of manoeuvre:

> The character and methods of manoeuvre in the course of attack have tangibly changed. While earlier the basic goal of manoeuvre was striving quickly and in an organised manner to transfer forces and place them in a more favourable position in relation to the enemy, now to this has been added the necessity for rapid advance into the depth for the swift use of the results of the nuclear strikes and for seizing enemy objectives. A completely new feature is manoeuvre with nuclear means, which permits carrying defeat to the enemy without altering the basic groupings of one's own troops. The wide use of airborne troops will also have an influence on manoeuvre – in the regions where they have been dropped, tank and motorised rifle units and subunits must be sent in swiftly.[15]

But in the very last sentence of the book the author observes:

> In working out methods of conducting battle in conditions of nuclear war, Soviet military science does not exclude the possibility of conducting combat operations with the use of only conventional means of fighting.[16]

Meanwhile, the theory was being practised.

Forty years previously, in 1935, 600 paratroops had been dropped from TB-3 bombers near Kiev; the invited foreign observers had been suitably

Above The Antonov An-22 was the Soviet Air Forces' first modern strategic transport.

Below The Il-76 Candid is steadily supplanting the An-12s in service with SAF transport units. (*Anton Wettstein*)

impressed. As the An-22 and An-12 entered service in the 1960s so airborne elements began once more to play a steadily increasing part in major exercises. During the night of August 20–21, 1968, Soviet airborne troops landed at Prague Airport, whence they moved swiftly into the centre of the city, seizing radio stations and parliament and other government buildings. The landings followed two major exercises in territory adjoining Czechoslovak borders during the previous month. They were apparently well co-ordinated, and when they were mounted the commanders could not have known that they would be unopposed. In Exercise Dvina in March 1970 some 8,000 paratroops and 160 combat vehicles are said to have been dropped in 22min.[17] Since then the An-12 Cub, which was the major contributor to Dvina, has been supplemented and in some units replaced by the four-jet Il-76 Candid. Candid can lift over a hundred paratroops or, in cramped conditions, some 140 troops in transit. Its nominal operating

range is in excess of 3,000 miles with a payload of 88,000lb.

Most exercises reported in the West as involving VTA and/or Aeroflot aircraft have been associated with the Army and Airborne Forces, but not all. In 1982 the Warsaw Pact Shield 82 manoeuvres included an attack by the Black Sea Fleet on the Bulgarian coast. Il-76s lifted troops, vehicles and equipment to small airfields in the exercise area. They also earned the commendation of Col-Gen A. Volkov, commander-in-chief of VTA, for the success of a large-scale air drop despite bad weather, and for the concentration in time of the air-landing operations. Helicopters were also used but were not accorded the same emphasis. In July the following year Minister of Defence Marshal Ustinov was reported to have taken command of a Guards Airborne unit during an air drop on manoeuvres in Byelorussia and the Baltic States. The air-dropped were

A Hungarian coach is used to demonstrate the payload and volume capabilities of the Il-76. (*Tass*)

tasked with acquiring up-to-date information on enemy air defences, destroying command posts, neutralising nuclear weapon stores, disrupting communications and capturing an airfield. On successful completion of the drop, a second wave of Il-76s landed heavy vehicles and equipment.[18]

Soviet belief in the value of the helicopter in support of the offensive in general and the operational manoeuvre group in particular was illustrated in Chapter 3. The Soviets distinguish clearly between the fixed-wing "airborne" forces and the largely helicopter-borne "air-mobile" forces. VTA is responsible for providing airlift for the former. Contemporary exercises illustrate the similarities and differences between the two:

They have transport which ensures the possibility to carry out broad and quick manoeuvre in the air over great distances and to penetrate into the enemy rear, ie they have a high air mobility. It consists in the capability of subunits, units and formations of the land forces to be airlifted by planes or helicopters and to use air space in carrying out combat missions. They also have much in common as regards their missions and methods of carrying them out.

The difference between them arises from their organisational structure, the tactical and technical characteristics of their means of transport and their combat capabilities. Inasmuch as airborne forces use combat planes for their transportation and are even united in airborne corps, while airmobile forces are lifted by helicopters and their largest organisational unit is a division, it is clear that the airborne forces can carry out operations of greater scope and in greater depth. Transport planes have a flying range of up to several thousand kilometres, whereas airmobile force helicopters have a range of only hundreds of kilometres. Airmobile forces are also distinguished by their specific missions such as tank fighting, covering operations, etc.[19]

Since 1979 airmobile helicopter exercises have assumed a new dimension, being located in mountainous areas. Instead of mass assaults or placements ahead of a penetrating OMG, assault landings are practised in the rear and flanks of smaller opposing numbers, not unlike those met in Afghanistan and possibly akin to those likely to be met in northern or southern flank operations against NATO. There is evidence to suggest that helicopter skills have been sharpened by such exercises:

The helicopter pilots crossed one mountain ridge, then another. It was still a long way to the target, yet the lead pilots reminded their wingmen, ''Be alert!'' The air is very dusty in the mountains, visibility is minimal, and one has to be particularly careful to avoid crashing into mountain peaks or coming under ''enemy'' fire from anti-aircraft weapons positioned in the hills. . . .

Before the pilots served in these areas they had had some experience working with other branches of troops. Here, however, in the mountainous desert region, this experience

The heavyweight Mi-26 has brought a new meaning to the term ''air-mobility'' for the Soviet forces.

clearly proved insufficient. For this reason, the squadron commanders and their deputies paid special attention to studying the tactics and specific features of co-operating with motorised rifle and assault units in the mountains. . . .

If there were some who had previously earned high-class ratings without training very diligently, they now had to do some serious work to improve their understanding and perfect their skills. The mountains only recognise skill of the highest standard. And today this skill was being tested.[20]

On September 22, 1982, *Red Star* carried an article praising the improvisation during such an exercise "in the mountains" of a medical officer with a Guards paratroop battalion air-landed by helicopter on the expected route of retreat of the enemy forces. A lack of medical equipment, shortage of water and inadequate shelter suggested that it was not just helicopter crew training that was becoming more realistic as a result of the move to the mountains. Western commentators naturally associate such activities with operations in Afghanistan as well as on NATO's flanks, but in fact they could have a much more wide-ranging application: as part of the development of air mobility not just in traditional theatres of war but across the Soviet Union's southern borders. Over the last 20 years the Soviet Union has steadily developed its ability to project military power well beyond its frontiers. The most visible expansion has been in the surface fleet developed by Admiral Gorshkov, but both strategic and tactical airlift have also assumed an increasingly significant role

Bears begin to fly

Immediately after the Arab-Israeli war of 1967 the London *Economist* carried a leading article entitled "Bears Can't Fly". It began:

It isn't just a little local difficulty that Mr Kosygin finds himself stuck with after the Middle East War. When he decided not to intervene on the Arabs' side he was admitting the central weakness of Russian policy:

its lack of strategic mobility. This is the problem that hampers the Russians everywhere outside the heart of the Eurasian land mass."[21]

Then followed references to Soviet incapacity to influence matters in the Congo in 1960 and the Hobson's choice between backing down and initiating nuclear war at the time of the Cuban crisis of 1962. The author could also have cited the Anglo-French landings at Suez, the US-British intervention in Lebanon and Jordan in 1958, and the British action in Kuwait in 1961. Russia, the article affirmed, was

. . . a giant that is able to bring its conventional forces to bear on problems immediately within its reach, or to crush opponents with nuclear power; but it is unable to use small mobile forces to further its policies in far-off parts of the world.[22]

Sokolovsky's views on the role of airborne forces was noted, but, the article went on, the Soviets lacked the right sort of forces, the necessary logistics support, and the friendly airfields necessary for rapid long-range intervention. The USA had made use of sea power, which was still important, but "the mobility which in Mahan's day was gained from sea power is still more effectively to be found in the air." After speculating on the goals of Soviet foreign policy, which could include the embarrassment of Western opponents and encouragement of revolutionary zeal in the Third World – the article concluded:

The combination of an offensive ideology with a defensive strategy is apt to produce such diplomatic defeats. To avoid more Cubas and Sinais the Russians will have either to resist the temptation to take on commitments in the Third World (which includes encouraging "wars of liberation") or else to acquire the military capacity this sort of policy calls for. This means building aircraft carriers and acquiring staging posts for airborne troops. It will be a bad omen for East-West relations if there are signs that they have chosen the second way out of their dilemma.[23]

In fact the decision had already been made and, even as the *Economist* article was written,

The last two decades have seen a number of massive Soviet resupply efforts involving many hundreds of An-12 sorties.

was being implemented. The development of aircraft carrier doctrine and deployment has already been examined in Chapter 4. As early as 1966 the USSR had secured permission for its military transport aircraft to overfly Yugoslavia. After the debacle in 1967 some 350 An-12 flights went via Yugoslavia and Iraq, carrying arms and equipment to the defeated Arab states. Later that year a further 170 flights went via Yugoslavia and Luxor in Egypt, carrying fighter aircraft and technicians to the republican faction in the North Yemeni civil war.[24]

But it was in the 1973 Arab-Israeli conflict that VTA made its most significant long-range contribution to date, and in so doing raised the temperature of US-Soviet relations. During October 1973 VTA carried out over 1,000 An-12 and An-22 resupply flights to Cairo and Damascus. On October 23 the tempo was suddenly reduced, and reports that the USSR was preparing to airlift some or all of its seven airborne divisions to intervene directly in the fighting between Egypt and Israel began to circulate in the West. The reports were persistent enough to prompt President Nixon to proclaim a Defence Condition 3 alert and to bring the 82nd Airborne Division in North Carolina to an advanced state of readiness. On this occasion the *Economist* missed a splendid opportunity to recall with satisfaction its speculation of six years before: the Bear could now fly and the impact was exactly as predicted.

In the subsequent decade VTA and Aeroflot extended Soviet reach deep into Africa and Asia. In 1975 and 1976 the communist MPLA forces in Angola were supplied with arms, equipment and Cuban troops by An-12s, An-22s and Aeroflot Il-62s. In the following year an even larger airlift was mounted in support of the Marxist government of Ethiopia, embroiled in a border war against Somalia and battling Eritrean guerrilla forces in the Ogaden Desert. The use of Aeroflot aircraft allowed the Soviet Union to avoid any overt infringement of neutral airspace, proven VTA routes via Yugoslavia, Syria and Iraq were also used. Over 200 aircraft are believed to have been involved, flying mainly from Odessa to Addis Ababa.

In December 1979 some 5,000 troops of the 105th Airborne Division were airlifted to Kabul from Kergona, with aircraft reportedly landing at Kabul Airport at a rate of one every ten minutes.

These troops were responsible for the overthrow of the existing Afghan regime and its replacement with a pro-Soviet faction. More recently, VTA and Aeroflot have flown regular missions to establish and support the Soviet bases at Da Nang and Cam Ranh Bay in Vietnam. By 1985 VTA had airfield access in Syria, Libya, Cuba, Guinea, Ethiopia, Angola, South Yemen and Vietnam, and the world's largest military transport, the An-124 Condor, had made its first international appearance, at the 1985 Paris Salon. Approximating in size to the USAF's C-5 Galaxy, Condor is estimated to be able to carry a payload of 125,000kg over a range of 3,400km.[25] Like the Galaxy, it has the volume to carry tanks, armoured personnel carriers and artillery. Without doubt it will fill an important gap in Soviet airlift capability.

The acquisition over just two decades of the ability to project power far beyond the national frontiers has been perhaps the most dramatic aspect of Soviet air power expansion. It has certainly made a significant contribution to the implementation of Soviet foreign policy. The centralised and co-ordinated relationship of the transport fleets seems to have led to much more effective command and control. Aeroflot's regular African network has expanded from five to 25 countries. Even the most generous assessments of revenue generated by these flights suggest that financial considerations were not uppermost when the decisions to open the new routes were made. Instead, they provide ready conduits for the movement of military advisers, students, political cadres travelling for indoctrination courses in the USSR, and KGB officials.

SS-1 Scud-A nuclear-tipped battlefield support missile is unloaded from an An-22 in a demonstration of the strategic potential of the SAF transport force. (*Tass*)

Left Boasting world record-breaking payload-range performance, the An-124 Condor will fill the gap in Soviet airlift capability created by the limitations of the An-22 force.

Below left Over 200 examples of the An-26 Curl short-haul transport are operated by state airline Aeroflot on behalf of the SAF. The type is particularly well endowed with built-in cargo-handling facilities. (*Tass*)

As in the Angolan and Ethiopian examples, they can also be used for the movement of troops without concern for neutral sensitivities about military overflights. The participation of Aeroflot aircraft in the twice-yearly roulement of conscripts between the USSR and Eastern Europe without interruption of scheduled flights indicates how much spare capacity the airline has. In a transition to war that capacity would be immediately and unobtrusively available for movement of units to forward positions within Warsaw Pact airspace or in friendly Middle Eastern countries. Similarly, while great attention is rightly paid to the development of rail and road communications between Western Russia and the eastern provinces, the USSR already possesses the ability to move by air large numbers of troops to the Chinese border areas should another Khalkin Gol or Amur River crisis occur.

Soviet air transport: strengths and weaknesses

In a race to intervene in the Third World the Soviet Union would possess an obvious advantage in the form of its location within the Eurasian landmass. In 1981 it was estimated that the US would require six days to lift a 16,500-man Marine amphibious brigade, excluding heavy equipment, to the Persian Gulf, whereas VTA and Aeroflot could move 20,000 troops in little over two days.[26] Such considerations underlay the United States' establishment of the Rapid Deployment Force and development of the C-17 long-range, rough-field transport to complement the C-5. Moreover, it is possible that Soviet transports might have technical advantages under such circumstances. Ever since Trotsky's intervention in the early 1920s Soviet transports have been designed to operate in the often primi-

tive conditions of the Russian hinterland. Their undercarriage tends to be rugged, and variable tyre pressures allow them to use either paved or unmade runways and airstrips. They are also much more self-contained, with on-board cargo-handling equipment and auxiliary power units for take-off from sparsely equipped airfields, and frequently carry ground engineers to deal with minor unserviceabilities. Whereas the majority of Western air forces rely on civilian aircraft of different types for crisis reinforcement, the commonality between Aeroflot and VTA – excluding the former's jet airliners – permits much greater interoperability. Groundcrew are familiar with the aircraft, and VTA and the airline have spares and servicing procedures in common. Nor would the Soviet Union have any problems in directing "civilian" aircraft and their crews into a war zone at short notice. It is therefore possible that in seeking to intervene in the Middle East or Southern Asia, the Soviet Union could capitalise on its geographical advantage by means of immediate civilian transport reinforcement and rapid turnrounds on unsophisticated airfields.

But Soviet advantages begin to diminish if the intervention is located further afield. Calculations in 1984[27] suggested that one division could in theory be moved from the Southern Caucasus to South Yemen in 24 hours only if all available cargo aircraft were used and if they spent no more than one hour on the ground at each end. A lift of one airborne division with all its equipment – armoured vehicles, guns, trucks, bowsers etc – over 3,000km would require the equivalent of 639 Il-76 sorties, more than the total number of An-12s, An-22s and Il-76s combined. Comparisons with or projections from the Czechoslovakian and Afghanistan operations are misleading. On both occasions a large amount of heavy equipment was already in each country or prepositioned on the frontiers. In the Gulf, on the other hand, it is the USA that has been able to preposition large amounts of heavy matériel. Moreover, the eight Soviet airborne divisions are widely dispersed in the Soviet Union, and moves to co-ordinate them at airheads, together with their increased readiness, would probably be swiftly detected by Western reconnaissance, as they were in 1973.

Left This An-22 is about to deliver earth-moving equipment to an oilfield in the Tyumen region of Siberia. The military implications of the big Antonov's ability to take heavy materiel into semi-prepared strips are obvious. (*Tass*)

Below left Hundreds of troops – probably equivalent to a Western battalion in strength – file aboard a quintet of Il-76s.

Below In wartime fixed-wing transports like the An-12 would probably be too heavily committed to the support of air-landed forces to be able to make much of a contribution to resupply from the rear. (*Tass*)

Matters would be different in Europe, however. In the event of a direct confrontation with NATO the ability of the Soviet Union to airlift troops to Eastern Europe, where heavy matériel is already prepositioned, would be a major factor in the balance of conventional forces. At a tactical level the availability of helicopters to shift strength laterally and concentrate it at selected positions before an offensive would be invaluable. How far these advantages would extend beyond the outbreak of hostilities is however a matter for speculation. Demands for air mobility, both fixed-wing and helicopter, would increase greatly. Soviet armoured divisions are to a certain extent logistically self-contained and would be supported by several hundred vehicles carrying ammunition, fuel and the innumerable other items required for a fast-moving offensive with a

high rate of fire. Helicopters would probably be used for priority loads and the resupply of units furthest forward, though on exercises their main roles are the provision of air mobility to troops and the enhancement of the offensive's firepower. Fixed-wing aircraft could capitalise on their greater range to resupply directly from stocks and bases deeper in the rear. But if exercise patterns are anything to go by, they would in fact be heavily committed to the support of airborne and air-dropped forces. It is significant that a repeated airborne objective in combined-arms exercises is the securing of airfields ahead of the land offensive. So, even in a benign environment free of the fierce air defences likely to be put up by NATO, the Soviet High Command would be faced with many difficult decisions on how and when to use its airlift capacity.

Fundamental to the success of Soviet air mobility is the winning of air supremacy. Without it, as has been explained earlier, the Soviet ground forces could expect to receive a severe mauling and offensive support would become problematical. For helicopters and, especially, lumbering transports, failure to establish air supremacy would spell disaster. Though there seems to be little explicit relationship between fighter and transport aircraft in Soviet doctrine, in the Czechoslovakian and Afghan incursions, and increasingly in exercises involving airborne forces, fighters have flown as escorts to the transports. But, as operations in the Second World War illustrated on many occasions, the escort force needs to be very large and with enough endurance to stay alongside or fight around the bombers or transports. The Bf 109 could not do it in 1940, in 1944 the P-51 could. A handful of Bulgarian MiG-21s and MiG-23s escorting Il-76s in an exercise over the Black Sea is one thing; the same mission over the battle zone and into NATO airspace would be something else again.

The vulnerability of helicopter-borne air assault forces is clearly recognised in the Soviet Union, although the recommended remedial action has on occasion perhaps been a little optimistic. For example, in one tactical air assault exercise in 1977 the ground troops generally acquitted themselves well, except in one vital respect:

But its air defence activity was not up to the mark because the Bn CO limited it to the covering action of the attached AA battery in the departure area. He also failed to attach due importance to the organisation of the air defence system during flight, in the landing and combat areas.[28]

In his explanation of his actions the battalion commander perhaps unwittingly indicated how far his faith in fixed-wing support differed from that of his critical superiors:

Major Krivolapov explained his miscalculations by the fact that he had relied on the umbrella fighters, saving his own air defence facilities for situations when the battalion was to act independently.[29]

The senior commander who directed the exercise, and the writer pointing the lessons, were in no doubt about the significance of aviation in such circumstances:

The senior commander . . . gave the battalion low marks for its inadequate appraisal of the "enemy" aircraft capabilities. The experience of modern local wars and exercises shows that aviation can play a decisive role in wearing out and destroying a landing force. The same is evidenced by the experience of the Great Patriotic War.[30]

In the planning of the operation, therefore, the battalion commander, in consultation with the specialist air defence staff officer, must ensure that:

. . . much thought is given to the problems of establishing co-operation between the anti-aircraft gunners on the one hand and the supported subunits and umbrella fighters on the other hand.[31]

While airborne the troops are expected to contribute to their own air defence:

Helicopters carrying a tactical air landing force fly at minimal altitude, the task of fighting the air "enemy" being assigned at that time to helicopters with motorised infantrymen in transport and to umbrella fighters. Experience shows that if a helicopter with a landing force aboard has perfectly organised small-arms fire, it can destroy air targets at a distance up to 1,500–2,000m in a vertical target sector of 45–60°. In the horizontal plane the only dead space is the aft hemisphere. But this inconvenience can be avoided by helicopters flying snaking manoeuvres.[32]

One wonders what the Soviet soldiers and helicopter crews think of such "perfectly organised" firepower and the "inconvenience" of vulnerability to attack from astern. But the above article was published in 1977, and since then there have been developments that make it more credible. In 1985 Western publications carried the first reports of two new helicopters, the Mi-28 Havoc and Ka-29(?) Hokum.[33] The former was categorised as an attack helicopter by official US sources, though one knowledgeable observer speculated that its primary role would be "the armed escort of troop and cargo helicopters."[34] There was no such equivocation about Hokum, said to offer a "rotary-wing air superiority capability."[35] In the light of the importance attached by the Soviet Union to air supremacy, these assessments are likely to prove well founded. If so, they would contribute greatly to the local command of the air that is essential to effective air mobility.

Other factors influencing the effectiveness of Soviet air transport are more difficult to quantify. The evolution of heavy-lift fixed-wing transport in the USSR has not been smooth. Production of the An-22 was stopped in 1974 after a very short run, and no successor came forward to replace it. Two An-22s were lost in overseas operations in the early 1970s, while another, reported to have 200 troops aboard, crashed soon after leaving Kabul Airport in October 1984, although on this occasion mujahideen ground fire may have been responsible. Entry into Aeroflot service of the wide-bodied Il-86 Camber was very slow in the late 1970s, and the ill-fated Tu-144, for which Khrushchev had such high hopes, was officially withdrawn from service in February 1983 because it was "too heavy and too inefficient" even for the Moscow–Alma Ata route to which it had apparently been restricted.[36]

Soviet heavy-lift helicopters are a different matter, frequently provoking the envy of Western operators. By 1985 over 600 examples of the Mi-6 Hook, first flown in 1957, were in service with VTA and a further 300 with Aeroflot and other civil agencies.[37] In 1977 Hook's hefty 26,400lb payload was surpassed by the 44,000lb of the Mi-26 Halo. By 1985 "several dozen"[38] Mi-26s were operational and production was continuing. In 1981 a modified Mi-8, with uprated engines and designated Mi-17, was demonstrated at the Paris Salon. Claimed improvements included higher speed and better

Antonov An-22: short production run and a chequered career.

Western air forces must covet the heavy-lift capacity of the Mi-6 Hook. (*Tass*)

single-engine capability. In sum, Soviet use of helicopters for tactical airlift and resupply owes little to Western example and seems to be one facet of air power in which the Soviet Union enjoys a clear-cut superiority.

Soviet transport aircrew effectiveness may compare favourably with that of their fast-jet counterparts. In August 1983 *Red Star* noted that one transport navigator, Lt-Col V. Gushchin, had completed 7,000hr flying and held the Order of the Red Banner and two Orders of the Red Star for his work on flying exercises. Co-ordination of VTA and Aeroflot, together with state manpower control, ensures that there is no haemorrhage of transport crews to civilian airlines of the

kind that perennially presents a challenge to the personnel management authorities of Western air forces. Experience gained in Afghanistan, where terrain, enemy opposition and the nature of the combat have forced reconsideration of formalised training and tactics and induced a greater reliance on aircrew initiative, must have increased the effectiveness of both the active-service aircrew and, by percolation, many others, especially in the helicopter regiments.

Crew effectiveness may be enhanced by the comprehensive training and improved career prospects enjoyed by navigators – occasionally regarded as second-class citizens in some Western air forces. While the most senior Soviet commanders in 1985 seemed to be pilots, the position of Chief Navigator of the Soviet Air Force was held by Lieutenant-General of Aviation Vladimir Bulov, and many one-star and other senior positions were held by navigators. Some 500 navigators are recruited annually, and all have to accept a 25-year active-duty commitment. They can attend senior Air Force academies and are eligible for the awards of Honoured Military (Combat) Navigator (inaugurated in 1965), Sniper Navigator (1972) and Distinguished Military Navigator of the USSR, the last awarded for "distinguished mastery of aviation technology and the training and education of flight cadres coupled with many years of accident-free flying."[39] On the other hand, while VTA navigators may be highly trained and long-serving on type, there is no reason to

believe that their nav systems compare any more favourably with those of the West than do the majority of contemporary Soviet avionics.

It is likely that the technical inferiority of Soviet fixed-wing transports – and presumably their lower serviceability – cannot be helped by the generally sub-Western standard of Soviet Air Force technician and engineering personnel. Occasional shreds of evidence suggest that fighter aviation is given priority over transport in the allocation of graduates of the Irkutsk Military Aviation School, and that there are insufficient flight engineers to meet demand, despite the commitment to the principle of simple design and minimum maintenance.[40] Serviceability problems may be responsible for the fact that only a small proportion of Aeroflot's fleet is engaged in normal operations at any one time,

The SAF's competent and well motivated transport aircrew could be frustrated by low serviceability rates. (*Tass*)

and could hamstring VTA during anything more than a short-period surge in time of crisis or actual hostilities. This would however be of less significance if the war were short and fought at a tempo dictated by the Soviet Union.

In spite of the shortcomings outlined above, the current outlook for VTA and the other elements conferring air mobility on the Soviet forces is bright. Capability is being steadily improved by the continued entry into service of Il-76 Candid. Wide-body capacity is being provided by Il-86 Camber, and a quantum improvement is promised by An-124 Condor. Hip and Hind provide a significant air assault capability, while Hook and Halo are available in increasing numbers for tactical resupply. Soviet capacity for unopposed long-range intervention beyond national frontiers has grown from virtually nothing in the 1950s to a level which first prompted US concern and then, in the Rapid Deployment Force, the allocation of extensive resources to counter it. And, regardless of the RDF, the Soviet Union can now support and

Above Flight deck of the An-22. The number of crew seats visible shows that there was little in the way of labour-saving avionics when it was built. (*Tass*)

Right The enormous cargo hold of the An-124 offers a potential for swift large-scale reinforcement of Soviet clients worldwide. (*Air Portraits*)

encourage its friends well beyond the Eurasian landmass. Should threats materialise in the Far East, VTA and Aeroflot could reinforce the Far Eastern theatre with a speed and volume far in excess of the capabilities of the previous generation. But above all, the Soviet ability to mount airborne and air assault attacks, to reinforce and resupply in any confrontation with NATO in Europe has raised even higher the stakes in the crucial competition for air supremacy. The success of that aspect of air power which has for so long been so unfashionable – air transport – now depends absolutely on the achievement of the oldest and most publicised: command of the air.

The An-72 Coaler STOL transport may now be entering series production as a replacement for the An-26. Coaler's short-field capability and low-pressure tyres make it particularly suitable for the tactical transport role. (*Air Portraits*)

Notes

1 *In The Sky – Military Transport Aviation*, Col V. Izgarshev, *Pravda*, January 4, 1979, page 6.
2 *Airborne Landings in War and Revolution*, A. N. Lapchinsky, Book 6, 1930.
3 *Upravlenie and Soviet Airborne/Air Landing Operations*, J. Erickson, University of Edinburgh 1980, page 195.
4 *Soviet Military Transport Aviation*, J. F. Besette, in *The Soviet Air Forces*, Murphy (ed.), McFarland 1984, page 193.
5 Sokolovsky op cit, page 158.
6 Sokolovsky ibid, page 131.
7 Sokolovsky ibid, page 318.
8 *Khrushchev Remembers*, Book Club Associates, London, page 395.
9 Ibid, page 36.
10 Kurochkin, *Red Star*, September 22, 1962.
11 *New Questions of Warfare*, M. N. Tukhachevsky, included in *Questions of Strategy and Operational Art in Soviet Military Works 1917–40*, page 122.
12 *The Growing Role of Airborne Troops in Modern Military Operations*, Cols I. I. Andrukhov and V.

Bulatnikov, *Military Thought* No 7, July 1966.
13 Krasovsky op cit, pages 197–198.
14 Andrukhov and Bulatnikov op cit, page 200.
15 Ibid.
16 Ibid.
17 *The Dramatic Impact of Soviet Airborne Operations*, M. Vego, *Defence and Foreign Affairs*, September 1980, page 31.
18 Extracts by Wg Cdr F. J. French RAF(Retd) from *Pravda*, July 1982, in correspondence with author.
19 Unattributed article in *Modern Battle: Questions and Answers*, series in *Soviet Military Review* 9/81, page 22.
20 *Helicopters Land Airborne Troops*, Capt V. Glezdenev, *Aviation and Cosmonautics*, 1982.
21 *The Economist*, London, June 24, 1967.
22 Ibid.
23 Ibid.
24 Vego op cit, page 41.
25 J. W. R. Taylor, quoting United States Department of Defence sources, in *Air Force Magazine*, March 1984, page 120.
26 *Soviet Projection Forces*, J. H.

Hansen, *Armed Forces Journal International*, October 1981, page 81–82.
27 *The Strategic Role of Soviet Airborne Troops*, Mark L. Urban, *Jane's Defence Weekly*, July 14, 1984.
28 *Air Defence of a Tactical Air Landing Force*, Col V. Subbotin, *Soviet Military Review* 5/1977, page 22.
29 Ibid.
30 Ibid.
31 Ibid.
32 Ibid, page 23.
33 *Soviet Military Power*, US DoD 1985, page 65.
34 *From Hind to Havoc*, Sergei Sikorsky, *Air Force Magazine*, March 1985, page 95
35 *Soviet Military Power* op cit.
36 First Deputy Minister of Civil Aviation Boris E. Panyukov, as reported in *Aviation Week and Space Technology*, February 15, 1983, page 31.
37 Sikorsky op cit, page 91.
38 Ibid.
39 *Navigators of the USSR*, Capt Donald W. Rightmyer USAF, *The Navigator*, Spring 1984, pages 15–17.
40 See for example *Lieutenants at the Crossroads*, Col A. Khorev, *Red Star*, June 2, 1979, page 2.

Part Two

Soviet military aircraft

Antonov An-12

NATO reporting name: **Cub**

The four-turboprop An-12BP has operated as a standard troop and freight transport with the VTA (Military Transport Aviation) service since 1959. About 750 were delivered, each equipped to carry 90 troops or 20 metric tonnes of cargo. The complete force could airlift two full army divisions, totalling 14,000 men, with all their equipment, over a radius of 650nm (1,200km; 750 miles). In reserve were a further 200 An-12s built for the state airline Aeroflot.

In terms of configuration, size and duty, the An-12BP can be regarded as the Soviet counterpart to the West's Lockheed C-130 Hercules; but it is less refined. The cargo hold lacks the Hercules' pressurisation and air-conditioning; and the An-12BP does not have an integral rear loading ramp. Instead, the undersurface of the upswept rear fuselage is composed of a pair of longitudinally divided doors which hinge up inside the fuselage. To facilitate direct loading from trucks, the undersurface aft of these doors consists of a further panel which is hinged at the rear to retract upward. With the doors up, 60 paratroops can be despatched from an An-12BP in under one minute.

Progressive re-equipment of An-12BP units with turbofan Il-76s has been under way since 1974, leaving about 225 of the Antonov aircraft still operational in their original form. Others, retired from transport duties, have been converted for a variety of tasks, and NATO reporting names allocated to five military variants of the An-12 may be listed:

Antonov An-12 modified as a testbed for advanced avionics.

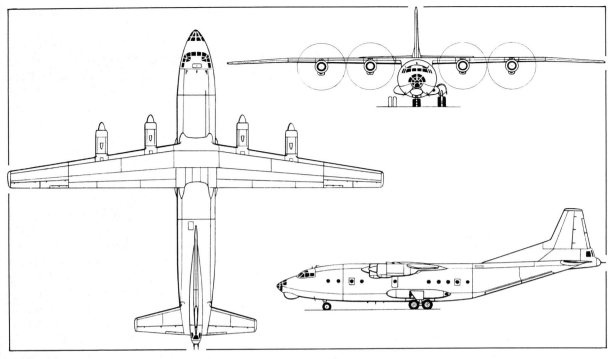

Antonov An-12BP Cub. (*Pilot Press*)

Cub Standard An-12BP transport. Manned gun turret in tail. Undernose radome enlarged on some aircraft.

Cub-A Electronic intelligence (elint) version. Generally similar to basic Cub transport, but with blade antennae on front fuselage, aft of flight deck, and other changes.

Cub-B Conversion of Cub transport for elint missions. Examples photographed over international waters each had two additional radomes under the forward- and centre-fuselage, plus other antennae. About 10 produced for Soviet Naval Air Force.

Cub-C ECM variant carrying several tons of electrical generation, distribution and control equipment in the cabin, and palletised jammers for at least five wavebands faired into the belly, plus ECM dispensers. Glazed nose and undernose radar of transport retained. An ogival "solid" fuselage tailcone, housing electronic equipment, is fitted in place of the former gun position. It is suggested that these aircraft would orbit at a height of more than 9,150m (30,000ft), at least 40nm (75km; 46 miles) on their own side of the border, at a time of tension or conflict, to jam the radars of NATO Hawk surface-to-air missile batteries.

Cub-D Another ECM variant, with different equipment to that of Cub-C, to extend active countermeasures capabilities.

Up to 40 Cub-C and D aircraft are believed to be in service with the Soviet Air and Naval Forces.

In addition to these operational variants, the An-12 has been used as a testbed for advanced avionics housed in a large blister fairing on each side of the fuselage, forward of the landing gear fairings, and in other containers under the front of the rear loading doors and rear turret.

Data for An-12BP (Cub)

Powerplant: Four 2,983kW (4,000ehp) Ivchenko AI-20K turboprops.

Accommodation: Crew of six. Up to 20,000kg (44,090lb) of freight, 90 troops or 60 parachute troops. Built-in freight handling gantry with capacity of 2,300kg (5,070lb).

Armament: Two 23mm NR-23 guns in manned tail turret.

Dimensions: **Wing span** 38.00m (124ft 8in); **length** 33.10m (108ft 7¼in); **height** 10.53m (34ft 6½in); **wing area** 121.70m² (1,310sq ft). Cargo hold: **length** 13.50m (44ft 3½in); **max width** 3.50m (11ft 5¾in); **max height** 2.60m (8ft 6¼in); **volume** 97.2m³ (3,433cu ft).
Weights: **Empty** 28,000kg (61,730lb); **normal T-O** 55,100kg (121,475lb); **max T-O** 61,000kg (134,480lb).
Performance: **Max level speed** 419 knots (777km/hr; 482mph); **max cruising speed** 361 knots (670km/hr; 416mph); **min flying speed** 88 knots (163km/hr; 101mph); **landing speed** 108 knots (200km/hr; 124mph); **max rate of climb** 600m (1,970ft)/min; **service ceiling** 10,200m (33,500ft); **T-O run** 700m (2,300ft); **landing run** 500m (1,640ft); **range with max payload** 1,942nm (3,600km; 2,236 miles); **range with max fuel** 3,075nm (5,700km; 3,540 miles).

Antonov An-22

NATO reporting name: **Cock**

This outsize four-turboprop transport was designed to carry the Soviet Army's mightiest fighting vehicles, including the T-62, T-72 and T-80 main battle tanks, and missile launchers like that for the Ganef SAM. The prototype flew for the first time on February 27, 1965, and became the star of the Paris Air Show a few months later. It was named *Antheus*, after the giant son of the Greek god Poseidon and Gaea, personification of the earth. This was an unfortunate, but perhaps prophetic, choice. Mythology relates that, as a wrestler, Antheus was invincible so long as he remained in contact with his mother earth. The An-22 was also more impressive when displayed on the ground than in everyday service. As a result, production ended in 1974, after about 75 had been delivered to the VTA and others to Aeroflot.

As in the case of the An-12, Antonov made no attempt to pressurise the cargo hold of the An-22, restricting pressurisation to the flight deck and a forward cabin for 28/29 passengers. A reinforced titanium floor and rear loading ramp/door met the needs of vehicle payloads. Four travelling gantries and two winches facilitated freight handling. In record attempts, a freight load of 100 metric tonnes was lifted to a height of 7,848m (25,748ft). Fifty metric tonnes were carried around a 2,000km course at 320 knots (593km/hr; 368mph). In a long-range overseas demonstration of the big freighter's capability, four An-22s airlifted relief supplies to Peru after a severe earthquake in July 1970; but one of them was lost over the Atlantic, south of Greenland. Subsequent missions have included the delivery of combat aircraft to foreign bases, including the MiG-25 reconnaissance aircraft which were operated from Egypt in the 1970s. More than 50 remain in service.

Antonov An-22 Antheus, NATO code-named Cock. (*Brian M. Service*)

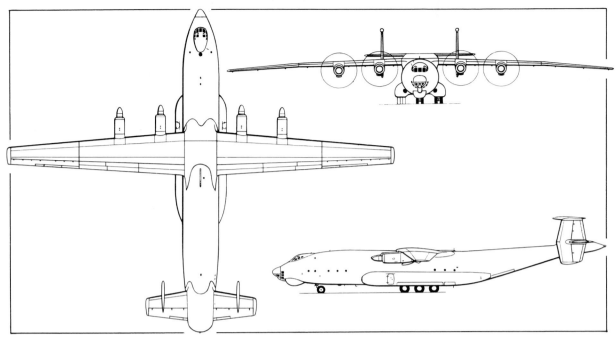

Antonov An-22 Cock. (*Pilot Press*)

Powerplant: Four 11,186kW (15,000shp) Kuznetsov NK-12MA turboprops, each driving a pair of four-blade contra-rotating propellers.

Accommodation: Crew of five or six. Cabin forward of main cargo hold for 28/29 passengers. Up to 80,000kg (176,350lb) of freight, including vehicles.

Armament: None.

Dimensions: **Wing span** 64.40m (211ft 4in); **length** 57.92m (190ft 0in); **height** 12.53m (41ft 1½in); **wing area** 345m² (3,713sq ft). Cargo hold: **length** 33.0m (108ft 3in); **max width** 4.4m (14ft 5in); **max height** 4.4m (14ft 5in).

Weights: **Empty** 114,000kg (251,325lb); **max T-O** 250,000kg (551,160lb).

Performance: **Max level speed** 399 knots (740km/hr; 460mph); **T-O run** 1,300m (4,260ft); **landing run** 800m (2,620ft); **range with max fuel and 45,000kg (99,200lb) payload** 5,905nm (10,950km; 6,800 miles); **range with max payload** 2,692nm (5,000km; 3,100 miles).

Antonov An-26

NATO reporting name: **Curl**

More than 200 of these pressurised twin-turboprop freighters, belonging nominally to Aeroflot, are available to supplement the Soviet military transport force. Max payload is 5,500kg (12,125lb), and conversion of the standard freight configuration to carry troops or stretchers takes only 20 to 30 minutes in the field. Versatility is enhanced by Oleg Antonov's unique rear loading ramp. This forms the underside of the rear fuselage when retracted, in the usual way, but can be slid forward under the rear of the cabin to facilitate direct loading on to the floor of the freight hold, or when the cargo is to be air-dropped. An OPB-1R sight is used to ensure pinpoint delivery into the dropzone.

Antonov An-26 Curl.

There are two versions of this aircraft:

An-26 Basic version, with electrically powered mobile hoist, capacity 2,000kg (4,410lb) to hoist crates through rear entrance and travel on a rail in the cabin ceiling to position payload in cabin. Electrically/manually operated conveyor built in flush with floor.

Antonov An-26 Curl. (*Pilot Press*)

An-26B Announced in 1981, this improved version is equipped to carry three standard freight pallets, each 2.44m (8ft) long, 1.46m (4ft 9½in) wide and 1.60m (5ft 3in) high. Rollgangs on floor, mechanism to move the pallets, and moorings enable two men to load or unload all three pallets in 30 minutes.

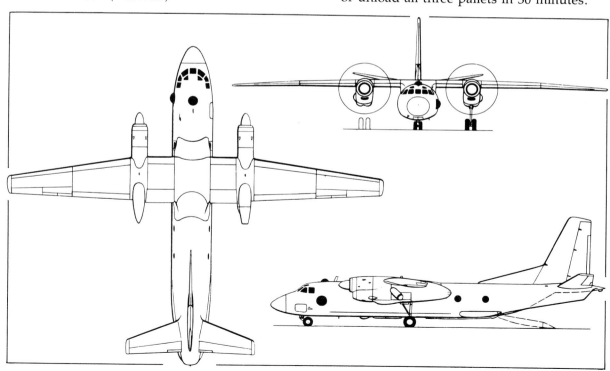

Powerplant: Two 2,103kW (2,820ehp) Ivchenko AI-24VT turboprops. One 7.85kN (1,765lb st) RU 19A-300 auxiliary turbojet in rear of starboard engine nacelle for use, as required, at take-off, during climb and in level flight, and for starting main engines.

Accommodation: Crew of five. Up to 5,500kg (12,125lb) of freight, or 40 paratroops. Ambulance version carries 24 litters.

Armament: None.

Dimensions: **Wing span** 29.20m (95ft 9½in); **length** 23.80m (78ft 1in); **height** 8.575m (28ft 1½in); **wing area** 74.98m² (807.1 sq ft). Cargo hold: **length** 11.50m (37ft 8¾in); **width of floor** 2.40m (7ft 10½in); **max height** 1.91m (6ft 3in).

Weights: **Empty** 15,020kg (33,113lb); **max T-O and landing** 24,000kg (52,911lb).

Performance: **Cruising speed** 237 knots (440km/hr; 273mph) at 6,000m (19,675ft); **landing speed** 102 knots (190km/hr; 118mph); **max rate of climb** 480m (1,575ft)/min; **service ceiling** 7,500m (24,600ft); **T-O run** 780m (2,559ft); **landing run** 730m (2,395ft); **range with max payload** 594nm (1,100km; 683 miles); **range with max fuel** 1,376nm (2,550km; 1,584 miles).

Antonov An-72/74

NATO reporting name: **Coaler**

The An-72 is often described as a smaller copy of Boeing's YC-14 prototype advanced medium STOL transport. However, it is a less refined design, and Oleg Antonov claimed that he adopted the high engine location primarily to avoid problems caused by foreign object ingestion. Their efflux is ejected over the wing upper surface and then down over large multi-slotted flaps, to provide maximum lift for short-field operation. Added to the low-pressure main landing gear, with two trailing-arm legs in tandem on each side, this enables the An-72 to operate from comparatively small unprepared airfields or from surfaces covered with ice or snow.

First jet built by the Antonov bureau, the aircraft was conceived as a replacement for the

Antonov An-72 Coaler.

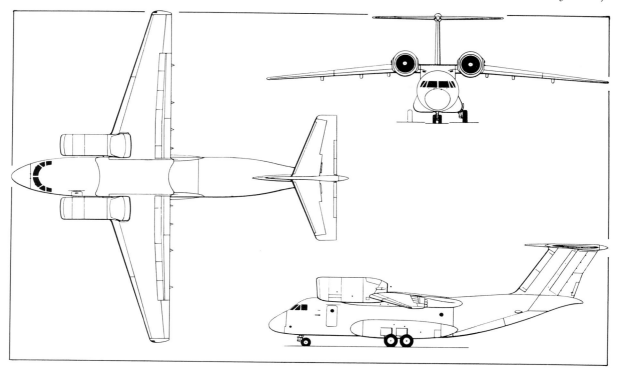

Antonov An-72 Coaler. (*Pilot Press*)

An-26. The first of two prototypes flew on December 22, 1977, and flight testing is said to have progressed well, if slowly. The Doppler based automatic navigation system, linked to an on-board computer, is pre-programmed before take-off, on a push-button panel to the right of a large map display on the flight deck. Production aircraft, which will probably be designated An-74, have a special "slide-forward" rear loading ramp of the kind fitted to the An-26 and optional wheel-ski landing gear.

Powerplant: Two Lotarev D-36 high bypass ratio turbofans, each rated at 63.74kN (14,330lb st). Thrust reversers standard.

Accommodation: Crew of two or three. Up to 10,000kg (22,045lb) of freight for normal operation, or 3,500kg (7,715lb) for STOL missions. Folding seats for 32 passengers along side walls of cabin, with provision for carrying 24 litters and attendant in ambulance configuration. All accommodation pressurised. Mobile winch, capacity 2,500kg (5,510lb), to assist loading of freight containers or pallets. Provision for roller conveyors in floor.

Armament: None.

Dimensions: **Wing span** 25.83m (84ft 9in); **length** 26.58m (87ft 2¼in); **height** 8.24m (27ft 0¼in); **wing area** approx 90m² (969sq ft).

Cargo hold: **length** 9.00m (29ft 6¼in); **width of floor** 2.10m (6ft 10¾in); **height** 2.20m (7ft 2½in).

Weights: **Max T-O** 26,500kg (58,420lb) from 1,000m (3,280ft) runway, 33,000kg (72,750lb) from 1,500m (4,925ft) runway.

Performance: **Max level speed** 410 knots (760km/hr; 472mph); **max cruising speed** 388 knots (720km/hr; 447mph); **T-O speed** 81–97 knots (150–180km/hr; 94–112mph) according to load; **landing speed** 89 knots (165km/hr; 103mph); **service ceiling** 11,000m (36,100ft); **T-O run** 470m (1,542ft); **range with max payload, 30 min reserves** 540nm (1,000km; 620 miles); **range with max fuel, 30 min reserves** 2,050nm (3,800km; 2,360 miles).

Antonov An-124

NATO reporting name: **Condor**

For once NATO chose an entirely appropriate reporting name when confronted with the An-124. Condors are the world's largest flying birds; the An-124 is the largest aeroplane currently to be seen in the air, in terms of wing span, with the heaviest maximum take-off weight of any aeroplane yet built. Development began in the mid-1970s to replace the disappointing An-22. The prototype flew on December 26, 1982 and three Condors had been flown by the time an example named *Ruslan* – after the giant hero of Russian folklore immortalised by Pushkin – made its public debut at the 1985 Paris Air Show. Production was then said to be well advanced, with entry into service scheduled for Summer 1986.

Except for having a low-mounted tailplane, the An-124's general configuration is similar to that of its US counterpart, the Lockheed C-5 Galaxy. It has an upward-hinged visor type nose and rear fuselage ramp-door for simultaneous front and rear loading/unloading. Advanced features include a fly-by-wire control system, titanium floor throughout the cavernous main hold, and 5,500kg (12,125lb) of composites, making up 1,500m² (16,150sq ft) of its surface area and giving a weight saving of 1,800kg (3,968lb). The 24-wheel landing gear enables the An-124 to operate from unprepared fields, hard packed snow and ice-covered swampland. Payloads include the largest Soviet battle tanks and complete SS-20 nuclear missile systems.

Introduction of the An-124 confirms that the Soviet Union has, at last, turbofan engines as powerful as those fitted in the latest Western

Antonov An-124 Condor. (*British Aerospace*)

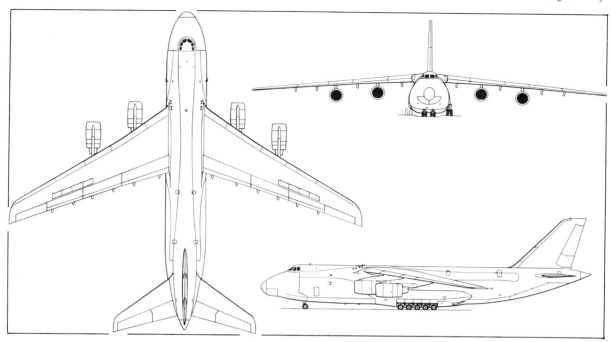

transport aircraft and with comparable fuel economy. They enabled one of the early Condors to set 21 official records on July 26, 1985, by lifting a payload of 171,219kg (377,473lb) to a height of 10,750m (35,269ft). This exceeded by 53% the previous record set by a C-5A Galaxy.

Antonov An-124 Condor. (*Pilot Press*)

Powerplant: Four Lotarev D-18T turbofans, each rated at 229.75kN (51,650lb st). Thrust reversers standard.

Accommodation: Crew of seven, plus reserve crew. Up to 88 passengers on upper deck, aft of wing. Freight on lower deck, which is pressurised to a lower differential than the upper deck and cannot be used normally for passenger carrying. Loads positioned by two electric travelling cranes with total lifting capacity of 20,000kg (44,100lb).

Armament: None on aircraft shown in public by Spring 1986.

Dimensions: **Wing span** 73.3m (240ft 5¾in);

length 69.5m (228ft 0¼in); **height** 22.5m (73ft 9¾in); **wing area** 628m² (6,760sq ft). Cargo hold: **length** 36.0m (118ft 1¼in); **max width** 6.4m (21ft 0in); **max height** 4.4m (14ft 5¼in).

Weights: **Max payload** 150,000kg (330,693lb); **max fuel** 230,000kg (507,063lb); **max T-O** 405,000kg (892,872lb).

Performance: **Max cruising speed** 467 knots (865km/hr; 537mph); **normal cruising speed** 432–459 knots (800–850km/hr; 497–528mph) at 10,000–12,000m (32,800–39,370ft); **approach speed** 124–140 knots (230–260km/hr; 143–162mph); **T-O field length** 3,000m (9,850ft); **landing run** 800m (2,625ft); **designed range with max fuel** 8,900nm (16,500km; 10,250 miles); **designed range with max payload** 2,430nm (4,500km; 2,795 miles).

Beriev M-12 (Be-12)
NATO reporting name: **Mail**

The uniqueness of this anti-submarine and maritime surveillance amphibian in a landplane age, as well as its capability, is shown by the fact that M-12s hold all 44 records listed by the Fédération Aéronautique Internationale for turboprop amphibians and flying-boats. About 100 were built. They entered service in the mid-1960s, and 80 remain operational, with no replacement in sight.

M-12s are deployed primarily at coastal air bases of the Soviet Northern and Black Sea Fleets, for operation out to some 200nm (370km; 230 miles) from shore. Their mission equipment includes a search/navigation radar in the nose, above the glazing of the navigator's station, and a long MAD (magnetic anomaly detection) tail-sting. The sharply cranked gull wing, and long strakes on each side of the front of the hull, keeps the turboprops clear of spray during take-off and landing on water.

Powerplant: Two 3,124kW (4,190ehp) Ivchenko AI-20D turboprops.
Accommodation: Crew of five.
Armament: Variety of weapons and stores for maritime search and attack carried in internal bay aft of step in bottom of hull and on four pylons under outer wings.
Dimensions: **Wing span** 29.71m (97ft 5¾in); **length** 30.17m (99ft 0in); **height** 7.00m (22ft 11½in); **wing area** 105m² (1,130sq ft).
Weight: **Max T-O** 29,450kg (64,925lb).
Performance: **Max level speed** 328 knots (608km/hr; 378mph); **normal operating speed** 172 knots (320km/hr; 199mph); **max rate of climb** 912m (2,990ft)/min; **service ceiling** 11,280m (37,000ft); **range with max fuel** 2,158nm (4,000km; 2,485 miles).

Right Beriev Be-12 Mail. (*Pilot Press*)

Below Beriev Be-12 of the Soviet Naval Air Force. (*Swedish Air Force*)

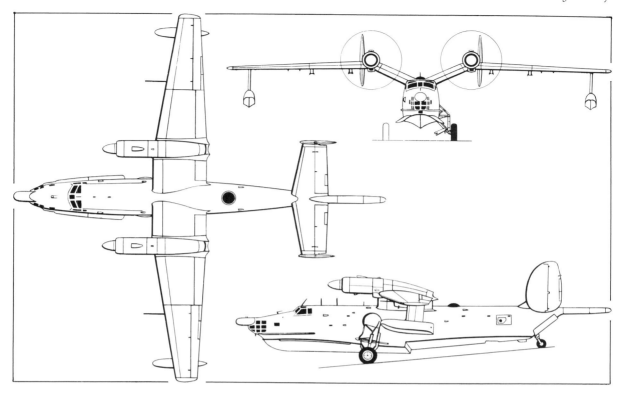

Ilyushin Il-20

NATO reporting name: **Coot-A**

More than 700 Il-18 four-turboprop airliners were built, the vast majority for operation by

Ilyushin Il-20 Coot-A is literally shadowed by a Royal Navy Sea Harrier. (*Royal Navy*)

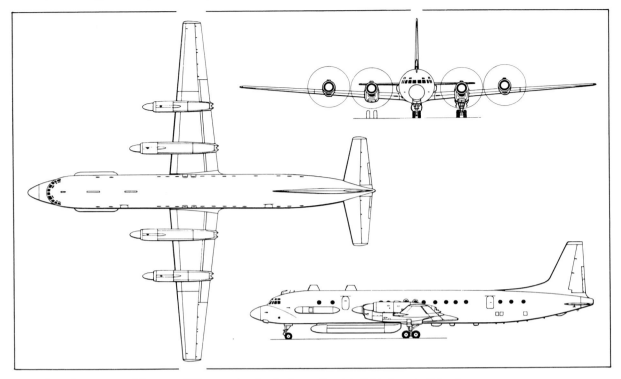

Ilyushin Il-20 Coot-A. (*Pilot Press*)

Aeroflot, from 1959. Those still in service include former passenger carrying aircraft converted into freighters. Others have been passed on to the Soviet Air Force and Naval Aviation, for a second career in specialised military configurations. One of these adaptations, first identified in 1978, is the Il-20 ECM or electronic intelligence (elint) aircraft known to NATO as Coot-A.

The basic airframe and powerplant seem to be little changed by comparison with the Il-18, but the Il-20 carries under its fuselage a container about 10.25m long and 1.15m deep (33ft 7½in × 3ft 9in) which is assumed to house side-looking radar (SLAR). Smaller containers on each side of the forward fuselage each contain a door over a camera compartment. About eight other anten-

nae and blisters can be counted on the undersurface of the centre and rear fuselage, plus two large plates projecting above the forward fuselage.

Powerplant: Four 3,169kW (4,250ehp) Ivchenko AI-20M turboprops.
Armament: None.
Dimensions: **Wing span** 37.42m (122ft 9¼in); **length** 35.9m (117ft 9in); **height** 10.17m (33ft 4in); **wing area** 140m² (1,507sq ft).

Ilyushin Il-38

NATO reporting name: **May**

This anti-submarine/maritime patrol aircraft was developed from the Il-18 airliner, in the same way that the US Navy's P-3 Orion was based on the Lockheed Electra. The lengthened cabin of the Il-38 has few windows, and the complete wing assembly is much further forward than on the Il-18, to offset the effect on the CG position of added internal equipment and stores. The origi-nal version has an undernose radome, a MAD tail-sting, other specialised electronic equipment, and internal weapons/stores bays fore and aft of the wing carry-through structure. On some aircraft the front weapon bay doors are replaced by a second, longer, blister fairing.

About 60 Il-38s are operational at shore bases of the Soviet Naval Air Force. They are encountered frequently over the northern waters of the Atlantic, over the Mediterranean from bases in Syria and Libya, and over the Red Sea, Gulf of

Il-38 photographed by an aircraft of the Royal Air Force.

Below Ilyushin Il-38 May. (*Pilot Press*)

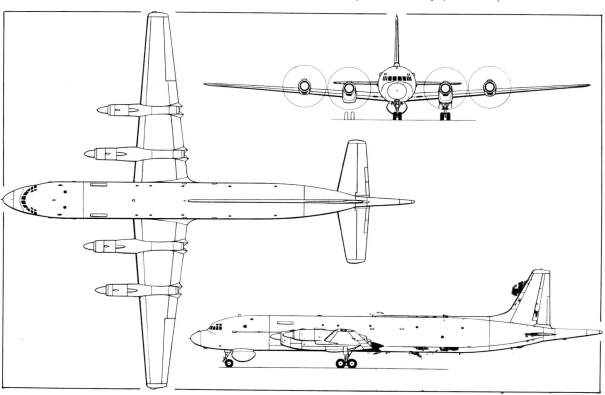

Aden and Arabian Sea from South Yemen. Flights from Ethiopia were suspended after Eritrean rebels destroyed two Il-38s on the ground at Asmara in May 1984, but two Il-38s were deployed to Mozambique in 1985.

Powerplant: Four 3,169kW (4,250ehp) Ivchenko AI-20M turboprops.
Accommodation: Crew of twelve.
Armament: Bombs, depth charges, torpedoes, sonobuoys and possibly mines can be housed in internal weapons bay.
Dimensions: **Wing span** 37.42m (122ft 9¼in); **length** 39.60m (129ft 10in); **height** 10.16m

(33ft 4in); **wing area** 140m² (1,507sq ft).
Weights: **Empty** 36,000kg (79,367lb); **max T-O** 63,500kg (140,000lb).
Performance: **Max level speed at 8,230m (27,000ft)** 347 knots (645km/hr; 400mph); **max cruising speed at 8,230m (27,000ft)** 321 knots (595km/hr; 370mph); **patrol speed at 600m (2,000ft)** 216 knots (400km/hr; 248mph); **min flying speed** 103 knots (190km/hr; 118mph); **T-O run** 1,300m (4,265ft); **landing run with reverse thrust** 850m (2,790ft); **range with max fuel** 3,887nm (7,200km; 4,473 miles); **patrol endurance with max fuel** 12 hours.

Ilyushin Il-76
NATO reporting name: **Candid**

In the second half of the 1960s, leadership of the Ilyushin Bureau began to pass from its founder to Genrikh V. Novozhilov. One of its major tasks at this period was to design a four-turbofan transport in the same class as the US Air Force's C-141A StarLifter, of which 285 had been ordered for delivery in 1964–68. Predictably, the two types proved to be similar in configuration, with the Soviet transport, designated Il-76, marginally larger overall. It was also given a wider and higher freight hold, and higher rated engines which, combined with full-span leading-edge slats and triple-slotted flaps, ensured a better field performance.

The first prototype flew for the first time on March 25, 1971. Its designers had been required to produce an aircraft that would haul 40 metric tonnes (88,185lb) of freight over a distance of 2,700nm (5,000km; 3,100 miles) in under six hours, in the harsh conditions of the USSR's

Ilyushin Il-76TD Candid-A. (*Anton Wettstein*)

Siberian regions. This implied that the Il-76 had to carry twice the payload of the An-12BP over five times the latter's range. Proof of its capability was revealed internationally in July 1975, when Il-76s set a series of 25 official records. They included a payload of more than 70 metric tonnes (154,590lb) lifted to a height of 11,875m (38,960ft), and a speed of 462.283 knots (856.697km/hr; 532.327mph) around a 2,000km circuit with 55 metric tonnes.

Design features of the Il-76 include rear loading ramp/doors, weather radar and a navigator's station in the glazed nose, ground mapping radar in a large undernose fairing, and a unique and complex 20-wheel landing gear. The entire accommodation is pressurised, making it possible to carry troops as an alternative to freight. Advanced mechanical handling systems are fitted for containerised and other freight. Equipment for all-weather operation includes a computer for automatic flight control and automatic landing approach. Versions identified to date are as follows:

Il-76 (Candid-A)   Initial basic production version.

Il-76T (Candid-A)   Developed version, with additional fuel tankage in wing centre-section above fuselage, and heavier payload. No armament.

Il-76M (Candid-B)   As Il-76T, but for military use, with rear gun turret containing two 23mm NR-23 guns, and with small ECM fairings between centre windows at front of navigator's compartment, on each side of the front fuselage, and on each side of rear fuselage. Turret and ECM not always fitted on export Il-76Ms.

Il-76TD (Candid-A)   Unarmed version, generally similar to Il-76T. Fully operational from July 1983, this version has Soloviev D-30KP-1 engines that maintain full power up to ISA + 27°C against ISA + 15°C for earlier models. Max T-O weight 190,000kg (418,875lb); payload increased by 8,000kg (17,635lb). Extra fuel increases max range by 648nm (1,200km; 745 miles).

Il-76MD (Candid-B)   Military version, generally similar to Il-76M but with same improvements as Il-76TD.

Built in Tashkent, Il-76s equipped about half of the 600-strong VTA transport force in early 1986, and will continue replacing An-12BPs at the rate of about 30 a year. They can be supplemented

Ilyushin Il-76M Candid-B. (*Pilot Press*)

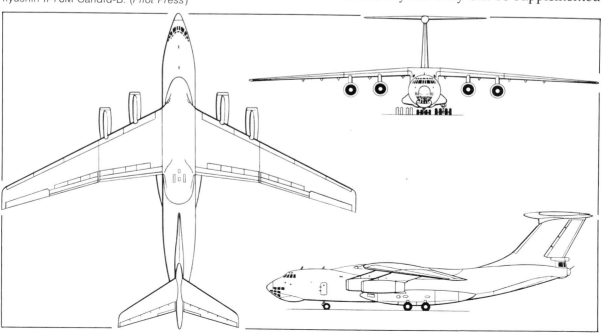

when necessary by the Il-76Ts and Ms of Aeroflot. A developed version is entering service with the Soviet Air Forces in an AEW&C role (see entry on Mainstay), and will be followed by Il-76 in-flight refuelling tankers (see Midas entry).

Data for Il-76M (Candid-B)
Powerplant: Four Soloviev D-30KP turbofans, each rated at 117.7kN (26,455lb st). Thrust reversers standard.
Accommodation: Crew of seven, including two freight handlers. Pressurised cargo hold has rear loading ramp and folding roller conveyors. Two overhead travelling cranes can utilise two hoists, each with capacity of 3,000kg (6,615lb), or four hoists, each with capacity of 2,500kg (5,510lb). Ramp can be used as additional hoist, with capacity of 30,000kg (66,140lb) to facilitate loading of large vehicles and those with caterpillar tracks. Loads can include containers, pallets, or three modules each able to accommodate 30 passengers in four-abreast seating, litter patients and medical attendants, or cargo. Max seating for 140 passengers.
Armament: Two 23mm NR-23 guns in tail turret.
Dimensions: **Wing span** 50.50m (165ft 8in); **length** 46.59m (152ft 10¼in); **height** 14.76m (48ft 5in); **wing area** 300m² (3,229sq ft). Cargo hold: **length, including ramp** 24.50m (80ft 4½in); **max width** 3.40m (11ft 1¾in); **max height** 3.46m (11ft 4¼in); **volume** 235.3m³ (8,310cu ft).
Weights: **Max payload** 40,000kg (88,185lb); **max T-O** 170,000kg (374,785lb).
Performance: **Max level speed** 459 knots (850km/hr; 528mph); **cruising speed** 405–432 knots (750–800km/hr; 466–497mph) at 9,000–12,000m (29,500–39,370ft); **T-O speed** 114 knots (210km/hr; 131mph); **approach and landing speed** 119–130 knots (220–240km/hr; 137–149mph); **T-O run** 850m (2,790ft); **landing run** 450m (1,475ft); **range with max fuel** 3,617nm (6,700km; 4,163 miles).

Ilyushin Il-76 AEW&C Variant
NATO reporting name: Mainstay

An airborne early warning and control (AEW&C) version of the Il-76 has been under development since the 1970s as a replacement for the Tu-126s operated by the Voyska PVO home defence force and Soviet tactical air forces. Known to NATO as Mainstay, it is said to have a conventional rotating "saucer" radome pylon mounted above the rear fuselage, lengthened fuselage forward of the wings, and a flight refuelling probe.

The US Department of Defence has stated in its *Soviet Military Power* booklet that Mainstay will improve substantially Soviet capabilities for early warning and air combat command and control. It is considered fully capable of detecting and tracking aircraft and cruise missiles flying at low altitudes over land and water, and could be used to direct fighter operations over European and Asian battle areas as well as to enhance air surveillance and defence of the USSR.

Tests and evaluation were continuing in 1985, by which time at least four Mainstays had been completed, with production expected to continue at the rate of five a year. They are intended primarily to operate with the new-generation MiG-29, MiG-31 and Sukhoi Su-27 fighters.

Ilyushin Il-76 Flight Refuelling Variant
NATO reporting name: **Midas**

This flight-refuelling tanker version of the Il-76 has been under development since the mid-1970s and was nearing deployment in 1986. It will support both strategic and tactical combat forces.

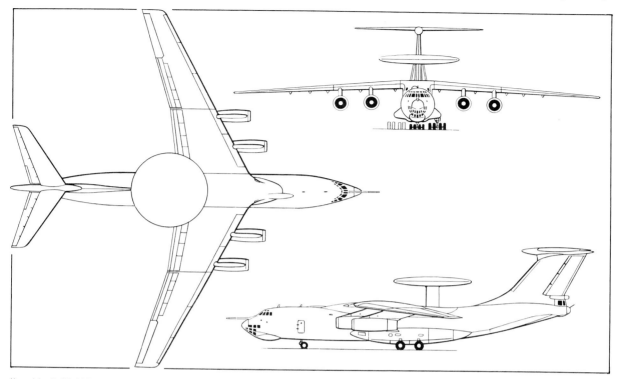

Ilyushin Il-76 (AEW&C) Mainstay. (*Pilot Press*)

Kamov Ka-25
NATO reporting name: **Hormone**

Because of the somewhat ungainly and cluttered appearance of most of the Kamov Bureau's helicopters, it is easy to undervalue their ingenuity and capabilities. In fact, by standardising on a compact twin-turbine/coaxial-rotor configuration the Kamov designers have been able to package extensive equipment permutations into aircraft small enough to operate from a wide variety of naval and merchant ships.

About 460 Ka-25s were manufactured in 1966–75, primarily to replace piston-engined Mi-4s in the Soviet Navy's ship- and shore-based force of 250 anti-submarine helicopters. Replacement with the similarly compact but vastly more effective Ka-27 is proceeding at an impressive rate, but about 125 Ka-25s were estimated to remain in Soviet Navy service in early 1986, in three identifiable versions:

Hormone-A Basic ship-based ASW version, with large flat-bottomed housing for under-nose search radar, and racks for small stores, including canisters of sonobuoys, on the starboard side of the fuselage. Other equipment varies from one aircraft to another. Some have an underfuselage weapon bay, which can be extended downward as a container for wire-guided torpedoes. Most have an infra-red jammer on the tailboom, under a "flower pot" housing with a transparent top, and a window of some kind in the undersurface of the boom. Each of the four wheels of the landing gear can be enclosed in an inflatable pontoon, surmounted by inflation bottles. The rear legs are pivoted, so that the wheels can be moved into a position where they offer least interference to signals from the nose radar. Dipping sonar is housed in a compartment at the rear of the cabin, but the Ka-25 is unable to operate with this at night or

in adverse weather. Ka-25s have been observed on cruisers of the Kara and Kresta classes, the nuclear-powered missile cruiser *Kirov* the carrier/cruisers of the *Kiev* class, each of which can carry about 19 Hormone-As and Bs; and the helicopter cruisers *Moskva*

Sensors visible on this Kamov Ka-25 Hormone-A include the undernose search radar and an infra-red jammer housed in the "flower pot" on the upper surface of the tailboom.

Kamov Ka-25 Hormone-A. (*Pilot Press*)

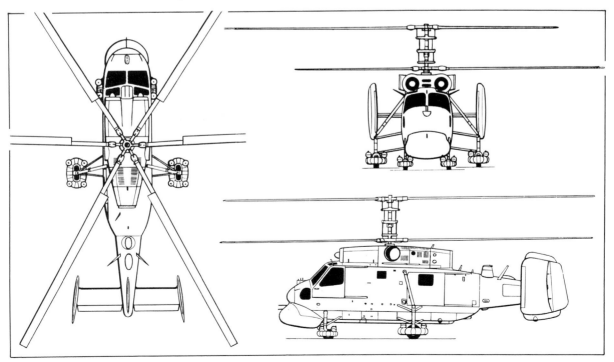

and *Leningrad*, each of which accommodates about 18 aircraft.

Hormone-B Special electronics variant able to provide over-the-horizon target acquisition and midcourse guidance for SS-N-3, SS-N-12 and SS-N-19 cruise missiles. Larger undernose radome with more spherical undersurface. Cylindrical radome under rear of cabin. Data link equipment.

Hormone-C Utility and search and rescue model generally similar to Hormone-A but with inessential operational equipment and weapons removed. This version sometimes has a yagi aerial mounted on the nose; it has been photographed in non-operational red and white paint finish.

Data for Ka-25 (Hormone-A)

Powerplant: Two 671kW (900shp) Glushenkov GTD-3F turboshafts (later aircraft have 738kW; 990shp GTD-3BMs).

Accommodation: Crew of two on flight deck.

Other crew in main cabin, which is large enough to contain 12 folding seats for passengers.

Armament: Anti-submarine torpedoes, nuclear depth charges and other stores in weapon bay, when installed. Some aircraft reportedly armed with small "fire and forget" air-to-surface missiles.

Dimensions: **Rotor diameter (each)** 15.74m (51ft 7¾in); **fuselage length** 9.75m (32ft 0in); **height** 5.37m (17ft 7½in).
Cabin, excluding flight deck: **length** 3.95m (12ft 11½in); **max width** 1.50m (4ft 11in); **max height** 1.25m (4ft 1¼in).

Weights: **Empty** 4,765kg (10,500lb); **max T-O** 7,500kg (16,535lb).

Performance: **Max level speed** 119 knots (220km/hr; 136mph); **normal cruising speed** 104 knots (193km/hr; 120mph); **service ceiling** 3,500m (11,500ft); **range with standard fuel** 217nm (400km; 250 miles); **range with external tanks** 351nm (650km; 405 miles).

Kamov Ka-27
NATO reporting name: **Helix**

According to its designer, S. V. Mikheyev, the Ka-27 was conceived as a completely autonomous "compact truck", able to stow in much the same space as a Ka-25 with its rotors folded, despite its much greater power and capability, and able to operate independently of ground support equipment. Titanium and composite materials are used extensively throughout the airframe, with special emphasis on resistance to corrosion at sea. The twin turboshaft engines are similar to those used in the Mi-24 gunship, and enable flight to be maintained on one engine at max take-off weight. Ease of handling, with a single pilot, is ensured by such features as a "mix" in the collective control system that maintains constant total rotor thrust during turns to reduce the pilot's workload when landing on a pitching deck and to simplify transition into hover and landing. The autopilot is capable of providing automatic approach and hover on a preselected course, using Doppler.

First photographs of the Ka-27 became available in 1981, after two of the new helicopters had been observed on the stern platform of the *Udaloy* ASW guided missile destroyer during the Warsaw Pact's *Zapad-81* exercises in the Baltic. The US Department of Defence had already stated that these "Hormone variants" could be carried inside a telescoping hangar on the *Sovremennyy* class of guided missile destroyers, and at least 16 were seen on the carrier/cruiser *Novorossiysk* during its maiden deployment in 1983. By then it was known also that the new Kamov Ka-32 civilian helicopter shared the same airframe.

Three versions of the military Ka-27 have been identified:

Helix-A Basic ASW version, with probable crew of three. Equipment includes under-nose radar, a ventral weapons bay for torpedoes and other stores, sonobuoys, IFF, two radar warning antennae above the tailplane, and an infra-red jammer above the tailboom. About 50 operational.

Helix-A's longer cabin and lack of central fin distinguish it
from the earlier Hormone.

Kamov Ka-27 Helix in utility transport form. (*Pilot Press*)

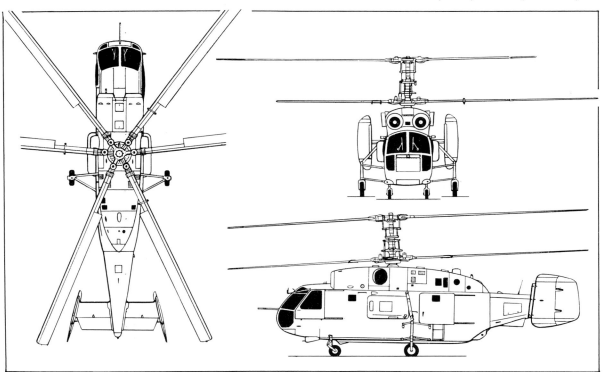

Helix-B   Infantry assault transport version. Different undernose radome.

Helix-C   Search and rescue and plane guard version. External fuel tank on each side of cabin and winch beside cabin door. Variant of this could provide an answer to the Soviet Navy's long-time need for a vertical replenishment shipboard helicopter.

Powerplant: Two 1,660kW (2,225shp) Isotov TV3-117V turboshafts.

Accommodation: Flight crew of two, with seat for third person. Folding seats along walls of main cabin for 16 passengers as alternative to mission equipment, litters or freight. Optional external load sling.

Armament: Not yet determined.

Dimensions: **Rotor diameter (each)** 15.90m (52ft 2in); **fuselage length** 11.30m (37ft 1in); **height** 5.40m (17ft 8½in).
Cabin: **length** 4.52m (14ft 10in); **max width** 1.30m (4ft 3in); **max height** 1.32m (4ft 4in).

Weights: **Max payload** 4,000kg (8,818lb) internal, 5,000kg (11,023lb) external; **normal T-O** 11,000kg (24,250lb); **max flying weight with slung load** 12,600kg (27,775lb).

Performance: **Max level speed** 135 knots (250km/hr; 155mph); **max cruising speed** 124 knots (230km/hr; 143mph); **service ceiling** 6,000m (19,685ft); **hovering ceiling out of ground effect** 3,500m (11,480ft); **range with max fuel** 432nm (800km; 497 miles); **endurance with max fuel** 4hr 30min.

Kamov Ka-?

NATO reporting name: **Hokum**

Helicopters perform so many key roles in modern warfare, over land and sea, that the need for effective anti-helicopter weapons has become increasingly urgent. Shoulder-fired and close-range surface-to-air missiles have to contend with ECM and other countermeasures, such as chaff and flares, carried by the aircraft. Most military helicopters are also fitted with infra-red suppressors, and their ability to fly just above the surface, taking advantage of natural cover,

Kamov Hokum. (*Pilot Press, provisional*)

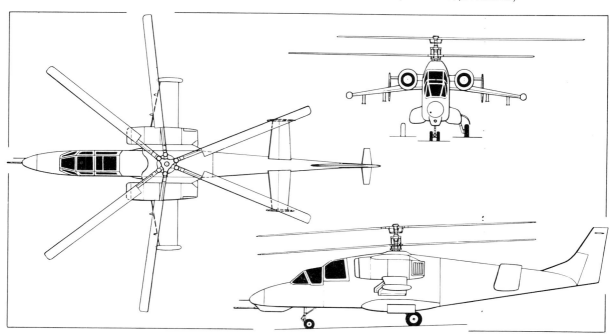

makes them difficult targets for fixed-wing aircraft.

Kamov's Hokum may represent the first attempt to produce an aircraft capable of both anti-helicopter and air-to-ground missions. Although it has been flying since 1984, all that is known with reasonable confidence is that it retains the traditional Kamov coaxial contra-rotating rotors, has a take-off weight in the 5,450kg (12,000lb) class, and carries a crew of two in tandem. Hokum has no Western counterpart,

and the US Department of Defense has commented that it "will give the Soviets a significant rotary-wing air superiority capability."

Dimensions: **Rotor diameter (each)** 14.0m (45ft 10in); **fuselage length** 13.5m (44ft 3½in); **height** 5.4m (17ft 8in).
Performance: **Max level speed** 189 knots (350km/hr; 217mph); **combat radius** 135nm (250km; 155 miles).

Mikoyan MiG-21
NATO reporting name: **Fishbed**

Still serving with 37 air forces in the mid-1980s, the single-seat MiG-21 remains the most widely-used jet fighter in history. It was designed on the basis of experience gained in jet-to-jet combat between MiG-15s and US aircraft during the Korean war. Emphasis was placed on good transonic and supersonic handling, high rate of climb, minimum size and light weight, using a turbojet of medium power. The first versions of the MiG-21 were, therefore, day fighters of limited range, with comparatively light armament and limited avionics. Subsequent development was concentrated on improvements in range, weapons, and all-weather capability, and the 600 MiG-21s still operational with Soviet tactical air forces are of the following, more capable, versions:

MiG-21PFMA (Fishbed-J) Multi-role all-weather fighter with Tumansky R-11-300 turbojet and radar (NATO Jay Bird) with a search range of 10.8nm (20km; 12.5 miles). Armament usually includes a GSh-23 twin-barrel 23mm gun. Four underwing hardpoints for two K-13A (NATO Atoll) close-range infra-red homing air-to-air missiles and either two external fuel tanks (supplementing underfuselage tank) or radar homing Advanced Atoll missiles. Additional

fuel tankage in deepened dorsal spine fairing above fuselage, giving total internal fuel capacity of 2,600 litres (572 Imp gallons; 687 US gallons).

MiG-21R (Fishbed-H) Reconnaissance version. Basically similar to MiG-21PFMA, but with a pod housing forward-facing or oblique cameras, infra-red sensors or ECM devices, and fuel, carried on the fuselage centreline pylon. Suppressed ECM antenna at mid-fuselage; optional ECM equipment in wing-tip fairings.

MiG-21MF (Fishbed-J) Differs from PFMA in having lighter-weight, higher-rated Tumansky R-13-300 turbojet. Entered service in 1970.

MiG-21RF (Fishbed-H) Reconnaissance version. Generally similar to MiG-21R, but based on MiG-21MF. Total of 50 Fishbed-Hs of both models estimated in service with Soviet tactical air forces.

MiG-21SMT (Fishbed-K) As MiG-21MF, but deep dorsal spine extends rearward as far as parachute brake housing to provide maximum fuel tankage and optimum aerodynamic form. Provision for ECM equipment in small removable wingtip pods. Deliveries believed to have started in 1971.

MiG-21*bis* (Fishbed-L) Third-generation multi-role air combat fighter/ground attack version, with wider and deeper dorsal fairing, updated avionics, and generally

MiG-21SMT Fishbed-K, with full-length dorsal fuel tank. (*Flug Revue*)

improved construction standards. Internal fuel capacity increased to 2,900 litres (638 Imp gallons; 766 US gallons).

MiG-21*bis* **(Fishbed-N)** Advanced version of Fishbed-L with Tumansky R-25 turbojet engine, rated at 73.6kN (16,535lb st) with afterburning. Enhanced avionics. Rate of climb at T-O weight of 6,800kg (15,000lb), with 50% fuel and two Atoll missiles, is 17,700m (58,000ft)/min. Armament uprated to two radar-homing Atolls and two Aphids.

There are also four two-seat training versions as follows:

MiG-21U (Mongol-A) Generally similar to MiG-21F short-range clear weather fighter,

with original smaller diameter nose air intake and centrebody. Two cockpits in tandem under a sideways-hinged double canopy and other, minor, changes. No gun.

MiG-21U (Mongol-B) As Mongol-A, but with wide-chord fin and deeper dorsal spine fairing.

MiG-21US (Mongol-B) As MiG-21U Mongol-B, but with flap blowing system to reduce landing speed, as on all current single-seaters, and retractable periscope for instructor.

MiG-21UM (Mongol-?) Trainer counterpart of MiG-21MF, with R-13 turbojet and four underwing hardpoints.

Mikoyan MiG-21SMT Fishbed-K. (*Pilot Press*)

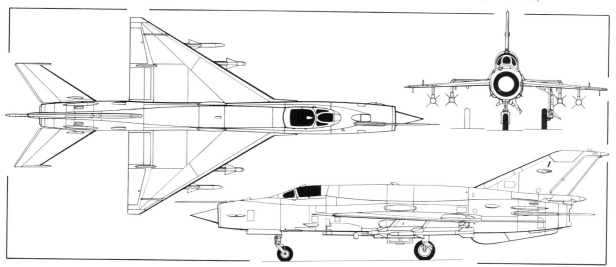

Data for MiG-21MF (Fishbed-J)

Powerplant: One Tumansky R-13-300 turbojet, rated at 64.73kN (14,550lb st) with afterburning. Internal fuel capacity 2,600 litres (572 Imp gallons; 687 US gallons). Provision for three 490 litre (108 Imp gallon; 130 US gallon) external tanks. Two jettisonable solid-propellant assisted take-off rockets can be fitted under rear fuselage.

Accommodation: Pilot only, on zero/zero ejection seat.

Armament: One GSh-23 twin-barrel 23mm gun with 200 rounds in belly pack. Four underwing hardpoints. Typical loads for interceptor role include two K-13A Atoll infra-red homing and two Advanced Atoll radar homing air-to-air missiles, with K-13As or UV-16-57 rocket packs (each sixteen 57mm rockets) as optional alternatives to Advanced Atolls. Ground attack loads include four UV-16-57s; two 500kg and two 250kg bombs; or four S-24 240mm rockets.

Dimensions: **Wing span** 7.15m (23ft 5½in); **length** 15.76m (51ft 8½in); **height** 4.50m (14ft 9in); **wing area** 23m² (247sq ft).

Weights: **T-O with four K-13As** 8,200kg (18,078lb), with two K-13As and three drop tanks 9,400kg (20,725lb).

Performance: **Max level speed** Mach 1.06 (701 knots; 1,300km/hr; 807mph) at low altitude, Mach 2.1 (1,203 knots; 2,230km/hr; 1,385mph) above 11,000m (36,000ft); **landing speed** 146 knots (270km/hr; 168mph); **service ceiling** 15,250m (50,000ft); **normal T-O run** 800m (2,625ft); **landing run** 550m (1,805ft); **combat radius** 200nm (370km; 230 miles) with four 250kg bombs, 400nm (740km; 460 miles) with four 250kg bombs and external fuel; **range with max internal fuel** 593nm (1,100km; 683 miles); **ferry range with three external tanks** 971nm (1,800km; 1,118 miles).

Mikoyan MiG-23

NATO reporting name: **Flogger**

First flown in mid-1967, the prototype of this variable-geometry (swing-wing) fighter had a Lyulka AL-7F-1 afterburning turbojet, as did the pre-production MiG-23S/SM (Flogger-A) versions. Current operational MiG-23s all have Tumansky turbojets. An estimated 2,100 form the backbone of the Voyska PVO air defence force and air combat elements of the Soviet tactical air forces; others are flown by all of the non-Soviet Warsaw Pact air forces and have been exported to at least ten further nations. The following versions are currently operational:

MiG-23M (Flogger-B) First series production version. Single-seat air combat fighter with Tumansky R-27 turbojet, rated at 100kN (22,485lb st) with afterburning, and considerably modified airframe compared with prototype and pre-production models. Deliveries began in 1972.

MiG-23MF (Flogger-B) Generally similar to MiG-23M, but with more powerful R-29 turbojet and uprated equipment, including J-band radar (NATO High Lark; search range 46nm; 85km; 53 miles, tracking range 29nm; 54km; 34 miles) in nose, ECM in fairings forward of starboard underwing pylon and above rudder, infra-red sensor pod beneath cockpit, and Doppler. Described as the first Soviet aircraft with a demonstrated ability to track and engage targets flying below its own altitude. Standard version for Soviet Air Force from about 1975 and for other Warsaw Pact air forces from 1978.

MiG-23UM/UB (Flogger-C) Tandem two-seaters for operational training and combat use. Identical to early MiG-23M (with R-27 engine), except for slightly raised second cockpit to rear, with retractable periscopic sight for occupant, and modified fairing aft of canopy.

MiG-23 (Flogger-E) Export version of Flogger-B, equipped to lower standard. Smaller radar (NATO Jay Bird; search range

MiG-23MF Flogger-G. (*Swedish Air Force*)

15nm; 29km; 18 miles, tracking range 10nm; 19km; 12 miles) in shorter nose radome. No infra-red sensor or Doppler. Armed with Atoll missiles and GSh-23 gun.

MiG-23BN (Flogger-F) Export counterpart of Soviet Air Forces' MiG-27 (Flogger-D) ground attack/interdictor. Has the nose shape, laser rangefinder, raised seat, cockpit external armour plate, and larger, low-pressure tyres of the MiG-27, but retains the powerplant, variable-geometry intakes, and GSh-23 twin-barrel gun of the MiG-23MF.

MiG-23MF (Flogger-G) First identified in Summer 1978. Basically similar to Flogger-B, but with much smaller dorsal fin, lighter-weight radar and, on some aircraft, an undernose sensor pod of new design.

MiG-23BN (Flogger-H) As Flogger-F, but with small avionics pod added on each side at bottom of fuselage, immediately forward of nosewheel doors.

MiG-23*bis* (Flogger-K) Latest version, announced in 1986, with pivoting weapon pylons under outer wings.

On all versions, wing sweep is variable manually, in flight or on the ground, to 16°, 45° or 72°. Full-span single-slotted trailing-edge flaps are each in three sections, permitting continued actuation of outboard sections when wings are fully swept. Upper-surface spoilers/lift dumpers operate differentially in conjunction with horizontal tail surfaces (except when cut out at 72° sweep), and collectively after touchdown. Leading-edge flap on outboard two-thirds of each main (variable-geometry) wing panel, coupled with trailing-edge flaps. Horizontal tail surfaces operate differentially and collectively for aileron and elevator functions respectively. Conventional rudder.

Data for MiG-23MF (Flogger-B)

Powerplant: One Tumansky R-29B turbojet, rated at 122kN (27,500lb st) with max afterburning. Variable-geometry air intakes and variable nozzle. Internal fuel capacity 5,750 litres (1,265 Imp gallons; 1,519 US gallons). Provision for 800 litre (176 Imp gallon; 211 US gallon) external fuel tank on centreline pylon, and two more under fixed wing panels. Attachment for assisted take-off rocket on each side of rear fuselage.

Accommodation: Pilot only, on ejection seat.

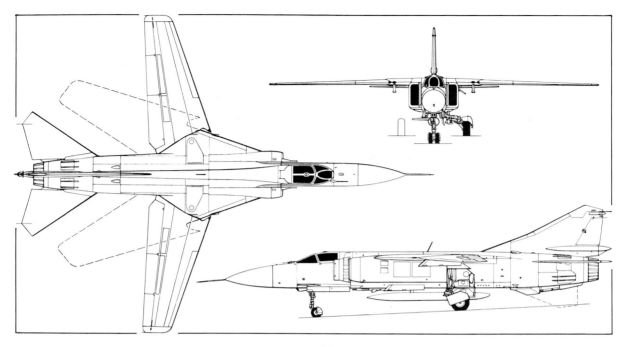

Mikoyan MiG-23MF Flogger-G. (*Pilot Press*)

Armament: One twin-barrel 23mm GSh-23 gun in belly pack. One hardpoint under centre-fuselage, one under each engine air intake duct, and one under each fixed inboard wing panel, for rocket packs, air-to-air missiles or other stores. Use of twin launchers under air intake ducts permits carriage of four Aphid missiles, in addition to two Apex on under-wing pylons.

Dimensions: **Wing span** 14.25m (46ft 9in) fully spread, 8.17m (26ft 9½in) fully swept; **length** 18.15m (59ft 6½in); **height** 4.50m (14ft 9in);

wing area 27.30m² (293.8sq ft) spread.

Weights: **Empty** 8,200kg (18,075lb); **max external weapon load** 2,000kg (4,410lb); **max T-O** 16,000–18,900kg (35,275–41,670lb).

Performance: **Max level speed** Mach 1.2 at S/L, Mach 2.35 at 11,000m (36,000ft); **service ceiling** 20,000m (65,600ft); **T-O and landing run** 900m (2,950ft); **combat radius** 485–700nm (900–1,300km; 560–805 miles).

Mikoyan MiG-25

NATO reporting name: **Foxbat**

The original MiG-25 interceptor was designed to counter the threat of the US Air Force's Mach 3 B-70 Valkyrie strategic bomber, for which North American Aviation was chosen as prime contractor in December 1957. Emphasis was placed on high speed, high altitude capability, and a radar/missile fit that would permit attack over a considerable range; manoeuvrability was less

important. When the B-70 was cut back to a research programme by President Kennedy, in March 1961, work on the MiG-25 continued, for both interception and reconnaissance missions.

Speed and height records set by MiG-25s, beginning in 1965, left no doubt that it was the fastest and highest flying combat aircraft ever produced for squadron service. Development of the interceptor has maintained its effectiveness despite the progressive NATO switch to low-level operations, and MiG-25s still equip

approximately one-quarter of the 1,200-strong Soviet home defence interceptor force. A further 130 interceptors and 170 reconnaissance MiG-25s fly with the tactical air forces; others operate under the national insignia of Algeria, India, Iraq, Libya and Syria. Five versions have been identified:

MiG-25 (Foxbat-A) Basic interceptor designed to attack high-flying targets. Built mainly of steel, with titanium only in places subject to extreme heating, such as the wing leading-edges. Slightly reduced wing sweep towards tips, which carry anti-flutter bodies housing ECM and CW target-illuminating radar. Nose radar (NATO Fox Fire) of MiG-25 examined in Japan in 1976, after the defection of its pilot, was the most powerful fitted to any interceptor of that period, but embodied vacuum tubes rather than modern circuitry, with emphasis on anti-jamming capability rather than range. Most operational Foxbat-As are being uprated progressively to Foxbat-E standard.

MiG-25R (Foxbat-B) Basic reconnaissance version, with five camera windows and various flush dielectric panels aft of very small dielectric nosecap for radar. Equipment includes Doppler navigation system and side-looking airborne radar (SLAR). No armament. Slightly reduced span. Wing leading-edge sweep constant from root to tip. Total of about 170 Foxbat-Bs and Ds estimated in service with Soviet tactical air forces.

MiG-25R Foxbat-D and B. Note the large flush dielectric panel aft of the nosecone on each aircraft.

MiG-25U (Foxbat-C) Two-seat trainer. New nose, containing separate cockpit with individual canopy, forward of standard cockpit and at a lower level. No search radar or reconnaissance sensors in nose.

MiG-25R (Foxbat-D) Similar to Foxbat-B, but with larger SLAR dielectric panel, further aft on side of nose, and no cameras.

MiG-25M (Foxbat-E) Converted Foxbat-A with changes to radar and equipment to provide limited lookdown/shootdown capability comparable with that of MiG-23MF (Flogger-B). Undernose sensor pod. Engines uprated to 137.3kN (30,865lb st) with afterburning. Developed via aircraft known as E-266M, which held the world absolute height record of 37,650m (123,524 ft) in early 1986.

Data for MiG-25 (Foxbat-A)

Powerplant: Two Tumansky R-31 turbojets, each rated at 120kN (27,010lb st) with afterburning. Internal fuel capacity approx 17,410 litres (3,830 Imp gallons; 4,600 US gallons).

Accommodation: Pilot only, on KM-1 zero-height/80 knot (150km/hr; 93mph) ejection seat.

Armament: Four air-to-air missiles. These may comprise one infra-red and one radar homing example of the missile known to NATO as

207

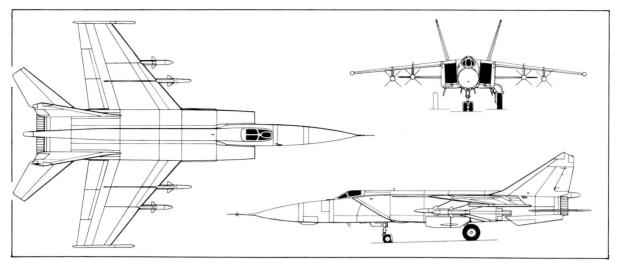

Acrid under each wing. Alternatively, one Apex and one Aphid or AA-11 can be carried under each wing.

Mikoyan MiG-25M Foxbat-E. (*Pilot Press*)

Dimensions: **Wing span** 13.95m (45ft 9in); **length** 23.82m (78ft 1¾in); **height** 6.10m (20ft 0¼in); **wing area** 56.83m² (611.7sq ft).

Weights: **Empty** over 20,000kg (44,100lb); **max T-O** 37,425kg (82,500lb).

Performance: **Never-exceed combat speed, with four Acrid missiles and 50% fuel,** Mach 2.83; **max level speed at S/L, with four Acrid mis-** siles **and 50% fuel,** Mach 0.85; **landing speed** 146 knots (270km/hr; 168mph); **max rate of climb at S/L** 12,480m (40,950ft)/min; **service ceiling** 24,400m (80,000ft); **T-O run** 1,380m (4,525ft); **landing run** 2,180m (7,150ft); **normal combat radius** 610nm (1,130km; 700 miles); **max combat radius** 780nm (1,450km; 900 miles).

Mikoyan MiG-27

NATO reporting name: Flogger

The MiG-27 is a single-seat ground attack aircraft which utilises the basic airframe of the MiG-23. The fuselage forward of the wing is redesigned to give the pilot the best possible field of view, to embody additional armour protection, and to house equipment for air-to-surface rather than air-to-air missions. The power plant is similar to that of the MiG-23MF, but with a fixed nozzle and fixed engine air intakes, consistent with the primary requirement of transonic speed at low altitude. Two versions are operational in Soviet tactical air forces:

Flogger-D Basic version. Instead of having an ogival radome, nose is sharply tapered in side elevation, with a small sloping window covering a laser rangefinder and marked target seeker. Additional armour on flat sides of cockpit. Seat and canopy raised to improve pilot's view. Six-barrel 23mm Gatling-type underbelly gun replaces GSh-23 of interceptor. Bomb rack under each side of rear fuselage in addition to MiG-23's five hardpoints. External stores can include tactical nuclear weapons and, probably, the air-to-surface missiles known to NATO as Kerry and AS-14. Provision for external fuel tank for ferry flights under each outer wing, which must be kept fully-forward when tanks are in place. Bullet-shape antenna above each glove pylon.

Flogger-J Identified in 1981. New nose shape, with lip at top and blister fairing below. No antennae above glove pylons. Wing-root leading-edge extensions on some aircraft. Armament includes two gun pods on underwing pylons, with gun barrels that can be depressed for attacking ground targets.

Most obvious difference between Flogger-J, shown here, and Flogger-D is the new nose shape.

Mikoyan MiG-27 Flogger-J. (*Pilot Press*)

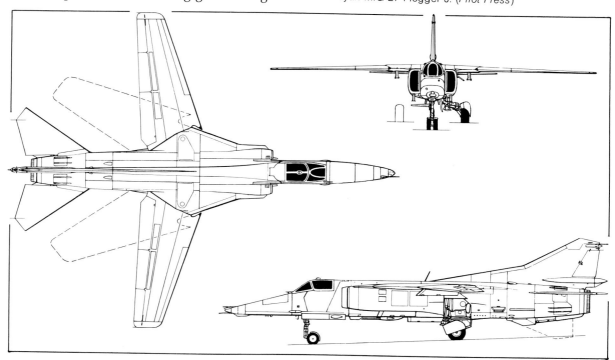

A total of about 730 Flogger-Ds and Js is deployed with Soviet tactical air forces, plus at least one squadron with the East German Air Force. The somewhat similar aircraft known to NATO as Flogger-F and H are MiG-23s. Both have been operated by Soviet units, but are basically export counterparts of the MiG-27, equipped to lower standards.

Data for MiG-27 (Flogger-D)
Powerplant: One Tumansky R-29B turbojet, rated at 112.8kN (25,350lb st) with afterburning. Internal and external fuel, and provision for assisted take-off rockets, as described for MiG-23MF.

Accommodation: Pilot only, on ejection seat.

Armament: Described above.

Dimensions: **Wing span** 14.25m (46ft 9in) spread, 8.17m (26ft 9½in) fully swept; **length** 16.00m (52ft 6in); **wing area** 27.30m² (293.8sq ft) spread.

Weights: **Max external load** 4,500kg (9,920 lb); **T-O weight** 15,500kg (34,170lb) clean, 20,100kg (44,313lb) max.

Performance: **Max level speed** Mach 1.1 at S/L, Mach 1.7 at height; **service ceiling** 16,000m (52,500ft); **T-O to 15m (50ft), clean,** 800m (2,625ft); **combat radius (lo-lo-lo) with four 500kg bombs, two Atoll missiles and centreline fuel tank** 210nm (390km; 240 miles); **ferry range with three external tanks** 1,350nm (2,500km; 1,550 miles).

Mikoyan MiG-29
NATO reporting name: **Fulcrum**

Operational since early 1985, the MiG-29 is expected to replace MiG-21s, Su-21s, and some MiG-23s in Soviet service. The basic version is a twin-engined single-seat fighter comparable in size to the USAF's F-16 Fighting Falcon. An important difference is that the MiG is fitted from the start with a large pulse-Doppler lookdown/shootdown radar that gives it day and night all-weather operating capability against low-

flying targets as well as freedom from the outmoded ground control interception techniques that restricted Soviet air defence effectiveness in the past.

References to this fighter first appeared in the Western press in 1979, after a prototype had been identified in photographs taken over

A pair of MiG-29s pictured on the occasion of the type's first public appearance in the West, at a Finnish air base in July 1986. (*Hasse Vallas*)

Ramenskoye flight test centre by a US reconnaissance satellite. From the start, it was plain that the MiG-29 (NATO Fulcrum) represented a concerted effort by the Soviet Union to close the technology gap with the West. Sustained turn rate is much improved over earlier Soviet fighters, and thrust-to-weight ratio is better than one. Although intended primarily as a counter-air fighter, it is likely to have a full dual-role air combat/attack capability, and a combat capable two-seater is also in production. Manufacture is centred at a factory in Moscow, from which more than 150 MiG-29s are believed to have been delivered by the Spring of 1986.

Powerplant: Two Tumansky R-33D turbofans, each rated at 81.4kN (18,300lb st) with afterburning.

Accommodation: Pilot only (tandem two-seater to follow).

Armament: Six AA-10 medium-range radar homing air-to-air missiles, or a mix of AA-10s and close-range AA-11s, or bombs, rocket pods, or other stores on two pylons under each wing and one under each engine air duct. At least one large-calibre gun is also likely.

Dimensions: **Wing span** 12.00m (39ft 4½in); **length** 17.66m (57ft 11¼in); **height** 2.75m (15ft 7¼in).

Weights: **Empty** 7,825kg (17,250lb); **max T-O** 16,500kg (36,375lb).

Performance: **Max level speed at S/L** Mach 1.06 (700 knots; 1,300km/hr; 805mph), **at height** Mach 2.2 (1,260 knots; 2,335km/hr; 1,450mph); **max unrefuelled combat radius** 620nm (1,150km; 715 miles).

Mikoyan MiG-29 Fulcrum. (*Pilot Press*)

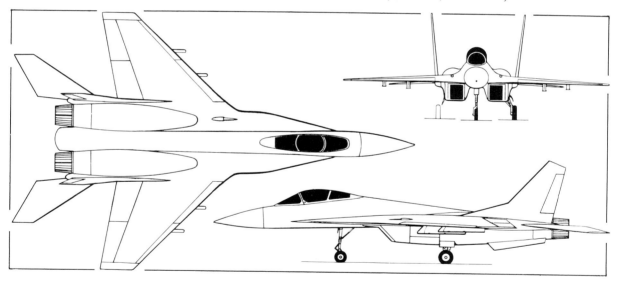

Mikoyan MiG/31

NATO reporting name: **Foxhound**

For some years the MiG-31 was regarded as, simply, a new-generation Foxbat. It is now known to be a very different aircraft from its

predecessor. The Mikoyan Bureau combined a well proven airframe configuration with new pulse-Doppler radar that offered true lookdown/shootdown and multiple-target engagement capability for the first time in a Soviet interceptor. Availability of the AA-9

The MiG-31 Foxhound is very much more than an updated Foxbat. (*Royal Norwegian Air Force*)

radar-homing long-range missile, already tested successfully against simulated cruise missiles, meant that the Mach 2.8 performance of the MiG-25 was no longer necessary.

Features evident in the first photographs of the MiG-31, taken (with undoubted Soviet approval) from an F-16 of the Royal Norwegian Air Force, include tandem cockpits for a two-man crew; an infra-red sensor under the front fuselage; underfuselage mountings for four AA-9s; multiple stores racks on the underwing

pylons that can presumably carry close-range missiles like Aphid; wing root leading-edge extensions not found on the MiG-25; and lengthening of both the air intake trunks forward of the wings and the engine tailpipes aft of the tailplane. The result presents a much more attractive appearance than that of Foxhound's predecessor, marred only by the fact that the underfuselage AA-9s are not recessed, as are the missiles carried by Western interceptors like the Tornado F.2.

Mikoyan MiG-31 Foxhound. (*Pilot Press*)

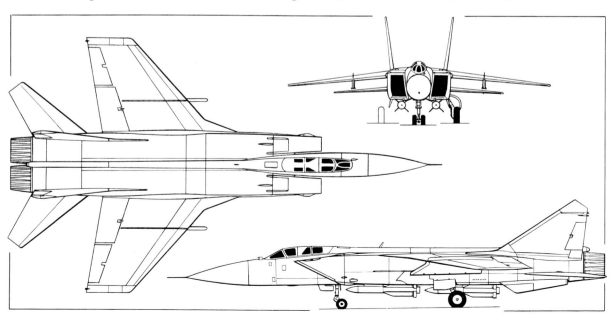

Deployment of MiG-31s with Voyska PVO air defence regiments has been under way for three years, and more than 100 were already known to be operational by the Spring of 1986, from the Arkhangelsk area near the USSR's western borders to Dolinsk on Sakhalin Island, north of Japan. Production, at a high rate, is centred at the Gorkiy airframe plant.

Powerplant: Two Tumansky turbojets, each rated at 137.3kN (30,865lb st) with afterburning.

Accommodation: Crew of two in tandem.
Armament: As described above.
Dimensions: **Wing span** 14.0m (45ft 11¼in); **length, excl nose-probe and tailplane** 21.50m (70ft 6½in).
Weights: **Empty** 21,825kg (48,115lb); **max T-O** 41,150kg (90,725lb).
Performance: **Max level speed** Mach 2.4 (1,375 knots; 2,550km/hr; 1,585mph) at height; **combat radius** 1,135nm (2,100km; 1,305 miles).

Mil Mi-6
NATO reporting name: **Hook**

Since Igor Sikorsky designed and flew the first four-engined aeroplane at Saint Petersburg (now Leningrad) in 1913, Russian engineers have always "thought big". The Mi-6 was, typically, the world's largest helicopter when it was revealed publicly in the Autumn of 1957. It was also the first Soviet production helicopter fitted with small fixed wings to offload the main rotor in cruising flight. These wings are normally removed when the aircraft operates in a flying crane role, carrying external freight. More than 860 production Mi-6s are believed to have been delivered for commercial and military service, the latter currently with the Soviet and five

Mil Mi-6 Hook in Egyptian markings.

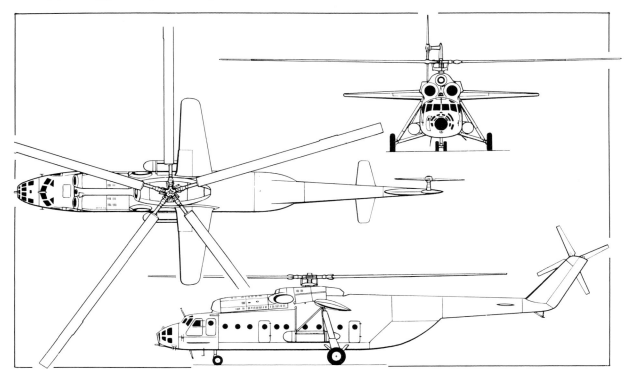

Mil Mi-6 Hook. (*Pilot Press*)

foreign air forces. Task of these helicopters is to haul guns, armour, vehicles, supplies, freight, or troops in combat areas. Loading and unloading are facilitated by the large clamshell doors and ramps at the rear of the hold, and by an 800kg (1,765lb) capacity electric winch and pulley block system.

Powerplant: Two 4,101kW (5,500shp) Soloviev D-25V turboshafts. Internal fuel tank capacity 7,895 litres (1,736 Imp gallons; 2,085 US gallons), supplemented by two external tanks on sides of hold, capacity 4,365 litres (960 Imp gallons; 1,153 US gallons). Provision for two ferry tanks inside cabin, capacity 4,365 litres (960 Imp gallons; 1,153 US gallons).

Accommodation: Crew of five; 12,000kg (26,450lb) of freight; or 70 combat equipped troops on removable tip-up seats along side walls and removable seats in centre of cabin; or 41 litters and two medical attendants.

Armament: Some aircraft have a 12.7mm machine-gun in the nose.

Dimensions: **Main rotor diameter** 35.00m (114ft 10in); **tail rotor diameter** 6.30m (20ft 8in); **fuselage length** 33.18m (108ft 10½in); **height** 9.86m (32ft 4in); **wing span** 15.30m (50ft 2½in).
Cabin: **length** 12.00m (39ft 4½in); **max width** 2.65m (8ft 8¼in); **max height** 2.01m (6ft 7in) at front, 2.50m (8ft 2½in) at rear; **volume** 80m³ (2,825cu ft).

Weights: **Empty** 27,240kg (60,055lb); **max payload** 12,000kg (26,450lb) internal, 8,000kg (17,637lb) on external sling; **max T-O with slung cargo at altitudes under 1,000m (3,280ft)** 38,400kg (84,657lb); **normal T-O** 40,500kg (89,285lb); **max for vertical T-O** 42,500kg (93,700lb).

Performance: **Max level speed** 162 knots (300km/hr; 186mph); **max cruising speed** 135 knots (250km/hr; 155mph); **service ceiling** 4,500m (14,750ft); **range** 334nm (620km; 385 miles) with 8,000kg (17,637lb) payload, or 540nm (1,000km; 621 miles) with external tanks and 4,500kg (9,920lb) payload; **max ferry range** 781nm (1,450km; 900 miles).

Mil Mi-8

NATO reporting name: **Hip**

Of 8,100 Mi-8s delivered for military and civilian use, from plants in Kazan and Ulan Ude, an estimated 1,615 support Soviet armies in the field. Teamed with Mi-24 gunships, they make up the most formidable helicopter attack force in the world. At army level alone, according to US Department of Defence estimates, there are some 20 helicopter attack regiments, each with up to 60 Mi-8s and Mi-24s. At division level, helicopter detachments are being expanded to squadrons. Primary combat mission for the Mi-8s is to set down assault troops, equipment and supplies behind enemy lines within 15 to 20 minutes of a nuclear or conventional ''softening up'' bombardment/strike. Specialised versions perform a variety of electronic warfare and support roles.

Equipment for all-weather operation by day and night includes an automatically controlled electro-thermal de-icing system on all rotor blades; Doppler radar; a radio altimeter with ground proximity warning; and a four-axis autopilot to give yaw, roll and pitch stabilisation under any flight conditions, stabilisation of altitude in level flight or hover, and stabilisation

of pre-set flying speed. The engine cowling side panels form maintenance platforms when open. Air stored in the main landing gear struts can be used to recharge the tyres in the field. Military Mi-8s can also be fitted with infra-red suppressors and infra-red decoy dispensers. Versions in service are as follows:

Hip-C Basic assault transport. Twin-rack for stores on each side of cabin, able to carry a total of 128 57mm rockets in four packs, or other weapons.

Hip-D For airborne communications role. Generally similar to Hip-C, but with canisters of rectangular cross-section on outer stores racks and additional antennae.

Hip-E Standard Soviet army support helicopter. One flexibly mounted 12.7mm machine-gun in nose. Triple stores rack on each side of cabin, able to carry up to 192 rockets in six suspended packs, plus four Swatter homing anti-tank missiles on rails above racks.

Hip-F Export counterpart of Hip-E. Missile

Hip-C, distinguished by twin stores carriers on each side of the cabin. (*Tass*)

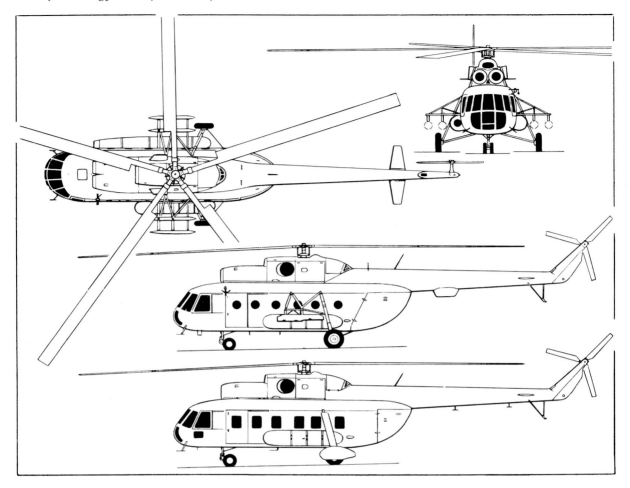

Mil Mi-8 Hip-C. Lower side view shows commercial version. (*Pilot Press*)

armament downgraded to six wire-guided Saggers.

Hip-G Airborne communications version. Rearward inclined antennae projecting from rear of cabin and from undersurface of tail-boom, aft of box for Doppler radar.

Hip-H See separate entry on Mi-17.

Hip-J ECM version, with additional small boxes on sides of fuselage, fore and aft of main landing gear legs.

Hip-K Communications jamming ECM version, with multiple antenna array on each side of cabin. No Doppler radar box under tailboom.

Data for Mi-8 (Hip-E)

Powerplant: Two 1,267kW (1,700shp) Isotov TV2-117A turboshafts. One internal fuel tank and two external tanks on sides of cabin, total capacity 1,870 litres (411.5 Imp gallons; 494 US gallons). Provision for one or two internal ferry tanks to raise max total capacity to 3,700 litres (814 Imp gallons; 977 US gallons).

Accommodation: Crew of two or three. Up to 32 passengers, but normal military configuration is for 24 combat equipped troops on tip-up seats along cabin side walls, with provision for quick adaptation to carry twelve litters and a medical attendant. Up to 4,000kg (8,820lb) of internal freight can be loaded via rear clamshell doors, with hook-on ramps for vehicles. A 200kg (440lb) capacity winch and pulley block system facilitates loading of heavy freight. Up to 3,000kg (6,614lb) can be carried on external cargo sling. Provision for 150kg (330lb) capacity rescue hoist at sliding door on port side of cabin at front.

Armament: Described under Hip-E model listing.

Dimensions: **Main rotor diameter** 21.29m (69ft 10¼in); **tail rotor diameter** 3.91m (12ft 9⅞in); **fuselage length** 18.17m (59ft 7⅜in); **height** 5.65m (18ft 6½in).

Weights: **Empty** 7,260kg (16,007lb); **normal T-O** 11,100kg (24,470lb); **max T-O** 12,000kg (26,455lb).

Performance (at normal T-O weight): **Max level speed** 135 knots (250km/hr; 155mph) at S/L, 140 knots (260km/hr; 101mph) at 1,000m (3,280ft); **max cruising speed** 122 knots (225km/hr; 140mph); **service ceiling** 4,500m (14,760ft); **hovering ceiling** 1,900m (6,235ft) in ground effect, 800m (2,625ft) out of ground effect; **range of cargo version with standard fuel** 251nm (465km; 289 miles); **ferry range** 647nm (1,200km; 745 miles).

Mil Mi-14

NATO reporting name: **Haze**

Comparison of photographs of this aircraft and the Mi-8 transport helicopter shows that the Mi-14 has shorter engine nacelles, with the intakes positioned above the mid-point of the sliding cabin door. Such nacelles, found also on the Mi-24 Hind and Mi-17, house TV3-117 turboshafts in place of the lower-rated TV2s of the Mi-8. Overall dimensions and dynamic components of the Mi-14 are generally similar to those of the Mi-8, from which it was

derived, except that the tail rotor is on the port side of the vertical stabiliser. New features to suit it for its overwater roles include a boat hull of the kind used on Western helicopters like the Sea King and a sponson on each side at the rear to confer a degree of amphibious capability. The landing gear is fully retractable. Operational

Mil Mi-14 Haze-A. The recesses visible at the rear of the planing hull are, from front to back, a retractable sonar housing and chutes for sonobuoys or signal flares.

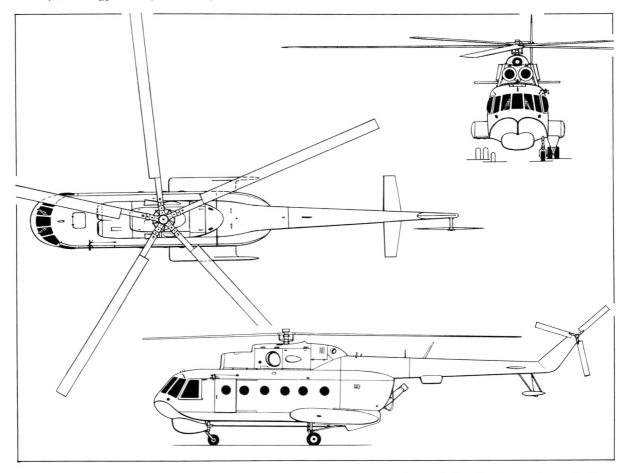

Mil Mi-14 Haze-A. (*Pilot Press*)

equipment of the primary anti-submarine version can be seen to include a large undernose radome; a retractable sonar unit housed in the starboard rear of the planing bottom, forward of what appear to be two sonobuoy or signal flare chutes; a towed magnetic anomaly detection (MAD) ''bird'' stowed against the rear of the fuselage pod; and a Doppler radar box under the tailboom. Weapons are carried in a weapons bay in the bottom of the hull.

The Mi-14 flew for the first time in 1973 and two versions have been identified by NATO reporting names:

Haze-A Basic anti-submarine version, as described in detail. About 100 in service with Soviet Naval Air Force. Others in Bulgaria,

Cuba, Libya, Poland, Romania and East Germany.

Haze-B Mine countermeasures version, identified by a fuselage strake and pod on the starboard side of the cabin, and no MAD. Ten in service.

Powerplant: Two 1,640kW (2,200shp) Isotov TV3-117 turboshafts.

Accommodation: Crew of four or five in Haze-A.

Armament: As described above.

Dimensions: **Main rotor diameter** 21.29m (69ft 10¼in); **tail rotor diameter** 3.91m (12ft 9⅞in); **length overall, rotors turning** 25.30m (83ft 0in); **height** 6.90m (22ft 7¾in).

Weight: **Max T-O** 14,000kg (30,865lb).

Performance: **Max level speed** 124 knots (230km/hr; 143mph); **max cruising speed** 108 knots (200km/hr; 124mph); **range** 432nm (800km; 497 miles).

Mil Mi-17

NATO reporting name: **Hip**

First seen in public at the 1981 Paris Air Show, and given the NATO reporting name Hip-H, the Mi-17 has the same basic airframe as the Mi-8 and the same uprated powerplant, short nacelles and port-side tail rotor as the Mi-14 and Mi-24. It could clearly perform the same variety of military roles as the Mi-8, with similar accommodation and operational loads. The engine air intakes can be fitted with domed particle separators to prevent the ingestion of sand, dust and other foreign objects at unprepared landing sites, as can those of the Mi-24, Mi-26 and Mi-28. If an engine fails, the power of the other is increased automatically to 1,640kW (2,200shp) for sustained single-engine flight.

Powerplant: Two 1,417kW (1,900shp) Isotov TV3-117MT turboshafts.

Dimensions: **Main rotor diameter** 21.29m (69ft 10¼in); **tail rotor diameter** 3.91m (12ft 9⅞in); **fuselage length** 18.43m (60ft 5⅜in); **height to top of main rotor head** 4.76m (15ft 7¼in).

Weights: **Empty** 7,100kg (15,653lb); **normal T-O** 11,100kg (24,470lb); **max T-O** 13,000kg (28,660lb).

Performance (at max T-O weight): **Max level speed** 135 knots (250km/hr; 155mph); **max cruising speed** 129 knots (240km/hr; 149mph); **service ceiling** 3,600m (11,800ft); **range with standard fuel** 251nm (465km; 289 miles).

Mil Mi-17 Hip-H. (*Pilot Press*)

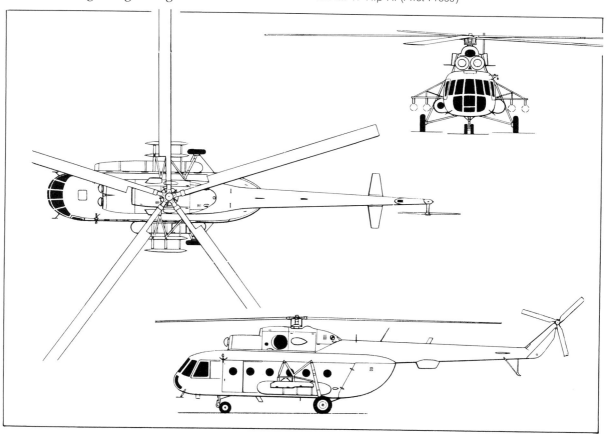

Mil Mi-24 and Mi-25
NATO reporting name: **Hind**

The Mi-24 was designed originally to deliver a squad of eight assault troops into a battlefield. Its weapons were intended then to clear a path past any tanks, anti-aircraft guns or other obstructions to its progress, but it was not long before training exercises caused a major change in tactics. Today, the Mi-24 is regarded as not only an anti-tank weapon, but capable itself of functioning as a high-speed, nap-of-the-earth "tank", and of destroying enemy helicopters in air-to-air combat. Other duties include escort of troop-carrying Mi-8s and ground attack, often partnered by Su-25 close-support aircraft. To reduce vulnerability to ground fire, steel and titanium have been substituted for aluminium in critical components, and glassfibre-skinned rotor blades have replaced the original metal blade-pocket design. Variants identified to date are as follows:

Hind-A   Armed assault transport, with large enclosed flight deck for crew of three, and places for up to eight fully-equipped troops in main cabin. Dynamic components and TV2-117 engines of Mi-8 fitted initially. Fully retractable landing gear. Auxiliary wings of this version have considerable anhedral. One 12.7mm machine-gun in nose, slaved to undernose sighting system; four hardpoints under stub wings for 32-round packs of 57mm rockets, up to 1,500kg (3,300lb) of chemical or conventional bombs, or other stores; four Swatter homing anti-tank missiles on wingtip launchers. Anti-torque rotor, originally on starboard side of offset tail pylon, repositioned to port side when TV2 engines were replaced by TV3s on later and converted aircraft. Initial series production Mi-24s were of this model.

Hind-B   Similar to Hind-A except that auxiliary wings have neither anhedral nor dihedral and carry only the two inboard weapon stations on each side. This version preceded Hind-A and was not built in quantity.

Hind-C   Generally similar to late-model Hind-A, but without nose gun and undernose blister fairing, and no missile rails at wingtips. For training duties.

Hind-D   Basically similar to late-model Hind-A, with TV3-117 engines and tail rotor on port side, but with front fuselage com-

Hind-E, upgunned by the addition of a twin-barrel 30mm cannon in place of the turret-mounted 12.7mm Gatling-type machine gun of earlier variants.

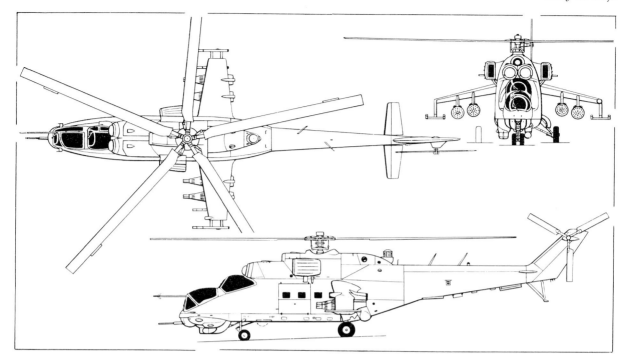

Mil Mi-24 Hind-D. (*Pilot Press*)

pletely redesigned and heavily armoured for primary gunship role, although transport capability retained. Tandem stations for weapon operator (in nose) and pilot have individual canopies, with rear seat raised to give pilot an unobstructed forward view. Probe fitted forward of top starboard corner of bullet-proof windscreen at extreme nose is part of low-airspeed sensing device to indicate optimum conditions for minimum dispersion of 57mm rockets. Under nose is a four-barrel Gatling-type 12.7mm machine-gun in a turret with a wide range of movement in azimuth and elevation, providing air-to-air as well as air-to-surface capability. Undernose pack for sensors, including radar and low-light-level TV. Wing armament of Hind-A retained. Many small antennae and blisters, including Odd Rods IFF. Infra-red jammer, suppressors and decoy dispensers optional.

Hind-E As Hind-D, for Soviet armed forces, but with up to 12 radio-guided Spiral tube-launched anti-tank missiles instead of Swatters, and enlarged undernose guidance pod on port side. Modified Hind-E, first shown in service with Soviet forces in photographs

published in 1982, has the nose gun turret replaced by a twin-barrel 30mm cannon mounted inside a semi-cylindrical pack on starboard side of fuselage, and the bottom of the nose smoothly faired above and forward of sensors.

Under the Soviet designation A-10, the Mi-24 has set a number of major FAI-approved records, including the current world speed record for helicopters of 198.9 knots (368.4km/hr; 228.9mph) over a 15/25km course.

Deliveries of all models of the Mi-24 exceed 2,400, from plants in Arsenyev and Rostov, with production continuing at the rate of more than 15 per month. In addition to the Soviet armed forces, operators include the air forces of Afghanistan, Algeria, Angola, Bulgaria, Cuba, Czechoslovakia, East Germany, Hungary, India, Iraq, Libya, Nicaragua, Poland, Vietnam and South Yemen. Some models, including those for India, are designated Mi-25, suggesting different equipment standards.

Data for Mi-24 (Hind-D)

Powerplant: Two 1,640kW (2,200shp) Isotov TV3-117 turboshafts.

Accommodation: Crew of two; eight troops or four litters in main cabin.

Armament: Described under individual model listings.

Dimensions: **Main rotor diameter** 17.00m (55ft 9in); **fuselage length** 17.50m (57ft 5in); **height** 6.50m (21ft 4in).

Weights: **Empty** 8,400kg (18,520lb); **normal T-O** 11,000kg (24,250lb).

Performance: **Max level speed** 173 knots (320km/hr; 199mph); **max cruising speed** 159 knots (295km/hr; 183mph); **max rate of climb at S/L** 900m (2,950ft)/min; **service ceiling** 4,500m (14,750ft); **hovering ceiling out of ground effect** 2,200m (7,200ft); **combat radius** 86nm (160km; 100 miles).

Mil Mi-26

NATO reporting name: **Halo**

When the Soviet armed forces first made known their requirement for a helicopter with a greater lifting capability than the Mi-6, in 1965, the Mil Bureau designed the Mi-12. To avoid years of development and the problems that might result from using an all-new dynamic system, they utilised two well-proven Mi-6 powerplant/rotor packages, mounted at the tips of long fixed wings. The fuselage of the Mi-12 was made large enough to accommodate missiles and other payloads of the kind carried by the huge An-22 freighter. The result was the largest and heaviest helicopter yet flown; but, although the Mi-12 lifted a world record payload of more than 40 metric tonnes, it did not progress beyond prototype testing.

Instead, in the early 1970s, Mil started work on the Mi-26. Western designers believed that if a

With the world's only operational eight-bladed rotor and a cargo hold as big as that of the Lockheed Hercules, the Mi-26 Halo is by a wide margin the best heavy-lift helicopter in service. (*Tass*)

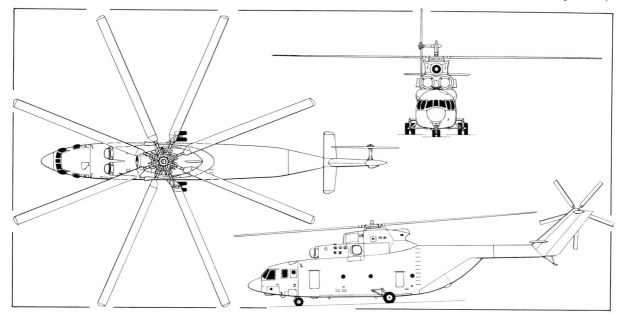

Mil Mi-26 Halo. (*Pilot Press*)

main rotor were fitted with more than seven blades efficiency would drop, because each blade would fly in the disturbed wake of the one too close in front. Marat Tishchenko, Mil's chief designer, knew better. He settled on eight blades for the main rotor of the Mi-26 and was able to meet the military specification with an aircraft of classical single-rotor configuration and uniquely attractive lines. With a payload and cargo hold comparable in size with those of a Lockheed C-130 Hercules transport, the Mi-26 was a success from the start.

The military had demanded that the helicopter should have an empty weight only 50% of its maximum permissible take-off weight. By designing a main gearbox of unprecedented efficiency, and using a high-pressure hydraulic system with very small rotor head control actuators; by making the rotor head itself of titanium, the blade skins of glassfibre, and adopting similar advances throughout the airframe, Mil achieved this requirement. Within a three-day period in February 1982 the Mi-26 set five world payload-to-height records. Only one year later it was in service with an air force development squadron, offering a payload far greater than the empty weight of the largest Western production helicopter.

For speedy loading and unloading, the rear of

the cabin is enclosed by large clamshell doors and a loading ramp/door. Two 2,500kg (5,510lb) capacity electric winches, on overhead rails, are used to transfer loads inside the hold. A device built into the main landing gear informs the flight engineer of the helicopter's loaded weight, so that an accident cannot be caused by overloading. The length of the main legs can be adjusted in flight to permit landing on a variety of surfaces, and on the ground to bring the floor of the hold nearer the surface. All equipment necessary for day and night operations in all weathers is standard, including weather radar, Doppler, a map display, horizontal situation indicator and automatic hover system. Closed circuit TV cameras enable the crew to observe slung payloads during attachment, release and in flight. Only the flight deck is pressurised, but it is seldom wise for modern military helicopters to fly at heights where pressurisation of the main hold would be essential.

Like all other modern Soviet military helicopters, the Mi-26 can be fitted with infra-red suppressors and decoy dispensers. There is, so far, no evidence of armament.

Powerplant: Two 8,500kW (11,400shp) Lotarev D-136 turboshafts.

Accommodation: Crew of five, including load-master. Four-seat passenger compartment aft of flight deck. About 20 tip-up seats along each side wall of hold. Max seating for about 85 combat-ready troops. Freight payload of up to 20,000kg (44,090lb) can include two air-borne infantry combat vehicles.

Dimensions: **Main rotor diameter** 32.00m (105ft 0in); **tail rotor diameter** 7.60m (24ft 11¼in); **fuselage length** 33.73m (110ft 8in); **height to top of main rotor head** 8.15m (26ft 8¾in).

Freight hold: **length, including ramp** 15.00m (49ft 2½in), **excluding ramp** 12.00m (39ft 4¼in); **width** 3.25m (10ft 8in); **height** 2.95 to 3.17m (9ft 8in to 10ft 4¾in).

Weights: **Empty** 28,200kg (62,170lb); **normal T-O** 49,500kg (109,125lb); **max T-O** 56,000kg (123,450lb).

Performance: **Max level speed** 159 knots (295km/hr; 183mph); **normal cruising speed** 137 knots (255km/hr; 158mph); **service ceiling** 4,600m (15,000ft); **hovering ceiling** 1,800m (5,900ft) out of ground effect; **range** 432nm (800km; 497 miles).

Mil Mi-28

NATO reporting name: **Havoc**

Because of its origins as an assault transport, the Mi-24 offers a large target for ground fire. When designing the Mi-28, the Mil Bureau began with a clean sheet of paper and produced a two-man attack helicopter with heavy armament but altogether slimmer and less vulnerable. The best illustration available in Spring 1986 is an artist's

impression released by the US Department of Defence. This shows an aircraft with a slim-as-practicable fuselage, slightly shorter than that of the Mi-24 and with the stepped cockpits, non-retractable tailwheel landing gear, weapon-

The Mil Mi-28 Havoc appears to incorporate the lessons learned from operations with the bulkier and more vulnerable Hind in Afghanistan. (*Department of Defence*)

carrying stub wings and undernose gun turret that have become the pattern for attack helicopters. The twin engines are almost certainly similar to those of the current Mi-17 and Mi-24. The slimness of the fuselage dictates side engine pods, and the DoD suggests upturned jet nozzles to minimise the infra-red signature.

Although the diameter of the main rotor appears to be much the same as that of the Mi-24, the rotor head is of new design, and the tail rotor is switched to the starboard side of the fin/pylon. The radar housed in an undernose pod on the Mi-24 appears to be transferred to a nose position on the Mi-28; but it might be dangerous to interpret the detail of the DoD drawing in such fine detail. It has been assumed generally that the stepped undernose glazing identifies an observer's station, providing an optimum forward/sideways/downward field of view. However, it seems more likely that the flat-plate sloping window at the front might enclose further sensors, such as low-light-level TV or a laser designator and marked target seeker.

Havoc is expected to be operational by 1987–88. Recognising its potential for popping up out of cover and using missiles to pick off armoured ground targets over long ranges, the US Army has already scrapped its Sgt York divisional air defence (DIVAD) radar guided gun, after spending around $1,800 million on this tracked weapon system.

Powerplant: Two unidentified turboshafts, probably related to the 1,640kW (2,200shp) Isotov TV3-117 engines of the Mi-24.
Accommodation: Co-pilot/gunner in front cockpit; pilot behind on elevated seat. Flat, non-glint transparencies.
Armament: Heavy-calibre gun in undernose turret. Pylon under each wing for external stores, including rocket pack. Wingtip pylons each capable of carrying two tube-launched missiles for air-to-air and air-to-ground use.
Dimensions: **Main rotor diameter** 17.00m (55ft 9in); **fuselage length** 17.40m (57ft 1in).
Performance: **Max level speed** 162 knots (300km/hr; 186mph); **combat radius** 130nm (240km; 149 miles).

Myasishchev M-4
NATO reporting name: **Bison**

The original version of the M-4, known to NATO as Bison-A, was the Soviet Union's first operational four-jet bomber, intended to carry only free-fall nuclear and conventional weapons and never adapted as a missile launcher. Design work began in 1951 and the prototype was first shown in a flypast over Moscow on May 1, 1954. Surprisingly, it proved to be a far less impressive bomber than Andrei Tupolev's turboprop Tu-95,

Myasishchev M-4 Bison-B, maritime reconnaissance version of the unsuccessful strategic bomber. (*Royal Air Force*)

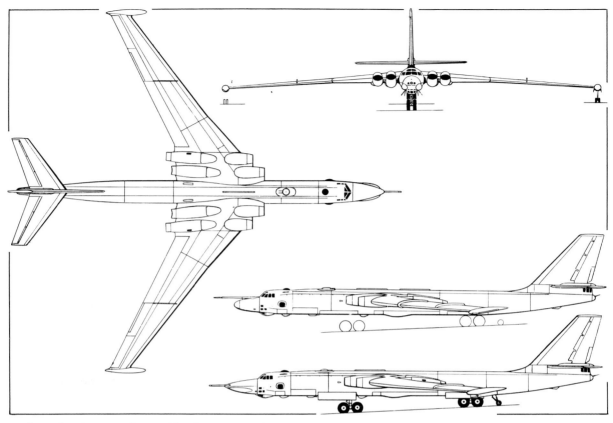

Myasishchev M-4 Bison-C. Upper side view shows Bison-B. (*Pilot Press*)

and production was limited by Soviet standards. Also, at a time when the RAF's jet-powered V-bombers were capable of penetrating enemy airspace without defensive armament, it was considered necessary to equip the M-4 with eight 23mm cannon in four turrets.

Bison-A was the Soviet counterpart to America's far superior B-52A Stratofortress. The later Bison-B and C were switched to maritime reconnaissance, with modified noses carrying a flight refuelling probe, and with reduced defensive armament. All had an unconventional landing gear, comprising two four-wheel main bogies in tandem, retracting into the fuselage, and small wingtip balancer wheels. About 75 Bisons remain available as bombers for maritime and Eurasian missions, and as probe-and-drogue flight refuelling tankers for the Backfire/Bear/Bison/Blinder attack force. Pending replacement, respectively, by Blackjacks and the Midas tanker version of the Il-76 transport, the M-4s are being phased out of service and placed in storage.

Data for M-4 (Bison-A)

Powerplant: Four Mikulin AM-3D turbojets, each rated at 85.3kN (19,180lb st).

Armament: Eight 23mm NR-23 guns in twin-gun turrets above fuselage forward of wing, under fuselage fore and aft of weapon bays, and in tail. Three weapon bays in centre-fuselage for free-fall weapons only.

Dimensions: **Wing span** 50.48m (165ft 7½in); **length** 47.20m (154ft 10in).

Weight: **Max T-O** 158,750kg (350,000lb).

Performance: **Max level speed** 538 knots (998 km/hr; 620mph) at 11,000m (36,000ft); **service ceiling** 13,700m (45,000ft); **combat radius** 3,025nm (5,600km; 3,480 miles); **range** 4,320nm (8,000km; 4,970 miles) at 450 knots (835km/hr; 520mph) with 5,450kg (12,000lb) of bombs.

Sukhoi Su-7

NATO reporting name: **Fitter-A**

The prototype of this large single-seat ground attack fighter flew for the first time more than 30 years ago, on September 8, 1955, but Su-7s remained in service with nine air forces in 1986 and have been used in action during the war against the Mujahideen in Afghanistan. Numbers in first-line deployment with Soviet tactical units have declined progressively with the introduction of newer types, but more than 125 were still operational in the mid-1980s, in the following versions:

Su-7BM Compared with the original Su-7B of the late 1950s, this model introduced a zero-altitude ejection seat, Sirena tail-warning radar, a second pair of underwing stores pylons, larger blast panels forward of wing roots, JATO attachments under rear fuselage, twin brake-chutes in a container at base of rudder, and an uprated engine.

Su-7BKL Introduced low-pressure nosewheel tyre, necessitating bulged doors to enclose it when retracted, and small extensible skid outboard of each mainwheel to assist operation from short, unprepared fields.

Su-7BMK As Su-7BKL, but with further equipment changes.

Above Sukhoi Su-7UM, two-seat operational training version of the Su-7BM Fitter-A.

Below Sukhoi Su-7BMK Fitter-A. (*Pilot Press*)

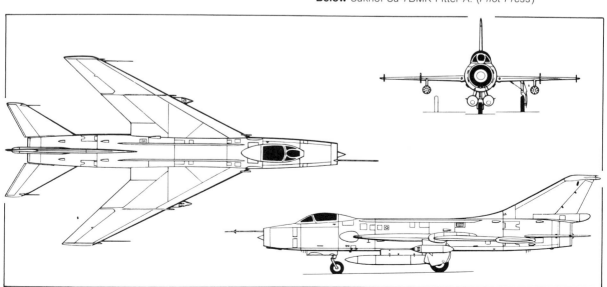

Tandem two-seat training versions of the BM and BMK are also in service, with the designations Su-7UM and Su-7UMK respectively. Their NATO reporting name is **Moujik**.

Data for Su-7BMK (Fitter-A)

Powerplant: One Lyulka AL-7F-1-100 turbojet, rated at 94.08kN (21,150lb st) with afterburning. Internal fuel capacity 2,940 litres (647 Imp gallons; 777 US gallons). Provision for two external tanks side by side under belly, combined capacity 1,200 litres (264 Imp gallons; 317 US gallons), and two ferry tanks on inboard wing pylons, combined capacity 1,800 litres (396 Imp gallons; 475 US gallons). Two assisted take-off rockets can be attached under rear fuselage to shorten take-off run.

Accommodation: Pilot only, on KS-4 zero-altitude rocket-powered ejection seat.

Armament: Two 30mm NR-30 guns in wing roots, each with 70 rounds; underwing pylons for two 750kg and two 500kg bombs, including nuclear weapons, or UV-16-57U rocket pods (each containing sixteen 57mm rockets), or S-24 250kg concrete piercing rockets. External weapons load is limited to 1,000kg (2,205lb) when underbelly fuel tanks are fitted.

Dimensions: **Wing span** 8.77m (28ft 9¼in); **length** 16.80m (55ft 1½in); **height** 4.80m (15ft 9in); **wing area** 23m² (247sq ft).

Weights: **Empty** 8,328kg (18,360lb); **normal T-O** 12,000kg (26,450lb); **max T-O** 13,440kg (29,630lb).

Performance: **Max level speed at S/L** 460 knots (850km/hr; 530mph) without afterburning, 625 knots (1,158km/hr; 720mph) with afterburning; **max level speed at 12,200m (40,000ft)** Mach 1.6 (917 knots; 1,700km/hr; 1,055mph) clean, Mach 1.2 (685 knots; 1,270km/hr; 788mph) with external stores; **T-O and landing approach speed** 195 knots (360km/hr; 224mph); **max rate of climb at S/L** 9,000m (29,525ft)/min; **service ceiling** 18,000m (59,050ft); **T-O run** 2,400m (7,875ft); **combat radius** 135–187nm (250–345km; 155–215 miles); **max range** 780nm (1,450km; 900 miles).

Sukhoi Su-15
(see Sukhoi Su-21)

Sukhoi Su-17, Su-20 and Su-22
NATO reporting names: **Fitter-C to K**

The original 1966 prototype of this family of aircraft, known to NATO as Fitter-B, was simply an Su-7 with about 4.2m (13ft 9in) of each wing pivoted outboard of a very large fence. By the time the Sukhoi Bureau had introduced also a more powerful engine and improved avionics, the variable-geometry Fitter was in a completely different class from Fitter-A. A doubled external load could be lifted from strips little more than half as long as those needed by the fixed-wing aircraft; it could then be carried about 30% farther and delivered with greater accuracy. As a result, the fighter was put into series production, and about 800 of the 2,350 ground attack aircraft now in service with Soviet tactical air forces are Su-17s. Soviet Naval Aviation has about 65 assigned to the Baltic Fleet for anti-shipping strike and amphibious support roles and has formed a further Su-17 unit in the Pacific. Variants in Soviet service are as follows:

Su-17 approaches with wings swept fully forward.

Su-17 (Fitter-C)   Basic single-seat attack aircraft for Soviet Air Forces, with Lyulka AL-21F-3 turbojet. Manual wing sweep control. Fuselage diameter constant between wing and tailplane. Curved dorsal fin between tail fin and dorsal spine fairing. Equipment said to include SRD-5M (NATO High Fix) I-band centrebody ranging radar, ASP-5ND fire control system, Sirena 3 omnidirectional radar homing and warning system, and SRO-2M IFF. Operational since 1971 in relatively small numbers. Serves also with Soviet Navy.

Su-17M (Fitter-D)   Generally similar to Fitter-C, but forward fuselage lengthened by about 0.25m (10in). Added undernose electronics pod for Doppler navigation radar. Laser rangefinder in intake centrebody.

Su-17UM (Fitter-E)   Tandem two-seat trainer for Soviet Air Force. Generally similar to Fitter-D, without electronics pod, but entire fuselage forward of wing drooped slightly to improve view from rear seat. Deepened dorsal spine fairing, almost certainly providing additional fuel tankage. Port wing root gun deleted.

Su-17 (Fitter-G)   Two-seat trainer variant of Fitter-H, with combat capability. Deepened dorsal spine fairing and drooped front fuselage like Fitter-E. Taller vertical tail surfaces.

Shallow ventral fin (removable). Starboard gun only. Laser target seeker fitted.

Su-17 (Fitter-H)   Improved single-seater for Soviet Air Forces. Basically as Fitter-C, but with wide and deep dorsal fairing aft of canopy, like Fitter E/G. Doppler navigation radar fitted internally in deepened undersurface of nose. Taller fin like Fitter-G. Removable ventral fin. Retains both wing root guns. About 200 Fitter-H/K equipped for tactical reconnaissance duties.

Su-17 (Fitter-K)   Latest single-seat version for Soviet Air Forces, identified in 1984. Dorsal fin embodies small cooling air intake at front.

It was deduced for some years that certain export versions of the variable-geometry Fitter series had different engines from the Su-17 variants listed above. Fitter-C/D/E/G/H/K operated by the Soviet Air Force and some other air forces have a rear fuselage of basically constant diameter and are powered by a Lyulka turbojet. Versions exported to Angola, Libya, Peru, Syria, Vietnam and North and South Yemen were seen to have a more bulged rear fuselage, now known to house a Tumansky R-29B turbojet, as fitted in the MiG-27, with re-arranged external air ducts and a shorter plain metal shroud terminating the rear fuselage. This change of power plant, and/or variations in equipment standard, is covered by the following changes to the Soviet type designation:

Su-20 (Su-17MK, Fitter-C)   Generally similar to Soviet Air Force Fitter-C, with Lyulka engine, but with reduced equipment standard. Supplied to Algeria, Czechoslovakia, Egypt, Iraq, Poland and Vietnam.

Su-22 (Fitter-F)   Export counterpart of Fitter-D, with modified undernose electronics pod. Tumansky R-29B turbojet, rated at 112.8kN (25,350lb st) with afterburning, in increased-diameter rear fuselage. Gun in each wing root. Weapons include Atoll air-to-air missiles. Aircraft supplied to Peru had Sirena 2 limited-coverage radar warning receiver, virtually no navigation aids, and IFF incompatible with that nation's SA-3 (NATO Goa) surface-to-air missiles.

Su-22 (Fitter-G)   Export counterpart of Su-17 Fitter-G, with R-29B engine.

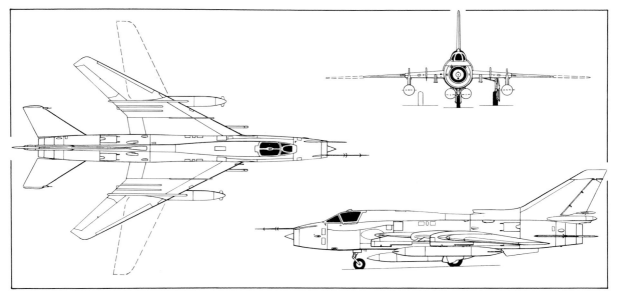

Su-22 (Fitter-J) Generally similar to Fitter-H, but with Tumansky engine. Internal fuel capacity 6,270 litres (1,379 Imp gallons; 1,656 US gallons). More angular dorsal fin. Atoll air-to-air missiles. Supplied to Libya.

There is also a two seat counterpart of Fitter-J that has no separate NATO reporting name.

Data for Su-17 (Fitter-C)

Powerplant: One Lyulka AL-21F-3 turbojet, rated at 110kN (24,700lb st) with afterburning. Internal fuel capacity 4,550 litres (1,000 Imp gallons; 1,200 US gallons). Up to four 800 litre (176 Imp gallon; 211 US gallon) drop tanks under fuselage and wings.

Accommodation: Pilot only, on ejection seat.

Armament: Two 30mm NR-30 guns in wing roots, eight pylons under fuselage and wings for more than 3,175kg (7,000lb) of bombs, including nuclear weapons, rocket pods and guided missiles such as the air-to-surface Kerry.

Dimensions: **Wing span** 13.80m (45ft 3in) spread, 10.00m (32ft 10in) fully swept;

Sukhoi Su-17 Fitter-K. (*Pilot Press*)

length 18.75m (61ft 6¼in); **height** 5.00m (16ft 5in); **wing area** 40m² (430sq ft) spread, 37m² (398sq ft) swept.

Weights: **Empty** 10,000kg (22,046lb); **T-O clean** 14,000kg (30,865lb); **max T-O** 17,700kg (39,020lb).

Performance (clean, with 60% internal fuel, except where stated): **Max level speed** Mach 1.05 (693 knots; 1,285km/hr; 798mph) at S/L, Mach 2.09 (1,200 knots; 2,220km/hr; 1,380mph) at height; **landing speed** 143 knots (265km/hr; 165mph); **max rate of climb at S/L** 13,800m (45,275ft)/min; **service ceiling** 18,000m (59,050ft); **T-O run at AUW of 17,000kg (37,478lb)** 1,000m (3,280ft); **landing run** 600m (1,970ft); **combat radius with 2,000kg (4,409lb) of external stores, including fuel: hi-lo-hi** 370nm (685km; 425 miles), **lo-lo-lo** 240nm (445km; 275 miles).

Sukhoi Su-21

NATO reporting name: **Flagon**

With deployment of the MiG-29 and MiG-31 gathering pace, the number of Flagons in first-line home defence units is believed to have diminished rapidly to fewer than 200 by early 1986. Those remaining are of two operational single-seat variants, which are so different from earlier, lower powered, Su-15 Flagon-As and Ds that their designation was reportedly changed to Su-21:

Flagon-E Longer-span wings than those of original Flagon-A, with compound sweep. Tumansky R-13F-300 turbojets, each rated at 64.73kN (14,550lb st), increasing speed and range. Uprated avionics. Major production version, operational since second half of 1973.

Flagon-F Last known production version, identified by ogival nose radome instead of conical type on earlier variants. Generally similar to Flagon-E, but with uprated engines.

Above Sukhoi Su-21 Flagon-F armed with Anab (outboard pylon) and Aphid (inboard) air-to-air missiles. (*Swedish Air Force*)

Below Sukhoi Su-21 Flagon-F. (*Pilot Press*)

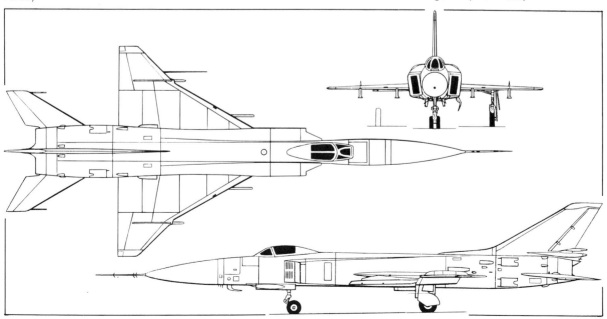

In addition, a tandem two-seat trainer version is in service, known to NATO as Flagon-C. This exists in two forms, corresponding to the single-seat Flagon-D and F.

Data for Su-21 (Flagon-F)

Powerplant: Two Tumansky R-13F2-300 turbojets, each rated at 70.6kN (15,875lb st) with afterburning.

Accommodation: Pilot only, on ejection seat.

Armament: Two pylons for external stores under each wing. One radar homing and one infra-red homing air-to-air missile (NATO Anab) on outboard underwing pylons; infra-red homing close-range missile (NATO Aphid) on each inboard pylon. GSh-23L 23mm gun pods or fuel tanks on two underbelly pylons.

Dimensions: **Wing span** 10.53m (34ft 6in); **length** 20.5m (68ft 0in).

Weight: **Max T-O** 16,000kg (35,275lb).

Performance: **Max level speed** Mach 2.1 (1,204 knots; 2,230km/hr; 1,386mph) above 11,000m (36,000ft); **service ceiling** 20,000m (65,600ft); **combat radius** 390nm (725km; 450 miles).

Sukhoi Su-24

NATO reporting name: **Fencer**

Best interdictor in the Soviet inventory, the Su-24 was the first modern Soviet fighter designed specifically for ground attack and the first to carry a weapon systems officer, in a side by side two-seat cockpit. Smaller and lighter than the USAF's F-111, its variable-geometry wings have a fully spread sweep of about 16°, fully swept angle of 68°, and intermediate sweep of 45°. The outer panels carry the first pivoting pylons that were seen on a Soviet variable-geometry aircraft. The primary pulse-Doppler radar dish appears to have a diameter of at least 1.25m (49in); other equipment is thought to include terrain avoidance radar and a laser rangefinder and marked target seeker. RAF assessment suggests that the Su-24 has five times the weapon load and five times the range of its immediate predecessor, enabling it to reach any target in England from East German advanced bases. A USAF senior officer has said that it can deliver ordnance within 55m (180ft) of its target in all weathers.

Known to NATO as Fencer, the Su-24 entered squadron service in December 1974 as a replacement for the Yak-28 Brewer. More than 700 are now serving with first-line squadrons, including 450 assigned to strategic missions. Two full

Sukhoi Su-24 Fencer-D.

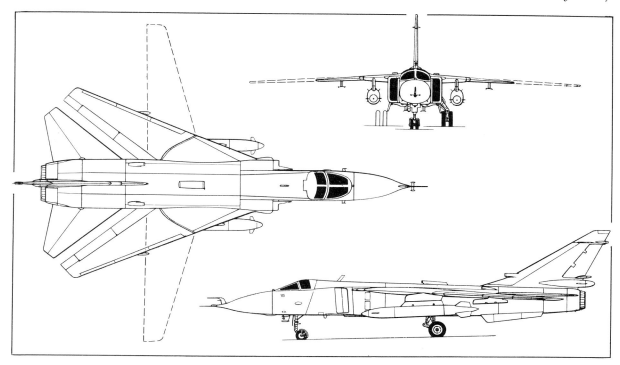

Sukhoi Su-24 Fencer-C. (*Pilot Press*)

regiments have been reported at Tukums in Latvia, near the Gulf of Riga and at Chernyakhovsk, near Kaliningrad on the Soviet Baltic coast. Two more are said to be stationed at Starokonstantinov and Gorodok in the Ukraine, and one in the Soviet Far East. First brief deployment beyond the Soviet borders was made to Templin Air Base, north of Berlin in East Germany, in July 1979. Su-24s have been standard equipment of the 16th Air Army in that country since 1982.

Four variants have been identified by NATO reporting names:

Fencer-A Identifiable by rectangular rear fuselage box enclosing jet nozzles.

Fencer-B Rear fuselage box around jet nozzles has deeply dished bottom skin between nozzles.

Fencer-C Introduced in 1981. Important equipment changes. Multiple fitting on nose instead of former simple probe. Triangular fairing forward of each fixed wing root, on side of air intake, presumably housing equipment of the kind seen on the fuselage sides, forward of the nosewheel doors, of ground attack MiG-23/27 Floggers.

Fencer-D First mentioned in 1986, when it was being deployed principally with strategic aviation regiments. DoD states that it was introduced into service in 1983. Strategic role suggests added flight-refuelling capability. Known features include slightly longer nose (approx 0.75m; 2ft 6in) forward of windscreen; large overwing fences integral with extended wing-root glove pylons, probably for AS-14 air-to-surface missiles; deletion of undernose aerials; addition of blister, probably for electro-optical sensor, aft of nosewheel bay; single long nose probe; and forward extension of fin leading-edge.

It is likely that an electronic warfare version of Fencer will replace the Yak-28 Brewer-E in due course. A reconnaissance variant is already in service.

Data for Su-24 (Fencer-C)

Powerplant: Two afterburning turbojets, believed to be related to Lyulka AL-21F fitted in Su-17. Internal fuel capacity estimated at 13,000 litres (2,860 Imp gallons; 3,435 US gallons). Provision for large drop tank on each glove pylon.

Accommodation: Crew of two, side-by-side on ejection seats.

Armament: No internal weapons bay. One gun on port side of belly. Eight pylons under fuselage, wing root gloves and outer wings for 11,000kg (24,250lb) of guided and unguided air-to-surface weapons, including nuclear weapons.

Dimensions: **Wing span** 17.25m (56ft 7in) spread, 10.00m (32ft 9½in) fully swept; **length** 21.29m (69ft 10in); **height** 5.50m (18ft 0in).

Weights: **Empty** 19,000kg (41,885lb); **max T-O** 39,500kg (87,080lb).

Performance: **Max level speed** Mach 1.2 (792 knots; 1,465km/hr; 912mph) at S/L, Mach 2.18 (1,250 knots; 2,315km/hr; 1,439mph) at height; **service ceiling** 16,500m (54,135ft); **combat radius: lo-lo-lo** over 174nm (322km; 200 miles), **lo-lo-hi** 515nm (950km; 590 miles) with 2,500kg (5,500lb) of weapons, **hi-lo-hi** 970nm (1,800km; 1,115 miles) with 2,000kg (4,400lb) of weapons.

Sukhoi Su-25

NATO reporting name: **Frogfoot**

The Su-25 single-seat ground attack aircraft is the Soviet counterpart to the US Air Force's A-10 Thunderbolt II. More significantly, it is a type of front-line combat aircraft that the Soviet Union pioneered with the Ilyushin Il-2 *Shturmovik* of the Second World War. The pilot is again protected by flat slabs of armour around his cockpit, and the Su-25 has big broad wings like the Il-2

This time they are fitted with ten weapon pylons for an estimated 4,500kg (9,920lb) of external stores, including chemical weapons. The flat fairings at the wingtips split at the rear to form airbrakes similar to those of the US Navy's A-6 Intruder.

Since 1982, in Afghanistan, the Soviet tactical air forces have been developing techniques for

Sukhoi Su-25 Frogfoot in Czechoslovak Air Force markings.

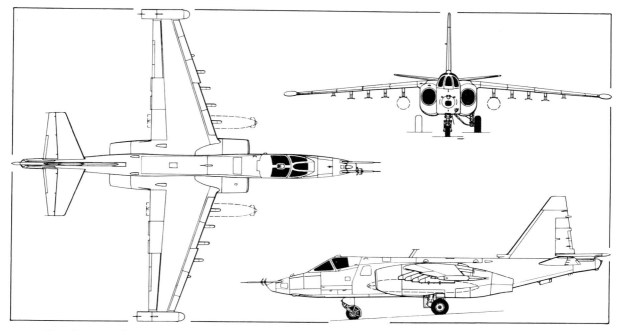

co-ordinating low-level close support by Su-25s operating in partnership with Mi-24 Hind helicopter gunships, notably against Mujahideen units in mountainous regions. On the basis of this experience, production appears to have been accelerated. After what seemed a slow start, Su-25s are now leaving the Tbilisi airframe factory in numbers adequate to re-equip not only Soviet tactical regiments but the air forces of Iraq and Warsaw Pact states, beginning with Czechoslovakia and Hungary.

The first good photographs of the Su-25, published in Czechoslovak journals, have revealed a variety of operational equipment including a large-calibre gun, SRO-2 (Odd Rods) IFF, a Sirena 3 radar warning system, a nose-mounted laser rangefinder and marked target seeker, and a flare dispenser in the tailcone. The aircraft's engines have also been confirmed as non-afterburning versions of the Tumansky turbojets that power late-model MiG-21s.

Sukhoi Su-25 Frogfoot. (*Pilot Press*)

Powerplant: Two non-afterburning Tumansky R-13-300 turbojets, each rated at 50kN (11,240lb st).

Accommodation: Pilot only.

Armament: One 30mm twin-barrel gun in port side of nose. Ten underwing pylons for external stores, including 57mm and 80mm rockets and 500kg incendiary, anti-personnel and chemical cluster bombs.

Dimensions: **Wing span** 15.50m (50ft 10in); **length** 14.50m (47ft 6in); **wing area** 37.60m² (404.7sq ft).

Weights: **Empty** 9,500kg (20,950lb); **max T-O** 18,120–19,200kg (39,950–42,330lb).

Performance: **Max level speed** 475 knots (880km/hr; 546mph); **combat radius** 300nm (556km; 345 miles).

Sukhoi Su-27

NATO reporting name: **Flanker**

Sukhoi's equivalent to the US Air Force's F-15 Eagle, the Su-27 Flanker is a supersonic all-weather counter-air fighter with lookdown/shootdown weapon systems and beyond-visual-range air-to-air missiles, and with a secondary ground attack role. The aircraft's range, thrust-to-weight ratio and manoeuvrability are all said to be improved by comparison with earlier Soviet fighters. Its large pulse-Doppler radar and heavy armament should also give it formidable potential against low flying aircraft and cruise missiles, particularly when it is deployed in partnership with the new Soviet AEW&C aircraft based on the Il-76 transport and known to NATO as Mainstay.

The only photographs of the Su-27 yet published are thought to show a prototype or pre-series model with curved wingtips. Production Su-27s have square tips, carrying launchers for air-to-air missiles; the twin tail fins are also moved outboard of the engine housings. Production is centred at a plant in Komsomolsk, Khabarovsk territory. The fighter was expected to achieve operational capability during 1986 and, with the MiG-31, to replace many of the MiG-21, MiG-23/27, Su-21 and MiG-25 aircraft in the 17 tactical air forces assigned to Soviet military districts and groups of forces.

Flanker has also been observed with various other types at Saki naval air base on the Black Sea. There, the Soviet Navy has a 297m (975ft) dummy flight deck, complete with arrester gear and barriers, as well as two ski-jump ramps, as part of the development programme for the 65,000 ton nuclear-powered aircraft carrier built at Nikolayev. This may suggest the eventual manufacture of a navalised version of the Su-27 to equip the ship's carrier air group.

Powerplant: Two unidentified turbofans, possibly related to the Tumansky R-31, each estimated to have a rating of 133.5kN (30,000lb st) with afterburning.

Accommodation: Pilot only, on ejection seat.

Armament: Six radar homing AA-10 air-to-air missiles, or a mix of AA-10s and close-range AA-11s, under fuselage and wings and on wingtip launchers. Able to carry up to 6,000kg (13,225lb) of external stores, including twelve 500kg bombs, for secondary attack role.

Dimensions: **Wing span** 14.50m (47ft 7in); **length** 21.00m (69ft 0in); **height** 5.50m (18ft 0in).

Weight: **Max T-O** 20,000 to 27,200kg (44,000 to 60,000lb).

Performance: **Max level speed** Mach 1.1 (725 knots; 1,345km/hr; 835mph) at S/L, Mach 2.0 (1,150 knots; 2,120km/hr; 1,320mph) above 11,000m (36,000ft); **combat radius** 810nm (1,500km; 930 miles).

Prototype or pre-series Su-27 Flanker, which differs from the service model in having curved wingtips, fins located above the engines, and no tailcone extension.

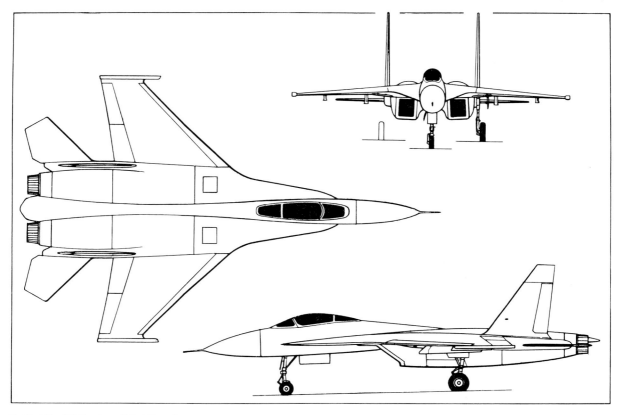

Sukhoi Su-27 Flanker. (*Pilot Press*)

Tupolev Tu-16
NATO reporting name: **Badger**

Anyone who questions the quality of Soviet combat aircraft need only consider the two Tupolev turbine-powered strategic bombers which made their public debut in Aviation Day flypasts over Moscow in the mid-1950s. The smaller of the pair, the Tu-16, is still in first-line service with both the medium-range bomber force and Soviet Naval Aviation, in a variety of forms, and continues in production in China. The larger Tu-95/142 is still in major production in the USSR after thirty years.

First flown in 1952, the Tu-16 entered production in the following year. About 2,000 were delivered, of which 260 are estimated to remain operational in the five Soviet strategic air armies,

supported by a few Tu-16 aerial refuelling tankers, more than 90 of various versions equipped for ECM duties, and 15 for reconnaissance. Soviet Naval Aviation is thought to have about 200 Tu-16 attack models, plus 75 tankers and up to 80 reconnaissance and ECM variants. The attack aircraft carry anti-ship cruise missiles with stand-off ranges varying from 90 to more than 300km (56 to 186 miles) and are often supplemented by air army Tu-16s in naval exercises. A squadron deployed to a permanent base at Cam Ranh Bay, Vietnam, comprises ten aircraft equipped for attack and six for reconnaissance missions, with a potential combat radius encompassing Thailand, the Philippines, Guam, most of Indonesia and southern China. Known versions of the Tu-16 are as follows:

Tupolev Tu-16 Badger-D maritime reconnaissance aircraft. (*Royal Navy*)

Badger-A Basic strategic jet bomber, able to carry nuclear or conventional free-fall weapons. Glazed nose, with small under-nose radome. Armed with seven 23mm guns. Some equipped as aerial refuelling tankers, using a unique wingtip-to-wingtip transfer technique to refuel other Badgers or a probe-and-drogue system to refuel Blinders. About 120 operational also with Chinese Air Force (still being built in China as Xian H-6).

Badger-B Generally similar to Badger-A, but equipped originally to carry two turbojet-powered aeroplane-type anti-shipping missiles (NATO Kennel) underwing. Still serves as conventional free-fall bomber.

Badger-C Anti-shipping version, first shown in 1961 Aviation Day flypast. Kipper winged missile carried in recess under fuselage, or Kingfish missiles underwing. Wide nose radome, in place of glazing and nose gun of Badger-A. No provision for free-fall bombs. Operational with Soviet Northern, Baltic, Black Sea and Pacific fleets.

Badger-D Maritime/electronic reconnaissance version, able to provide midcourse electronic guidance for missiles launched by other Badgers. Nose like that of Badger-C. Larger undernose radome. Three blister fairings in tandem under centre-fuselage.

Badger-E Similar to Badger-A, but with cameras in bomb-bay.

Badger-F Basically similar to Badger-E, but with electronic intelligence pod on pylon under each wing.

Badger-G Similar to Badger-A, but fitted with underwing pylons for two rocket-powered air-to-surface missiles (NATO Kelt) that can be carried to a range greater than 1,735nm (3,220km; 2,000 miles). Free-fall bombing capability retained. Majority serve with anti-shipping squadrons of the Soviet Naval Air Force. A few were passed on to Iraq.

Badger-G modified Specially equipped carrier for Kingfish air-to-surface missiles. Large radome, presumably associated with missile operation, under centre-fuselage. Total of about 85 standard and modified Badger-Gs believed operational with Soviet Northern, Black Sea and Pacific fleets.

Badger-H Stand-off or escort ECM aircraft to protect missile-carrying strike force, with primary function of chaff dispensing. The chaff dispensers (max capacity 9,075kg; 20,000lb) are probably located in the weapons-bay area. Hatch aft of weapons-bay. Two teardrop radomes, fore and aft of weapons-bay. Two blade antennae aft of weapons-bay.

Badger-J Specialised ECM jamming aircraft to protect strike force, with at least some of the equipment located in a canoe-shape radome protruding from inside the weapons-bay. Anti-radar noise jammers operate in A to I bands inclusive. Glazed nose like Badger-A.

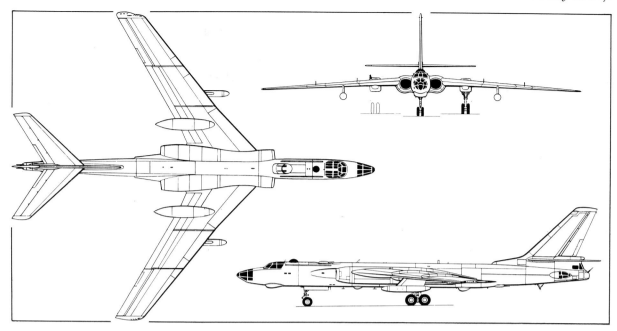

Tupolev Tu-16 Badger-F. *(Pilot Press)*

Badger-K Electronic reconnaissance variant with nose like Badger-A. Two teardrop radomes, inside and forward of weapons-bay.

Data for Tu-16 (Badger-A)

Powerplant: Two Mikulin AM-3M turbojets, each rated at 93.19kN (20,950lb st). Internal fuel capacity 45,450 litres (10,000 Imp gallons; 12,000 US gallons). Provision for underwing auxiliary fuel tanks and for flight refuelling. Tu-16 tankers trail hose from starboard wing-tip; receiving equipment is in port wingtip extension.

Accommodation: Crew of six.

Armament: Seven 23mm NR-23 guns in twin-gun turrets above front fuselage, under rear fuselage, and in tail, with single gun on starboard side of nose. Up to 9,000kg (19,800lb) of bombs in internal weapons-bay.

Dimensions: **Wing span** 32.93m (108ft 0½in); **length** 34.80m (114ft 2in); **height** 10.80m (35ft 6in); **wing area** 164.65m² (1,772.3sq ft).

Weights: **Empty** 37,200kg (82,000lb); **normal T-O** 72,000kg (158,730lb).

Performance: **Max level speed** 535 knots (992km/hr; 616mph) at 6,000m (19,700ft); **service ceiling** 12,300m (40,350ft); **range** 2,605nm (4,800km; 3,000 miles) with 3,790kg (8,360lb) of bombs; **max unrefuelled combat radius** 1,565nm (2,900km; 1,800 miles).

Tupolev Tu-95 and Tu-142

NATO reporting name: **Bear**

Seven examples of Andrei Tupolev's huge Tu-95 four-turboprop bomber took part in the 1955 Aviation Day flypast, less than a year after the first flight of the prototype. Western analysts failed to recognise the potential of the aircraft that NATO named Bear, feeling that it could never match the estimated capabilities of the four-jet M-4 Bison that had been seen over Moscow in 1954. In fact, the Tu-95 could achieve

Maritime reconnaissance Bear with US Navy Phantom in close attendance. (*US Navy*)

speeds 100mph (87 knots; 160km/hr) faster than anyone had expected a propeller-driven aircraft to fly, and offered such an astonishing range that the Soviet air forces had no hesitation in preferring it to the M-4. Production has now been continuous for more than thirty years, for a variety of duties. Fifteen years after the last of the original bomber variants left the assembly line, an entirely new version (Bear-H) entered series production, at Kuybyshev, as the first vehicle for the Soviet Union's new-generation AS-15 long-range air-launched cruise missiles with nuclear warheads and range of 1,620nm (3,000km; 1,865 miles). The complete list of variants to which reference may be made is as follows:

Bear-A Tu-95 long-range strategic bomber. Chin radome. Internal stowage for two nuclear or a variety of conventional free-fall weapons. Defensive armament of six 23mm guns in pairs in remotely-controlled rear dorsal and ventral turrets, and manned tail turret.

Bear-B As Bear-A, but able to carry large air-to-surface winged missile (NATO Kangaroo) under fuselage, with associated radar in wide undernose radome replacing glazed nose. Defensive armament retained. A few Bs operate in maritime reconnaissance role, with flight refuelling nose probe, and, sometimes, a streamlined blister fairing on the starboard side of the rear fuselage.

Bear-C Third strike version, with ability to carry Kangaroo, first observed near NATO ships in 1964. Differs from Bear-B in having a streamlined blister fairing on each side of its rear fuselage. Has been seen with a faired tail as mentioned under Bear-D entry. Refuelling probe standard.

Bear-D Identified in 1967, this maritime reconnaissance version is equipped with I-band surface search radar in a large blister fairing under the centre-fuselage. Glazed nose like Bear-A, with undernose radome and superimposed refuelling probe. Rear fuselage blisters as on Bear-C. Added fairing at each tailplane tip. I-band tail-warning radar in enlarged fairing at base of rudder. Carries no offensive weapons, but tasks include pinpointing of maritime targets for missile launch crews on board ships and aircraft that

are themselves too distant to ensure precise missile aiming and guidance.

A Bear-D photographed in 1978 had in place of the normal tail turret and associated radome a faired tail housing special equipment.

Bear-E Reconnaissance bomber. Generally as Bear-A, but with rear fuselage blister fairings and refuelling probe as on Bear-C. Six or seven camera windows in bomb-bay doors. Few only.

Bear-F First deployed by Soviet Naval Aviation in 1970 and since upgraded, this is a much refined anti-submarine version known in the Soviet Union as Tu-142. Originally, it had enlarged and lengthened fairings aft of its inboard engine nacelles for purely aerodynamic reasons, but current aircraft have reverted to standard size fairings. The undernose radar of Bear-D is missing on some aircraft; others have a radome in this

Tupolev Tu-142 Bear-F. (*Pilot Press*)

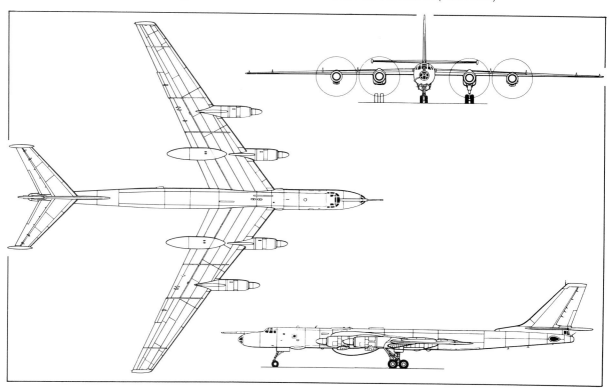

position, but of considerably modified form. On both models the main underfuselage I-band radar housing is considerably farther forward than on Bear-D and smaller in size; the forward portion of the fuselage is longer; the flight deck windscreens are deeper, giving increased headroom; there are no large blister fairings under and on the sides of the rear fuselage; and the nosewheel doors are bulged prominently, suggesting the use of larger or low-pressure tyres. Bear-F has two stores bays for sonobuoys, torpedoes and nuclear depth charges in its rear fuselage, one of them replacing the usual rear ventral gun turret and leaving the tail turret as the sole defensive gun position. Some aircraft have an MAD "sting" projecting from the rear of the fin tip. Production resumed in the mid-1980s.

Bear-G Generally similar to Bear-B/C, but reconfigured to carry two highly supersonic AS-4 (Kitchen) air-to-surface missiles instead of one AS-3 (Kangaroo), on a large pylon under each wing root. Other new features include a small thimble radome under the in-flight refuelling probe and a solid tailcone similar in shape to that on some Bear-Ds.

Bear-H This new production version, based on the upgraded airframe of Bear-F, is equipped with pylons under the inboard wing panels to carry long-range cruise missiles, including the AS-15. It achieved initial operational capability in 1984, and 40 were in service by Spring 1986. Features include a larger and deeper radome built into the nose and a small fin-tip fairing. There are no blister fairings on the sides of the rear fuselage and the ventral gun turret is deleted.

Most of the 150 Bears now serving with the five Soviet strategic air armies are of the new G and H models. Soviet Naval Aviation units have about 45 Bear-Ds and 55 Bear-Fs. Their duties include regular deployments to staging bases in Cuba and Angola, and eight are stationed permanently at Cam Ranh in Vietnam. Three Bear-Fs have been transferred to the Indian Navy.

Data for Tu-142 (Bear-F)

Powerplant: Four 11,033kW (14,795shp) Kuznetsov NK-12MV turboprops. Internal fuel capacity 72,980 litres (16,540 Imp gallons; 19,280 US gallons). Equipped for flight refuelling.

Armament: Described under individual model listings.

Dimensions: **Wing span** 51.10m (167ft 8in); **length** 49.50m (162ft 5in); **height** 12.12m (39ft 9in).

Weight: **Max T-O** 188,000kg (414,470lb).

Performance: **Max level speed** 500 knots (925km/hr; 575mph) at 12,500m (41,000ft); **max unrefuelled combat radius** 4,475nm (8,285km; 5,150 miles).

Tupolev Tu-22

NATO reporting name: **Blinder**

As the first Soviet bomber able to fly at supersonic speed for short periods of time, the Tu-22 caused a sensation when it appeared briefly in the 1961 Aviation Day flypast over Moscow. While some people in the West credited it with capability it never possessed, the Soviet leadership recognised the facts and limited production to – by their standards – the small total of about 250 aircraft. While building them, they authorised the Tupolev design bureau to begin thinking again; the result was the highly superior Tu-22M or Tu-26 Backfire, which is described separately.

The Tu-22 itself was not a total debit. The USSR had been quick to realise that replacement of free-fall bombs by long-range air-launched missiles would preserve aircraft like the Tu-16 and Tu-95 from the need to penetrate the close defences of their targets. Equally, such missiles could extend the attack radius of the Tu-22, which had proved particularly disappointing in terms of range. So, by the time 22 of the supersonic bombers flew over Moscow on Aviation Day 1967, most of them were fitted with flight refuelling probes and carried a Kitchen supersonic nuclear missile recessed into their

weapons-bay. This missile was to prove so good that it is now in large-scale service, in several forms, on one of the latest versions of the Tu-95 as well as the Tu-22 and Tu-26.

More than half of the production Tu-22s are believed to remain operational with medium-range bomber units of the Soviet air armies. Of the rest, the Soviet Navy has about 35 bombers and 20 equipped for maritime reconnaissance and ECM duties, based mainly in the southern Ukraine and Estonia to protect the sea approaches to the USSR. Their NATO reporting names are as follows:

Blinder-A Original reconnaissance bomber version, first seen in 1961, with fuselage weapons-bay for free-fall nuclear or conventional bombs. Limited production only.

Blinder-B Similar to Blinder-A, but equipped to carry air-to-surface missile (NATO Kitchen) recessed in weapons-bay. Larger radar and partially-retractable flight refuelling probe on nose. About 135 Blinder-As and Bs remain in service with Soviet air armies, including 15 equipped for reconnaissance,

Tupolev Tu-22 Blinder-B. The outline of the Kitchen air-to-surface missile which is the type's main armament can be seen on the weapon-bay doors. (*Tass*)

and others with Soviet Naval Aviation. The Libyan and Iraqi Air Forces each have about seven.

Blinder-C Maritime reconnaissance version, with six camera windows in weapons-bay doors. New dielectric panels, modifications to nosecone, etc, on some aircraft suggest added equipment for ECM and electronic intelligence roles.

Blinder-D Training version. Cockpit for instructor in raised position aft of standard flight deck, with stepped-up canopy. Used by Soviet and Libyan Air Forces.

Powerplant: Two Koliesov VD-7 turbojets, each rated at 137.5kN (30,900lb st) with afterburning.

Accommodation: Crew of three, in tandem, on ejection seats.

243

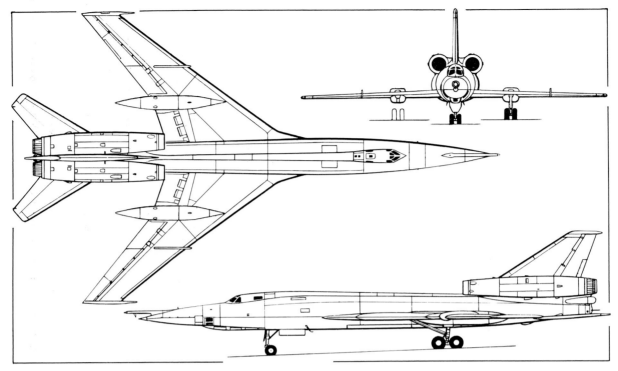

Armament: Single 23mm NR-23 gun in radar directed tail turret. Other weapons as described for individual versions.

Dimensions: **Wing span** 23.75m (78ft 0in); **length** 40.53m (132ft 11½in); **height** 10.67m (35ft 0in).

Weight: **Max T-O** 83,900kg (185,000lb).

Performance: **Max level speed** Mach 1.4

Tupolev Tu-22 Blinder-A. (*Pilot Press*)

(800 knots; 1,480km/hr; 920mph) at 12,200m (40,000ft); **service ceiling** 18,300m (60,000ft); **max unrefuelled combat radius** 1,565nm (2,900km; 1,800 miles).

Tupolev Tu-26
NATO reporting name: **Backfire**

Soviet delegates to the SALT II strategic arms limitation treaty talks referred to this strategic bomber as the Tu-22M. Addition of the suffix M to a Soviet designation sometimes implies that the aircraft is a modification of an earlier type (eg MiG-25M is an uprated MiG-25). This led to suggestions that the original version, known to NATO as Backfire-A, embodied Tu-22 Blinder major components. In fact, apart from having

large landing gear fairing pods on the wing trailing-edges, there was little confirmed similarity between Blinder and Backfire-A, which was first observed on the ground at Kazan manufacturing plant, in Central Asia, in July 1970 and subsequently equipped a single development squadron.

It soon became clear that the hoped-for major improvement in performance compared with Blinder had not been achieved. Tupolev undertook an extensive redesign, increasing the wing span and eliminating the drag-producing land-

Backfire-B photographed over the Baltic. (*Swedish Air Force*)

Backfire-B Basic production model, as illustrated. Air intake trunks of rectangular section, with splitter plates, inclined slightly forward.

ing gear pods except for shallow underwing fairings. The main wheels were made to retract inward into the bottom of the engine air intake trunks. The much improved bomber was then put into series production, reportedly as the Tu-26. It is known to exist in two versions:

Tupolev Tu-26 Backfire-B. (*Pilot Press*)

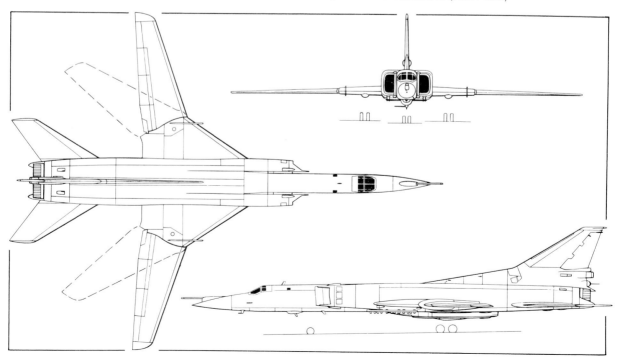

Backfire-C Generally as Backfire-B, but with wedge type engine air intakes, like those of MiG-25.

About 300 Backfires were in service by 1986. Two-thirds of them oppose NATO in Europe and over the Atlantic, with the others in the far east of the Soviet Union. The latter are observed frequently over the Sea of Japan, and 30 of them are believed to be drawn from the 125 Backfire-Bs and Cs deployed in a maritime role by Soviet Naval Aviation.

The 1985 edition of the US Department of Defence's *Soviet Military Power* document refers to Backfire as "a long-range aircraft capable of performing nuclear strike, conventional attack, anti-ship and reconnaissance missions", adding later that "Although Soviet spokesmen have stated (that Backfire) does not have an intercontinental role, the aircraft has the capability to strike the US on one-way intercontinental missions with forward recovery (in non-hostile territory such as Cuba). Using Arctic staging bases and in-flight refuelling, the Backfire could achieve similar target coverage on two-way missions. If staged, but not refuelled in flight, it could conduct strike missions against some targets in the US."

Production is expected to continue at the current rate of 30 a year into the 1990s, with progressive design changes to enhance performance. Backfires have been used for development launches of new-generation cruise missiles, but are not considered likely to become designated AS-15 carriers.

Data for Tu-26 (Backfire-B)

Powerplant: Two unidentified engines, reported to be uprated versions of the Kuznetsov NK-144 afterburning turbofans developed for the now-abandoned Tu-144 supersonic transport, for which they were each rated at 196.1kN (44,090lb st). Removable flight refuelling nose probe.

Accommodation: Crew of four, in two side-by-side pair of seats.

Armament: Twin 23mm guns in radar-directed tail mounting. Nominal weapon load 12,000kg (26,450lb). Primary armament of one or two Kitchen air-to-surface missiles semi-recessed in the underside of the centre-fuselage and/or carried under the fixed centre-section panel of each wing. Backfire can also carry the full range of Soviet free-fall nuclear and conventional weapons, and can have multiple racks for external stores under the front of the air intake trunks. Soviet development of decoy missiles has been reported, to supplement very advanced ECM and ECCM.

Dimensions: **Wing span** 34.45m (113ft) spread, 24.00m (78ft 9in) fully swept; **length** 42.5m (140ft); **height** 10.50m (34ft 6in).

Weight: **Max T-O** 130,000kg (286,600lb).

Performance: **Max level speed** Mach 0.9 (594 knots; 1,100km/hr; 684mph) at low altitude, Mach 1.92 (1,100 knots; 2.040km/hr; 1,267mph) at height; **max unrefuelled combat radius** 2,160nm (4,000km; 2,485 miles).

Tupolev Tu-28P/Tu-128

NATO reporting name: **Fiddler**

Contemporary with the Tu-22, this two-seat interceptor was first displayed in public during the July 1961 flypast over Tushino Airport, Moscow. NATO allocated the reporting name Fiddler-A, but this was changed to Fiddler-B for the improved production version, which took part in the last of the big Aviation Day shows, at Domodedovo in 1967. Largest purpose-designed interceptor ever put into service, it is normally designated Tu-28P in the Western press, although the US Department of Defence prefers Tu-128. Which is correct may soon be of mere academic interest, as the number of operational Fiddler-Bs had declined to 90 by 1986.

Powerplant: Two unidentified afterburning turbo-jets, each estimated to give about 120kN (27,000lb st).

Accommodation: Crew of two in tandem, on ejection seats.

Armament: Four air-to-air missiles (NATO Ash) under wings, two radar homing, two infra-red homing.

Dimensions: **Wing span** 18.10m (59ft 4½in); **length** 27.20m (89ft 3in).

Weight: **Max T-O** 45,000kg (100,000lb).

Performance: **Max level speed** Mach 1.65 (950 knots; 1,760km/hr; 1,090mph) at 11,000m (36,000ft); **service ceiling** 20,000m (65,600ft); **max range** 2,690nm (4,990km; 3,100 miles).

This pair of Tu-28P Fiddlers was photographed during a public display at Moscow's Domodedovo Airport. (*Novosti*)

Tupolev Tu-28P Fiddler-B. (*Pilot Press*)

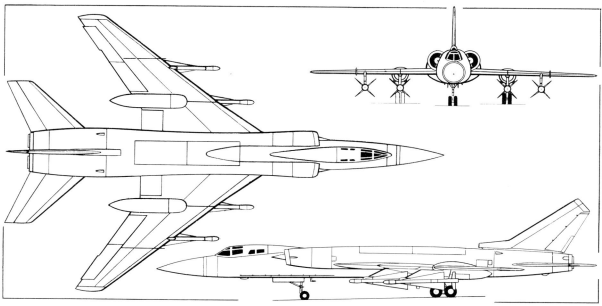

Tupolev Tu-126
NATO reporting name: **Moss**

This counterpart to the US Air Force's E-3 AWACS (airborne warning and control system) was first observed in an officially released Soviet documentary film shown in the West in 1968. About nine are operational, with airframe and powerplant based on those of the now-retired Tu-114 turboprop airliner rather than the smaller-fuselage Tu-95 bomber. The 11m (36ft) diameter rotating radar "saucer" above the fuselage is 1.83m (6ft) larger than that of the E-3; however, the Tu-126 is said to have only limited effectiveness in the warning role over water and to be ineffective over land. Its replacement by the Il-76 Mainstay has begun.

Powerplant: Four 11,033kW (14,795shp) Kuznetsov NK-12MV turboprops. Internal fuel capacity 76,000 litres (16,715 Imp gallons; 20,075 US gallons). Equipped with flight refuelling probe.
Accommodation: Crew of twelve.

Above Tu-126 Moss. Note the large strake beneath the rear fuselage, fitted to offset the extra keel area of the rotodome and its supporting structure.

Below Tupolev Tu-126 Moss. (*Pilot Press*)

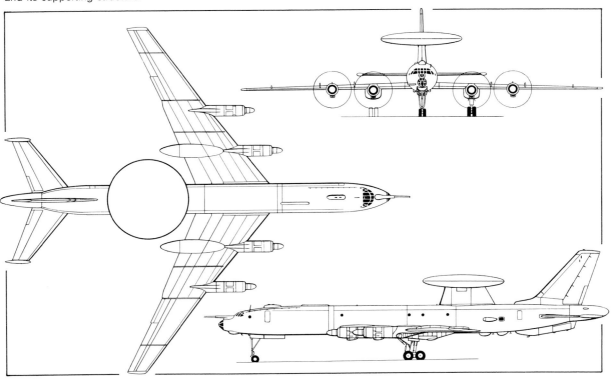

Armament: None.
Dimensions: **Wing span** 51.20m (168ft 0in); **length** 55.20m (181ft 1in); **height** 16.05m (52ft 8in); **wing area** 311.1m² (3,349sq ft).
Weight: **Max T-O** 170,000kg (374,785lb).

Performance: **Max level speed** 459 knots (850km/hr; 528mph); **normal operating speed** 351 knots (650km/hr; 404mph); **max unrefuelled range** 6,775nm (12,550km; 7,800 miles).

Tupolev Tu-?
NATO reporting name: **Blackjack**

Expected to attain operational capability by 1988, this long-awaited replacement for the M-4 Bison and Tu-95 Bear is longer than a US Air Force B-52, is 50% faster than a B-1B, and has a range that offers much the same target coverage as Bear. Apart from one poor-quality reconnaissance photograph taken over Ramenskoye flight test centre on November 25, 1981, only US Department of Defence artists' impressions are available to show that Blackjack is in no way a simple scale-up of Tupolev's earlier Backfire.

Common features include low-mounted variable-geometry wings and large vertical tail surfaces with a massive dorsal fin, but Blackjack's horizontal tail surfaces are mounted higher, at the intersection of the dorsal fin and main fin. The fixed root panel of each wing seems to be long and very sharply swept, like the inboard section of the delta wing of the now-retired Tu-144 supersonic airliner. The engine installation also seems to resemble that of the

Blackjack launches an AS-15 cruise missile in this Defence Department artist's impression.

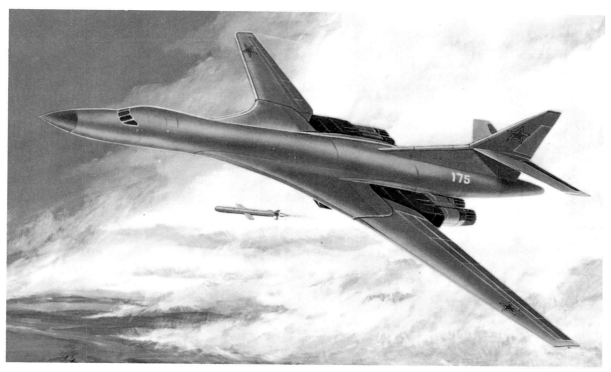

airliner rather than Backfire, leading to suggestions that Blackjack might be powered by four Koliesov single-shaft turbojets of the kind that gave the developed Tu-144D an increased range (and which might be related to the Type 57 engines tested in an experimental aeroplane known as Aircraft 101).

Such assessments should be regarded with caution, as the Tu-144D was designed to cruise at around Mach 2 throughout its flight, whereas the bomber would need to cruise at subsonic speed to conserve fuel and accelerate to supersonic speed at high altitude, or transonic speed at penetration height, only as it approached and left the target area. Major differences in flight profile normally call for different engines. However, it is Soviet policy to uprate or adapt an existing engine for a new aircraft rather than develop a new design, whenever this is possible. If the engines are mounted in pairs inside two divided underwing ducts, as on the Tu-144, the

gap between the ducts will determine the type and size of weapons that Blackjack can carry. Five prototype and pre-production examples were in advanced flight test by 1986, and the Department of Defence expects the Soviet Union to build a production series of at least 100 in a new complex added to the Kazan airframe plant. The AS-15 air-launched cruise missile and supersonic BL-10 missile, each with a range of 1,620nm (3,000km; 1,850 miles), will be Blackjack's primary weapons.

Powerplant: Possibly four Type 57 engines, each rated at 196.1kN (44,090lb st) with afterburning.
Armament: Up to 16,330kg (36,000lb) of free-fall bombs or air-launched cruise missiles.
Dimensions: **Wing span** 52.00m (172ft) spread, 33.75m (110ft) fully swept; **length** 50.625m (166ft); **height** 13.75m (45ft).
Weight: **Max T-O** 250,000kg (551,000lb).
Performance: **Max level speed** Mach 2.1 (1,200 knots; 2,230km/hr; 1,385mph) at height; **max unrefuelled combat radius** 3,940nm (7,300km; 4,535 miles).

Tupolev Blackjack. (*Pilot Press*)

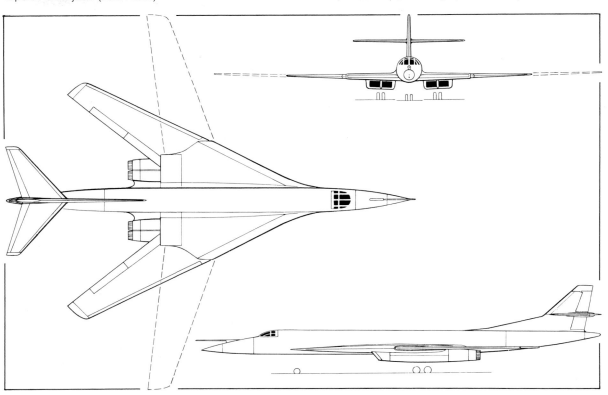

Yakovlev Yak-28
NATO reporting names: **Brewer and Firebar**

First seen in substantial numbers in the 1961 Soviet Aviation Day flypast over Moscow were three variants of a two-seat supersonic multi-purpose aircraft, identified subsequently as Yak-28s. Tactical attack versions known to NATO as Brewer-A, B and C have been retired from service. Versions of the Yak-28 still operational in 1986 are as follows:

Brewer-D Reconnaissance aircraft, carrying cameras or other sensors, including side-looking airborne radar, instead of weapons in its internal bomb-bay. Blister radome under fuselage forward of wings. About 150 operational.

Brewer-E Deployed in 1970 as the first Soviet operational ECM escort aircraft, with an active ECM pack built into its bomb-bay, from which the pack projects in cylindrical form. No radome under front fuselage, but many additional antennae and fairings. Chaff dispensers, anti-radiation missiles, or rocket packs can be carried under the outer wings, between the external fuel tank and balancer wheel housing. About 30 estimated in service.

Firebar With the Soviet designation Yak-28P, about 90 of these all-weather interceptors are

Above Yak-28P Firebar armed with Anab air-to-air missiles.
(*Flug Revue*)

Yakovlev Yak-28P Firebar. (*Pilot Press*)

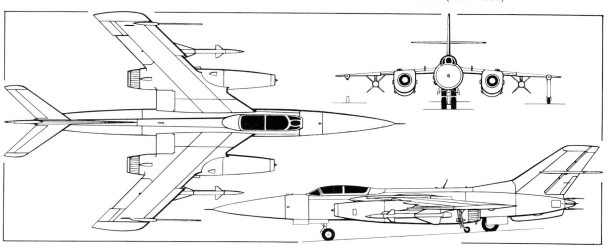

thought to remain operational in the Voyska PVO fighter force. The longer nosecone fitted retrospectively to some aircraft does not indicate any increase in radar capability or aircraft performance, but simply a change of material and shape.

There is also a trainer version of Firebar, known as the Yak-28U (NATO Maestro), with two individual single-seat cockpits in tandem.

Data for Yak-28P (Firebar)

Powerplant: Two Tumansky R-11 turbojets, each rated at 58.35kN (13,120lb st) with afterburning.

Accommodation: Crew of two in tandem.
Armament: Two air-to-air missiles (NATO Anab) under outer wings, with alternative infra-red or semi-active radar homing heads.
Dimensions: **Wing span** 12.95m (42ft 6in); **length (long nosecone)** 23.00m (75ft 5½in); **height** 3.95m (12ft 11½in).
Weight: **Max T-O** 20,000kg (44,000lb).
Performance: **Max level speed** Mach 1.88 (1,080 knots; 2,000km/hr; 1,240mph) at 10,670m (35,000ft); **cruising speed** 496 knots (920km/hr; 571mph); **service ceiling** 16,750m (55,000ft); **combat radius** 500nm (925km; 575 miles).

Yakovlev Yak-38

NATO reporting name: **Forger**

The Soviet Navy's Yak-38 is the only jet combat aircraft that shares the BAe Harrier's V/STOL capability, but it requires three engines, rather than one, to achieve this. Its single large propulsion turbojet exhausts through a pair of rotating nozzles aft of the wing roots. Two lift-jets are mounted in tandem aft of the cockpit, inclined at an angle so that their thrust is exerted upward and slightly forward. All three engines are used for take-off, which was always vertical when first observed on board the carrier/cruiser *Kiev* during

the ship's maiden voyage through the Mediterranean and North Atlantic in July 1976. More recently, the vertical take-off technique has been superseded by a STOL type with a short forward run, which can be assumed to offer improved payload/range performance. This has been made practicable by an automatic control system which ensures that the lift engines are brought into use, and the thrust vectoring rear nozzles

Yak-38 Forger-A photographed during the last stages of its approach to the parent ship.

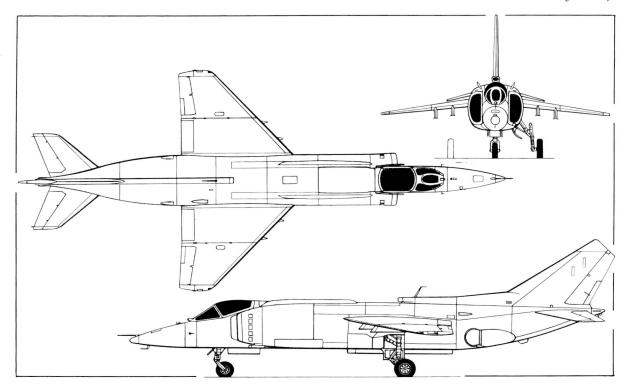

Yakovlev Yak-38 Forger-A. (*Pilot Press*)

rotated, at the optimum point in the take-off run.

Landing procedure begins with a gradual descent from far astern, with the last 400m (1,300ft) flown essentially level, about 30m (100ft) above the water. The aircraft crosses the ship's stern with about a 5 knot (10km/hr; 6mph) closure rate, 10–14m (35–45ft) above the flight deck, then flares gently to a hover and descends vertically. Precise landings are ensured by the automatic control system, perhaps in association with laser devices lining each side of the rear deck. Puffer-jets at the wingtips and tail help to give the Yak-38 commendable stability during take-off and landing. The outer wing panels fold upward for stowage on board ship.

With small refinements, the Yak-38, known to NATO as Forger, has become standard equipment also on the *Kiev's* three sister ships. There are two operational versions:

Forger-A Basic single-seat combat aircraft. Prototype was completed in 1971 and production began in 1975. Twelve appear to be operational on each Soviet carrier/cruiser, in addition to about 19 Kamov Ka-25 or Ka-27 helicopters. Primary operational roles are

reconnaissance, strikes against small ships, and fleet defence against shadowing, unarmed maritime reconnaissance aircraft. Production probably totals about 70 aircraft.

Forger-B Two-seat trainer, of which two are deployed on each carrier/cruiser. Second cockpit forward of normal cockpit, with its ejection seat at lower level, under a continuous canopy. Rear fuselage lengthened to compensate for longer nose. No ranging radar or weapon pylons. Overall length about 17.68m (58ft 0in).

Data for Yak-38 (Forger-A)

Powerplant: One Lyulka AL-21 non-afterburning turbojet (rated at 80kN; 17,985lb st), exhausting through two vectored-thrust nozzles that can rotate up to 10° forward of vertical for VTOL. Two Koliesov lift-jets, each rated at 35kN (7,875lb st).

Accommodation: Pilot only, on ejection seat.

Armament: Four pylons under inner wings for 2,600–3,600kg (5,730–7,935lb) of external stores, including Kerry short-range air-to-surface missiles, armour piercing anti-ship missiles, Aphid close-range air-to-air missiles, gun pods each containing a 23mm twin-barrel GSh-23 cannon, rocket packs, bombs and auxiliary fuel tanks.

Dimensions: **Wing span** 7.32m (24ft 0in); **width, wings folded** 4.88m (16ft 0in); **length** 15.50m (50ft 10¼in); **height** 4.37m (14ft 4in); **wing area** 18.5m² (199sq ft).

Weights: **Basic operating (including pilot)** 7,485kg (16,500lb); **max T-O** 11,700kg (25,795lb).

Performance: **Max level speed** Mach 0.8 (528 knots; 978km/hr; 608mph) at S/L, Mach 0.95 (545 knots; 1,009km/hr; 627mph) at height; **max rate of climb at S/L** 4,500m (14,750ft)/min; **service ceiling** 12,000m (39,375ft), **combat radius with max weapons: lo-lo-lo** 130nm (240km; 150 miles), **hi-lo-hi** 200nm (370km; 230 miles).

Soviet air-to-air, air-to-surface and surface-to-air missiles

Air-to-air

AA-2 (NATO **Atoll**)
Designated K-13A in the USSR, Atoll is the Soviet counterpart to the American Sidewinder 1A (AIM-9B), to which it is almost identical in size, configuration and infra-red guidance. It has long been standard armament on home and export versions of the MiG-21 and is carried by export models of the MiG-23 and Sukhoi Su-22. A solid-propellant rocket motor and 13lb fragmentation warhead are fitted.

Dimensions: **Length** 9ft 2in; **body diameter** 4.72in; **fin span** 1ft 8¾in.
Weight: 154lb.
Performance: **Cruising speed** Mach 2.5; **range** 3 to 4 miles.

Atoll carried by an East German MiG-21.

AA-2-2 (NATO **Advanced Atoll**)
The multi-role versions of the MiG-21 (NATO Fishbed-J, K, L, and N) can carry a radar-homing version of Atoll on the outer stores pylon under each wing, in addition to a standard infra-red-homing Atoll on the inboard pylon. The radar version is known as Advanced Atoll. Length is increased to at least 9ft 10in.

AA-3 (NATO Anab)

This solid-propellant air-to-air missile was first observed as armament of the Yak-28P all-weather fighters that took part in the 1961 Aviation Day display at Tushino. Subsequently it became standard also on Sukhoi Su-15/21 interceptors. Each aircraft normally carries one Anab with an I/J-band semi-active radar seeker and one with an infra-red homing head.

Dimensions: **Length** 13ft 5in (IR) or 13ft 1in (SAR), **body diameter** 11in, **wing span** 4ft 3in.
Performance: **Range** over 10 miles.

Infra-red and radar-homing versions of Anab under the port and starboard wings respectively of an Su-21 Flagon.

AA-5 (NATO Ash)

Several thousand of these large air-to-air missiles were produced as armament for the Tu-28P interceptors of *Voyska* PVO. The version with infra-red homing head is normally carried on the inboard pylon under each wing of the Tu-28P, with an I/J-band semi-active radar-homing version on each outboard pylon.

Dimensions: **Length** 17ft 4½in (IR) or 17ft 0in (SAR); **body diameter** 12in; **wing span** 4ft 3in.
Performance: **Range** 18.5 miles.

Tu-28P Fiddlers each armed with two AA-5 Ash.

AA-6 (NATO **Acrid**)

This air-to-air missile was identified during 1975 as one of the weapons carried by the Foxbat-A interceptor version of the MiG-25. Its configuration is similar to that of Anab but it is considerably larger, with a 220lb warhead. Photographs suggest that the version of Acrid with an infra-red-homing head is normally carried on each inboard underwing pylon, with a radar-homing version on each outer pylon. The wingtip fairings on the fighter, different in shape from those of Foxbat-B, are thought to house continuous-wave target-illuminating equipment for the radar-homing missiles.

Dimensions: **Length** 20ft 7½in (radar version), 19ft 0in (IR version).
Weight: 1,650lb.
Performance: **Cruising speed** Mach 2.2; **range** at least 23 miles.

AA-7 (NATO **Apex**)

This long-range air-to-air missile is one of the two types carried as standard armament by interceptor versions of the MiG-23 and is reported to be an alternative weapon for the MiG-25. Apex has a solid-propellant rocket motor and is deployed in both infra-red and semi-active radar-homing versions. Warhead weight is 88lb.

Dimensions: **Length** 15ft 1¼in; **body diameter** 8.75in; **wing span** 3ft 5½in.
Weight: 705lb.
Performance: **Range** 20 miles.

Foxbat-E armed with infra-red-homing Acrids on the inboard pylons and the radar-homing version on the outers.

ogger-B carries a single AA-7 Apex and a pair of AA-8
hids on each side. (*Swedish Air Force*)

AA-8 (NATO **Aphid**)

Second type of missile carried by the MiG-23, and also by late-model MiG-21s, Su-15/21s and Yak-38s, Aphid is a highly manoeuvrable close-range solid-propellant weapon with infra-red-homing guidance and a 13.2lb warhead.

Dimensions: **Length** 7ft 2½in; **body diameter** 4.75in; **wing span** 1ft 3¾in.
Weight: 121lb.
Performance: **Range** under 1,650ft min, 3–4.3 miles max.

AA-9

This radar-homing long-range missile is reported to have achieved successes against simulated cruise missiles after lookdown/shootdown launch from a MiG-25M interceptor. It is standard armament on the MiG-31.

Performance: **Range** 25–28 miles at height, 12.5 miles at S/L.

AA-10

The AA-10 has capabilities generally similar to those of the AA-9, but is intended for use over medium ranges. It forms the basic interception armament of the MiG-29 and Sukhoi Su-27 counterair fighters.

AA-11

Close-range weapon carried by Su-27, MiG-25 and MiG-29 to complement medium-range AA-10.

Anti-helicopter Grail

In addition to AT-3 anti-tank missiles, Gazelle helicopters licence-built by SOKO for the Yugoslav Air Force carry SA-7 Grail tube-launched IR-homing missiles for use against other helicopters. A similar installation on some Mi-24 helicopters has been reported.

This MiG-31 Foxhound is armed with four AA-9s. (*Royal Norwegian Air Force*)

Air-to-surface

AS-2 (NATO **Kipper**)

First seen 24 years ago, at the 1961 Aviation Day display, this aeroplane-configuration missile, with underslung turbojet engine, was described by the commentator at Tushino as an anti-shipping weapon. Radar is carried in the nose of the Tu-16 carrier aircraft, and guidance is believed to comprise pre-programmed flight under autopilot control, with optional command override, and active-radar terminal homing. A 2,200lb high-explosive warhead is fitted.

Dimensions: **Span** 15ft 0in; **length** 32ft 10in.
Weight: 9,260lb.
Performance: **Max speed** Mach 1.2; **range** 132 miles.

AS-3 (NATO **Kangaroo**)

Kangaroo was a standard air-to-surface missile on Tu-95 Bear strategic bombers from the early 1960s. It is replaced by the faster AS-4 Kitchen on aircraft uprated to Bear-G standard.

AS-4 (NATO **Kitchen**)

Developed as a standoff weapon for the Tu-22 strategic bomber, and now carried also by the Tu-95 (Bear-G) and variable-geometry Backfire, the AS-4 was first seen on a single Tu-22

Kipper carried by a Tu-16 Badger.

(Blinder-B) in 1961. Most of the 22 Tu-22s which participated in the 1967 Aviation Day display at Domodedovo carried an AS-4, semisubmerged in the fuselage, and production up to 1976 was stated by the UK Defence Minister to total

Several variants of AS-4 Kitchen are known to have been operated with Backfire-B.

around 1,000. The missile, which has been seen in more than one form, has an aeroplane configuration, with stubby delta wings and cruciform tail surfaces. Powerplant is believed to be a liquid-propellant rocket motor. Alternative nuclear (200kT) or 2,200lb high-explosive warheads can be assumed.

Guidance: Inertial, with radar terminal homing.
Dimensions: **Span** 9ft 10in; **length** 37ft 0in.
Weight: 13,225lb.
Performance: **Max speed** above Mach 3; **range** 185 miles at low altitude.

AS-5 (NATO **Kelt**)

According to the UK Minister of Defence, well over 1,000 AS-5s had been delivered by the spring of 1976. About 25 were used operationally during the October 1973 war between Israel and the Arab states, when Tu-16s from Egypt launched them against Israeli targets. Only five eluded the air and ground defences.

The transonic AS-5 has a similar aeroplane-type configuration to that of the turbojet-powered AS-1 (Kennel), which it superseded. The switch to liquid rocket propulsion eliminated the need for a ram-air intake and permitted the use of a larger radar inside the hemispherical nose fairing. Guidance is said to be by autopilot on a pre-programmed flightpath, with radar terminal homing that can be switched from active to passive as required. A 2,200lb high-explosive warhead is standard.

Dimensions: **Span** 14ft 1¼in; **length** 28ft 2in.
Weight: 7,715lb.
Performance: **Max speed** Mach 0.9 at low altitude, Mach 1.2 at 30,000ft; **range** 100 miles at low altitude, 200 miles at height.

AS-6 (NATO **Kingfish**)

This advanced air-to-surface missile was first photographed by the pilot of a Japan Air Self-Defence Force F-86F in December 1977 under the port wing of a Tu-16 (Badger). It is standard armament of modified Badger-Gs, which carry a Kingfish under each wing. Propulsion is said to be by liquid-propellant rocket motor, with inertial midcourse guidance and active-radar terminal homing, giving exceptional accuracy. The warhead can be either nuclear (200kT) or 2,200lb high-explosive.

Badger with a single AS-6 Kingfish beneath its port wing.

Dimensions: **Span** 8ft 2½in; **length** 34ft 6in.
Weight: 11,000lb.
Performance: **Max speed** Mach 3; **range** 135 miles
at low altitude.

AS-7 (NATO **Kerry**)

Carried by the Su-17 Fitter, Su-24 Fencer and
Yak-38 Forger, this tactical air-to-surface missile
is said to have a single-stage solid-propellant
rocket motor, radio command guidance system,
and 220lb high-explosive warhead.

Dimension: **Length** 11ft 6in.
Weight: under 880lb.
Performance: **Max speed** Mach 0.6; **max range**
7 miles.

AS-X-9

A reported anti-radiation missile, with a range of
50–56 miles, to arm the Su-24 (Fencer).

AS-10

This is a semi-active laser-homing weapon with
a solid-propellant rocket motor. It is said to be
operational on MiG-27, Su-17 and Su-24 attack
aircraft.

Dimension: **Length** 9ft 10in.
Performance: **Max speed** Mach 0.8; **max range**
6.2 miles.

AS-12

Anti radiation missile in service on tactical
aircraft.

AS-14

Missile in the class of the US Maverick, carried by
the MiG-27 and, probably, other Soviet attack
aircraft.

AS-15

After at least six years of development testing,
including launches from Backfire bombers, the
Soviet Union began deployment of its new-
generation AS-15 long-range air-launched
cruise missiles on Bear-H strategic bombers in
1984. The AS-15 will also arm the new supersonic Blackjack bomber, providing the Soviet

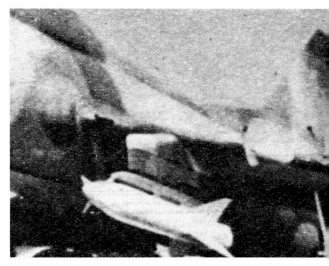

AS-7 Kerry on the wing-root pylon of an Su-17 Fitter-H.

strategic attack force with greatly improved
capabilities for low-level and standoff attack in
both theatre and international operations.
Configuration of the AS-15 is similar to that of
the USAF's much smaller General Dynamics
Ground-Launched Cruise Missile. Submarine-
launched and ground-launched versions are
under development as the SS-NX-21 and
SSC-X-4 respectively. All have a guidance system similar to the US Tercom, making possible a
CEP of about 150ft, and a nuclear warhead.

Dimensions: **Span** 10ft 8in; **length** 23ft 0in.
Performance: **Range** 1,850 miles.

AT-2 (NATO **Swatter**)

This standard Soviet anti-tank weapon formed
the original missile armament of the Mi-24
(Hind-A and D) helicopter gunship and is carried by the Hip-E version of the Mi-8. The solid-
propellant Swatter is steered in flight by means
of elevons on the trailing edges of its rear-
mounted cruciform wings and embodies terminal homing.

Dimensions: **Span** 2ft 2in; **length** 3ft 9¾in.
Weight: 65lb.
Performance: **Cruising speed** 335mph; **range**
1,640–11,500ft.

AT-2 Swatters arm a Czechoslovak Air Force Hind-D.

AT-3 (NATO **Sagger**)

In conformity with the Soviet practice of not supplying advanced equipment on its export aircraft, the wire-guided Sagger replaces Swatter on the Hip-F version of the Mi-8, as well as arming the Polish-built Mi-2, and Gazelles of the Yugoslav services.

Dimensions: **Span** 1ft 6in; **length** 2ft 10¼in.
Weight: 25lb.
Performance: **Speed** 270mph; **range** 1,650–9,850ft.

AT-6 (NATO **Spiral**)

Unlike previous Soviet helicopter-launched anti-tank missiles, Spiral does not appear to have a surface-launched application. Few details are yet available, except that it is tube-launched and radio-guided. It equips the Hind-E version of the Mi-24 and is said to have a range of 4.3 to 6.2 miles.

Surface-to-air

ABM-1 (NATO **Galosh**) and
ABM-2 (NATO **Gazelle**)

Keeping within the terms of the SALT I agreement, as amended by the 1974 Moscow Summit meeting, the USSR maintains around Moscow the world's only operational ABM (anti-ballistic missile) system. Its purpose is to provide a measure of protection for Soviet military and civil central command authorities during a nuclear war, and this has required major upgrading of the system in the past five years. When fully operational, perhaps by next year, it will provide a two-layer defence based on a total of 100 silo-based launchers for long-range modified

ABM-1 Galosh interceptors designed to engage targets outside the atmosphere and high-acceleration Gazelle interceptors to engage targets within the atmosphere. The launchers may be reloadable and will be supported by engagement and guidance radars, plus a large new radar at Pushkino designed to control ABM engagements.

Missiles purported to be Galosh have been paraded through Moscow inside containers about 65ft long with one open end on frequent occasions since 1964. No details of the missile could be discerned, except that the first stage has four combustion chambers. A single nuclear warhead is fitted. Missile range is said to be more than 200 miles.

ABM-X-3

The Soviet Union is believed to have at least two new ABM development programmes under way. One, designated ABM-X-3 by DoD, is said to be a rapidly deployable system using a phased-array radar, missile-tracking radar, and a new missile. Its availability would permit the Soviets to deploy a nationwide ABM system relatively quickly, should they decide to do so. In addition, the SA-10 and SA-X-12 surface-to-air missiles may be capable of intercepting some types of US strategic ballistic missiles.

SA-2 (NATO **Guideline**)

This land-mobile surface-to-air missile has been operational since 1959 and continues in first-line service in some 22 countries. It was used extensively in combat in North Vietnam and the Middle East and has been improved through

SA-2 Guideline, the "flying telegraph pole" of Vietnam War legend. (*Tass*)

several versions as a result of experience. SA-2 launchers are thought to remain operational at 350 sites in the Soviet Union, although the number declines annually. Data for export version:

Powerplant: Liquid-propellant sustainer, burning nitric acid and hydrocarbon propellants; solid-propellant booster.
Guidance: Automatic radio command, with radar tracking of target. Some late versions employ radar terminal homing.
Warhead: High-explosive, weight 288lb.
Dimensions: **Length** 34ft 9in; **body diameter** 1ft 8in; **wing span** 5ft 7in.
Launching weight: 5,070lb.
Performance: **Max speed** Mach 3.5; **slant range** 31 miles; **effective ceiling** 82,000ft.

SA-3 (NATO **Goa**)
Soviet counterpart of the American Hawk, the SA-3 is deployed by the Soviet Union at more than 300 sites and by about 24 of its allies and friends as a mobile low-altitude system (on two, three and four-round launchers) to complement the medium/high-altitude SA-2. As the SA-N-1, it is also a widely used surface-to-air missile in the Soviet Navy; in this application it is fired from a roll-stabilised twin-round launcher.

Powerplant: Two-stage solid-propellant.
Guidance: Radio command, with radar terminal homing.
Warhead: High-explosive, weight 132lb.
Dimensions: **Length** 22ft 0in; **body diameter** 1ft 6in; **wing span** 4ft 0in.
Launching weight: 1,402lb.
Performance: **Max speed** Mach 2; **slant range** 15–18.5 miles; **effective ceiling** over 43,000ft.

SA-4 (NATO **Ganef**)
Ramjet propulsion gives this anti-aircraft missile a very long range. Its usefulness is further enhanced by its mobility, as it is carried on a twin-round tracked launch vehicle that is itself air-transportable in the An-22 military freighter.

SA-4 Ganefs on review in Red Square.

The SA-4 was first displayed publicly in 1964 and is a standard Soviet weapon (approx 1,400 launchers) for defence of combat areas. It is operational also with Bulgarian, East German, Hungarian, Polish and Czechoslovak forces.

Powerplant: Ramjet sustainer, four wrap-around solid-propellant boosters.
Guidance: Radio command, with semi-active radar terminal homing.
Warhead: High-explosive, weight 220–300lb.
Dimensions: **Length** 28ft 10½in; **body diameter** 2ft 8in; **wing span** 7ft 6in.
Launching weight: approx 5,500lb.
Performance: **Max speed** Mach 2.5; **slant range** 43 miles, **effective ceiling** 80,000ft.

SA-5 (NATO **Gammon**)

The SA-5 is described by DoD as a surface-to-air weapon to provide long-range, high-altitude defence for Soviet targets. A drawing released in Washington suggests that its configuration is unusual for a Soviet missile, with long-chord cruciform delta wings, small tail surfaces, and four wrap-around jettisonable boosters. More than 2,000 SA-5s are said to be deployed at more than 100 sites, with significant deployments outside the USSR in Eastern Europe, Libya, Mongolia and Syria.

Powerplant: Two-stage solid-propellant, possibly with terminal propulsion for warhead.
Guidance: Semi-active radar homing.
Dimensions: **Length** 34ft 9in; **body diameter** 2ft 10in; **wing span** 9ft 6in.
Performance: **Max speed** above Mach 3.5; **slant range** 185 miles; **effective ceiling** 95,000ft.

SA-6 (NATO **Gainful**)

This mobile weapon system took an unexpectedly heavy toll of Israeli aircraft during the October 1973 war. Its unique integral all-solid rocket/ramjet propulsion system was a decade in advance of comparable Western technology, and the US-supplied ECM equipment that enabled Israeli aircraft to survive attack by other missiles proved ineffective against the SA-6. First shown on its three-round tracked transporter/launcher in Moscow in November 1967, the missile has

since been produced in very large quantities. Export models have been acquired by many nations, including Algeria, Angola, Bulgaria, Cuba, Czechoslovakia, Egypt, East Germany, Guinea, Hungary, India, Iraq, Kuwait, Libya, Mozambique, Peru, Poland, Romania, Syria, Tanzania, Vietnam, North and South Yemen, Yugoslavia and Zambia.

Powerplant: Solid-propellant booster. After burnout, its empty casing becomes a ramjet combustion chamber for ram air mixed with the exhaust from a solid-propellant gas generator.
Guidance: Radio command, semi-active radar terminal homing.
Warhead: High-explosive, weight 176lb.
Dimensions: **Length** 20ft 4in; **body diameter** 1ft 1.2in.
Launching weight: 1,212lb
Performance: **Max speed** Mach 2.8; **range** 18.5 miles; **effective ceiling** 59,000ft.

SA-7 (NATO **Grail**)

This Soviet counterpart to the US shoulder-fired, heat-seeking Redeye first proved its effectiveness in Vietnam against slower, low-flying aircraft and helicopters. It repeated the process during the 1973 Arab-Israeli war, despite countermeasures. In addition to being a standard weapon throughout the Warsaw Pact forces since 1968, it has been supplied to about 39 other nations and is used by various guerrilla/terrorist movements. Designed for use by infantry, the tube-launched SA-7 is also carried by vehicles, including ships, in batteries of four, six and eight, for both offensive and defensive employment, with radar aiming. Some are deployed on helicopters for anti-helicopter use.

Powerplant: Solid-propellant booster/sustainer.
Guidance: Infra-red homing with filter to screen out decoy flares.
Warhead: High-explosive, weight 5.5lb.
Dimensions: **Length** 4ft 3in; **body diameter** 2.75in.
Launching weight: 20lb.
Performance: **Max speed** Mach 1.5; **slant range** 5–6 miles; **effective ceiling** 5,000ft.

SA-8B Gecko. The earlier SA-8A vehicle carries two fewer rounds on unprotected launchers.

SA-8 (NATO Gecko)

First displayed publicly during the parade through Moscow's Red Square on November 7, 1975, this short-range, all-weather system is unique among Soviet tactical air defence weapons in that all components needed to engage a target are on a single vehicle. In the original SA-8A version two pairs of exposed missiles were carried, ready to fire; the later SA-8B system has six missiles in launcher-containers. Missile configuration is conventional, with canard control surfaces and fixed tail fins. Fire-control equipment and the four/six-round launcher are mounted on a rotating turret carried by a three-axle six-wheel amphibious vehicle. The surveillance radar, with an estimated range of 18 miles, folds down behind the launcher, permitting the weapon system to be airlifted. The tracking radar is of the pulsed type, with an estimated range of 12–15 miles. The SA-8B uses the same missile as the well estab-

lished but enigmatic naval SA-N-4. Each vehicle carries up to six reload missiles. About 700 SA-8 vehicles are thought to be in Soviet service; export customers include Angola, Guinea, India, Jordan, Kuwait, Libya, Poland and Syria.

Powerplant: Probably dual-thrust solid-propellant.
Guidance: Command guidance by proportional navigation. Semi-active radar terminal homing.
Warhead: High-explosive, about 90–110lb weight.
Dimensions: **Length** 10ft 6in; **body diameter** 8.25in.
Launching weight: 440lb.
Performance: **Range** 6–8 miles; **effective ceiling** 20,000ft.

SA-9 (NATO Gaskin)

This weapon system, deployed initially in 1968, comprises a BRDM-2 amphibious vehicle carrying a box launcher for two pairs of infra-red-homing missiles. The launcher rests flat on the rear of the vehicle when not required to be ready for launch. Four reload rounds are stowed in the BRDM-2. In addition to the Soviet Union, operators include most Warsaw Pact states and 11 other nations (see also SA-13).

Dimensions: **Length** 5ft 9in; **body diameter** 4.33in.
Launching weight: 66lb.
Performance: **Range** 5 miles; **effective ceiling** 16,400ft.

SA-10 (NATO **Grumble**)
If press reports are to be believed, this weapon threatens the viability of US cruise missiles. A single-stage rocket motor is said to accelerate the SA-10 at 100g to a cruising speed of Mach 6. A range of up to 60 miles and all-altitude capability are suggested, with active-radar terminal homing and multiple target engagement capability. Reported dimensions are a length of 23ft 6in and body diameter of 17.7in. By the Spring of 1986, the SA-10 was operational at more than 60 sites in the USSR, with 520 launchers and four missiles per launcher. At least 30 more sites are being prepared. A landmobile version, carried on a four-axle truck, was being deployed in 1986.

SA-11 (NATO **Gadfly**)
This new weapon system comprises a four-rail tracked launch vehicle for Mach 3.5 radar-guided missiles with a reported ability to deal with targets at altitudes between 100ft and 46,000ft and at ranges up to 18.5 miles. SA-11s are being deployed alongside SA-6s. Missile length is 18ft.

SA-12
This formidable container-launched weapon is considered capable of dual-mode operation against aircraft and intermediate-range and submarine-launched missiles. The SA-12 is in production and was nearing operational capability in Spring 1986. Little reliable information is available, but a DoD drawing has suggested a missile of fairly conventional configuration and about the same size as the SA-10. A complete fire unit could include two twin-round erector-launchers, a reload vehicle, two planar-array radar vehicles, and a command vehicle, all tracked. A range of 60 miles is expected.

SA-13 (NATO **Gopher**)
Deployed on a tracked vehicle in the late 1970s, the SA-13 is a replacement for the SA-9, providing improved capability in rough terrain and increased storage for reload missiles. Together with the ZSU-23-4 tracked gun vehicle, it equips the anti-aircraft batteries of motorised rifle and tank regiments. Range is about 5 miles at altitudes between 165ft and 16,500ft.

SA-14 (NATO **Gremlin**)
This new shoulder-fired infantry missile is believed to have a more powerful motor, giving higher speed and an effective ceiling of about 14,000ft. It may use a laser beam for beam-riding guidance.

SA-N-1 (NATO **Goa**)
Ship-launched variant of SA-3, carried on roll-stabilised twin launchers by 43 ships of the Soviet Navy.

SA-N-2 (NATO **Guideline**)
Ship-launched version of SA-2. On cruiser *Dzerzhinski* only.

SA-N-3 (NATO **Goblet**)
The twin-round surface-to-air missile launchers fitted to many of the latest Soviet naval vessels, including *Kiev*-class carrier/cruisers, helicopter cruisers *Moskva* and *Leningrad*, and Kara and Kresta II cruisers, carry a newer and more effective missile than the SA-N-1 (Goa). This is said to have an anti-ship capability and to carry an 88lb high-explosive warhead. The original version has a range of 18.6 miles and effective ceiling of 82,000ft. A later version has a range of 34 miles.

Dimension: **Length** 19ft 8in.
Weight: 1,200lb.

SA-N-4

This naval close-range surface-to-air weapon system is operational on at least nine classes of Soviet Navy ship. The retractable twin-round pop-up launcher is housed inside a bin on deck. The missiles are similar to those of the land-based mobile SA-8B system.

SA-N-5

At least 169 small Soviet ships have this simple air-defence system, which carries four SA-7 Grail launch tubes in a framework that can be slewed for aiming.

SA-N-6

This missile is housed in 12 vertical launch tubes under the foredeck of the Soviet battle cruiser *Kirov* and is also carried by *Slava*-class cruisers. It is assumed to have the same multiple-threat role as the US Navy's Aegis area defence system. No authentic information on the SA-N-6 missile is available, although some relationship with the land-based SA-10 seems likely. Best estimates suggest a length of about 23ft, effective ceiling of at least 100,000ft, and range of 37 miles at Mach 6, carrying a 200lb warhead. Likely features include multiple target detection and tracking, midcourse guidance, terminal homing, and high resistance to ECM and jamming.

SA-N-7

Two single-rail launchers for this new missile are fitted in each ship of the *Sovremennyy* class of guided missile destroyers. The sophistication and rapid-fire potential of the weapon system is indicated by a fit of no fewer than six associated fire-control/target-illuminating radars. The SA-N-7 itself is thought to be the naval equivalent of the land-based SA-11.

SA-N-8

Almost nothing is known about this vertically launched missile system carried by the new *Udaloy* class of anti-submarine ships.

SA-NX-9

The battlecruiser *Kirov* carries SA-N-4 and SA-N-6 surface-to-air missile systems. Sister ship *Frunze* also has provision for a total of 128 shorter-range SA-NX-9 missiles. These will be shared between two rows of four vertical launchers on each side of the stern helicopter pad, and two rectangular groups of four launchers on the forecastle. No other details are available.

Bibliography

Books

The Penkovsky Papers, Oleg Penkovsky, Collins 1965
Khrushchev Remembers, Deutsch 1971
Khrushchev Remembers, The Last Testament, Deutsch 1974
The Mind of the Soviet Fighting Man, R. A. Gabriel, Greenwood 1984
The Soviet Air and Rocket Forces, ed Asher Lee, Weidenfeld & Nicholson 1959
A History of Soviet Air Power, R. A. Kilmarx, Faber and Faber 1957
Military Strategy, Soviet Doctrine and Concepts, Sokolovsky, Praeger 1963
Soviet Power and Europe 1945–1970, T. W. Wolfe, Johns Hopkins 1970
The Soviet Air Forces, ed P. J. Murphy, McFarland 1984
Soviet Strategic Power and Doctrine, The Quest for Superiority, M. E. Miller; AISI 1982
The Soviet Air Force Since 1918, A. Boyd, Macdonald and Jane's, 1977
Soviet Military Policy, R. L. Garthoff, Faber and Faber 1966
The Threat, A. Cockburn, Hutchinson 1983
Soviet Decision Making for National Security, ed Valenta and Potter, Allen and Unwin 1984
American and Soviet Military Trends, J. M. Collins, Georgetown University 1978
Weapons and Tactics of the Soviet Army, D. C. Isby, Jane's 1981
Soviet Military Power and Performance, ed Erickson and Feuchtwanger, Macmillan 1979
Soviet Helicopters, J. Everett-Heath, Jane's 1983
The Impact of Air Power, ed Emme, Van Nostrand 1959

Soviet Air Power and The Pursuit of New Military Options, P. A. Petersen, US Government 1979
The Aim of a Lifetime, A. S. Yakovlev, Moscow 1968
Soviet Combined Arms, Theory and Practice, J. Erickson, Texas A & M University 1981
Stalin Means War, G. A. Tokaev, Weidenfeld and Nicholson 1951
Soviet Strategy Towards Western Europe, ed Moreton and Segal, Allen and Unwin 1984
Soviet Aviation and Air Power, ed Higham and Kipp, Westview 1977
Air Power and Warfare, ed Hurley and Ehrhart, US DoD 1979
Air Power in the Next Generation, ed Mason and Feuchtwanger, Macmillan 1979
Air Power in the Nuclear Age, Mason and Armitage, Macmillan 1983
Russian Aircraft Since 1940, J. Alexander, Putnam 1975
Soviet Air Power in Transition, R. P. Berman, Brookings 1978
Soviet Military Strategy in Europe, J. D. Douglass, Pergamon 1980
Soviet Strategy In the Nuclear Age, R. L. Garthoff, Atlantic 1958
Soviet Air Power 1917–76, K. R. Whiting, USAF Air University 1976
Worldwide Soviet Military Strategy and Policy, T. W. Wolfe, Rand 1973
Concept, Algorithm, Decision, Druzhinin and Kontorov, Moscow 1972
The Officer's Handbook, S. N. Koslov, Moscow 1971
The Offensive, A. A. Sidorenko, Moscow 1970
The Revolution in Military Affairs, ed N. A. Lomov, Moscow 1973

Operational Art and Tactics, V. Ye. Saukin,
    Moscow 1972
Long Range, Missile Equipped, B. A. Vasily'ev,
    Moscow 1972
MiG-Pilot, J. Barron, Reader's Digest 1985
The Liberators, V. Suvorov, Hamish Hamilton
    1981
Measuring Military Power, J. M. Epstein, Taylor
    & Francis UK 1985

Soviet press, selected translations from:
Aviation and Cosmonautics
Red Star
Air Defence Herald
Military Herald
Military-Historical Journal
Banner Bearer
Military Review
Pravda

Western journals and periodicals
Defense Electronics

International Defense Review
Interavia
Aviation Week and Space Technology
Flight International
Defence
Military Technology
Jane's Defence Weekly
Air Force Magazine
Air University Review
IISS Military Balance
IISS Strategic Survey
Soviet Armed Forces Review Annual
Soviet Military Power
Survival
Military Review
The Navigator
USN Institute Proceedings
The Economist
Naval War College Review
Royal United Services Institute Journal
Defence Attaché

Index

Italic numerals refer to captions